AAP & DOWN

AAP & DOWN

An Insider's Story of India's Most Controversial Party

MAYANK GANDHI

with

SHREY SHAH

SIMON & SCHUSTER

London · New York · Sydney · Toronto · New Delhi

First published in India by Simon & Schuster India, 2018
This edition published by Simon & Schuster India in 2025

1 3 5 7 9 10 8 6 4 2

Simon & Schuster India
818, Indraprakash Building,
21, Barakhamba Road,
New Delhi 110001

www.simonandschuster.co.in

PB ISBN: 978-93-86797-14-8
eBook ISBN: 978-93-86797-15-5

Typeset in India by SÜRYA, New Delhi

Printed and bound in India by Replika Press Pvt. Ltd.

To

My guru and the extraordinary lineage of gurus who harness divine intelligence through us, ordinary mortals

My parents for their genes and sanskara

My wife, children, friends and family for encouraging me to dance to my own music and for keeping me safe within a bubble of love, security and freedom

My country, the likes of which there is none other

Badi kashmakash hai zindagi mai
Timir se roushni vajr si ban gayi hai
Ki kaate kiran ki nahi katt rahi hai
Tumhe khud ko indhan banna padega

(Life is full of intense struggle
Minor troubles seem like thunderbolts
Even the rays of the sun have failed to cut through a
veil of pessimism
One will have to dedicate oneself to mankind)

—*Swami Vimuktananda*

CONTENTS

Preface

Last month, we had a long meeting with the doyen of Indian industry, the Chairman Emeritus of Larsen & Toubro, on the possibility of working together with his trust and our not-for-profit trust (Global Vikas Trust—GVT) to increase farmer incomes in South Gujarat. The meeting went well, and my heart swelled with anticipation as I prepared to present my book to a man I deeply admired.

'Naik sir,' I said with great excitement, signing my message with 'Nation first, always' before extending the book toward him. 'I would like to gift you my book, *AAP & Down*. While thousands of books chronicle our independence struggle, this crucial chapter of history—the IAC movement and AAP's birth—needed to be documented. Lakhs of people invested their hopes in this movement, and they deserve to know what transpired.'

He smiled warmly and reached for the book. But as his eyes fell upon the cover, his expression transformed. He withdrew his hand as if scalded. 'I will not take this book as this man, Kejriwal, is on the cover,' he declared, his voice thick with contempt. My heart sank. Noting my crestfallen expression, this sensitive leader called for a pair of scissors and, with unexpected kindness, suggested I remove Kejriwal's image from the cover. Only then did he accept my autographed book.

This visceral revulsion to Kejriwal has become a familiar sight in my encounters. The resentment runs deep in every heart I meet, stemming from a profound sense of personal betrayal. Those who had supported the movement, making tremendous sacrifices, now realise they were deceived into believing he and his party were different—that they could change India. They witnessed his betrayal of many senior members of the movement, including Anna, and watched in dismay as he systematically dismantled every principle that had earned him their support, all in his ruthless pursuit of power. If Lord Acton's words 'absolute power corrupts absolutely' needed a face in contemporary India, Kejriwal has volunteered his own. He has become the embodiment of treachery, and the nation's anger has become deeply personal.

The title *Aap & Down* carries a deeper meaning than mere electoral fortunes. The 'up' in AAP symbolises a battle for the nation's soul, for integrity itself. Electoral victories have never been my measure of success or failure. A party that stands for truth, regardless of consequences, is inherently 'up'. The 'down' signifies the tragic loss of moral compass. In 2018, I had clung to hope that the party's moral and political descent might be arrested, that it might find its way back to its founding principles. Today, that hope has vanished as AAP's downward spiral accelerates.

This book chronicles more than just a political journey—it documents the betrayal of an entire nation's dream.

Mayank Gandhi,
November 2024

Introduction

Six Years Hence

MUCH WATER HAS FLOWN SINCE I WROTE THE FIRST EDITION of this book in 2018.

Today, I stand heartbroken, my self-confidence shattered. I carry a burden that will haunt me for the rest of my life—the guilt of having betrayed my beloved country. I am ashamed that I failed to see through this false façade of patriotism, ashamed for having waved the Indian tricolour alongside those who saw the movement merely as a steppingstone to personal power, not a path to national redemption.

The reality of Arvind, my erstwhile friend and idol, having compromised all values and principles still feels surreal. Wrestling with the devastating truth of 'absolute power corrupts absolutely', my mind grapples with persistent questions: 'Is he being framed?', 'Was he always like this, and I was blind to it, or has power transformed him?', 'Are his formidable adversaries painting him in false colours?', 'Are the cases against him and his colleagues merely fabrications by the BJP and the institutions under their control?'

Determined to find answers, I embarked on an objective

investigation of each serious allegation, leveraging my connections with media, political commentators, and analysts. While I examined all accusations, three proved decisive—one involving corruption, and two deeply personal matters.

The reality of Indian elections is stark and sobering—a massive exercise in cash flow that operates largely in the shadows. In 2014, when I contested the Lok Sabha elections, each candidate was permitted to spend Rs 70 lakh per constituency. I held myself to this limit, not just because it was the law, but because it aligned with our movement's principles. Yet, from my ringside view, I watched in dismay as candidates, particularly from major parties, casually deployed a princely amount or more per constituency—mostly to buy votes in villages and urban slums.

My team and I weren't mere passive observers. Time and again, we received frantic calls about cash distribution in slums. We would alert the police, only to witness a carefully choreographed dance: party workers would create diversions and obstruct the police, buying precious minutes for the main operatives to vanish with their bags of cash. It was street theatre with devastating implications for democracy.

But these individual candidate expenses were merely the tip of the iceberg. The real money lay in the party machinery—grand rallies that transformed dusty maidans into temporary cities, advertisement blitzkriegs across every possible medium, forests of hoardings that sprouted overnight, public meetings with their elaborate staging, and relentless social media campaigns that flooded every screen. Political analysts, speaking in hushed tones, estimate that in

Gujarat alone, allegedly each major party's spending crossed Rs 3,000 crores—most of it being untraceable cash.

In this big-money game, AAP matched the established players stride for stride, particularly during the 2022 Gujarat assembly elections. It unleashed similarly aggressive campaigns in Goa and Punjab among other states, and even in Lok Sabha battles. The suspected expenditure runs into thousands of crores. Here's what troubles me deeply: Allegedly, AAP's legal donations have all but evaporated since they stopped their once-celebrated practice of publishing donation details online. The question that haunts me, that should haunt every citizen who believed in our movement, is simple yet devastating: Where is this torrent of cash coming from?

During our days in the India Against Corruption (IAC) movement, we conducted a forensic examination of political corruption, particularly its manifestation in electoral politics. What we uncovered was a sophisticated ecosystem of power and money, operating with clockwork precision. Politicians, armed with sweeping decision-making powers, orchestrate a carefully calibrated dance of favours—bestowing benefits upon industrialists, builders, and businessmen with calculated generosity, always with the implicit understanding of reciprocity.

The mechanics of this exchange are both elegant and disturbing. When industrialists receive their promised benefits, they respond with generous cash payments to their political benefactors. Here, politicians reveal their true colours. The supposedly 'honest' ones direct the entire sum to the party treasury, while others—perhaps more honest about their dishonesty—carve out their personal share before passing the remainder upward. This is why I've maintained throughout this book that 'honest politician' is perhaps the most glaring oxymoron in Indian public life. You can be honest, or you can be a politician—never both. The only variable is the ratio: how much flows to personal coffers versus party coffers.

But this machinery of corruption requires meticulous documentation. Every policy deviation, every rule modification designed to benefit business interests must be recorded in official files. This necessity draws the bureaucracy into the web, requiring their complicity—secured either through a share in the spoils or through other means. Delhi presents a particularly complex case study with its dual power structure: the state government on one side, and the Lieutenant Governor (LG) representing the Centre on the other. It's an open secret that many bureaucrats maintain direct lines to Narendra Modi and Amit Shah. In this environment, every contentious decision, every significant file faces potential scrutiny from a combative LG, hand-picked by the Home Minister or Prime Minister for precisely this oversight role.

The irony is striking—Kejriwal now battles to change Delhi's constitutional structure, the very framework under which he fought and won. His desperate bid to secure unlimited powers for the Delhi government has found little sympathy, even in courts. Yet, he's played his cards craftily. As Chief Minister, he held no ministry portfolio himself but pulled every ministerial string. He's replicated this playbook in Punjab, where his iron grip extends over the Chief Minister, cabinet, and bureaucracy alike. A masterclass in wielding absolute power while maintaining plausible deniability.

Something wasn't adding up. The party's election

spending was astronomical, yet formal donations had dried to a trickle. With my years in the system, I sensed that big money was changing hands somewhere. Then came July 2022, and with it, the liquor gate scandal. My old investigative instincts kicked in. Was this where one of the missing pieces of the puzzle lay? While the case remains sub judice, certain red flags were impossible to ignore:

1. The Delhi government's reaction was telling—it yanked the 2021–22 excise policy faster than a guilty hand withdrawing from a cookie jar, the moment questions were raised.
2. It's own admission was damning: the new policy had bled the state exchequer while gifting 'windfall gains' to select liquor traders. Fewer shops, more profit—the math was suspicious.
3. Media reports painted a staggering picture: Approximately Rs 2,500 crore. That's allegedly what the public lost while private license holders laughed their way to the bank.
4. The party's defence was paper-thin. 'No money found in Sisodia's house,' they claimed. The court's retort was scathing: Non-recovery of cash didn't amount to proof of no corruption.
5. The Central government moved like a chess player, each arrest a calculated move—Satyendra Jain, Vijay Nair, Manish Sisodia, and finally, Kejriwal. Three liquor businessmen turned approvers. They were building their case methodically, knowing arresting Kejriwal without ironclad evidence would be political suicide.
6. The courts' consistent rejection of bail pleas, after

examining the evidence, speaks volumes.

The case continues its journey through our legal labyrinth. I find myself wondering: Will time prove my instincts right? Is this another political witch hunt? The answers might reshape not just AAP's future, but the very narrative of political corruption in India.

When Amit Shah announced on Twitter that about eight more cases were waiting to be filed against the Kejriwal government, the irony wasn't lost on me. The same PM Modi whom Kejriwal had once brazenly labeled a 'coward and psychopath' now leads the charge through various central agencies, methodically excavating every potential case of corruption. The AAP government's path and Kejriwal and his core team's journey ahead looks thorny indeed.

You know what's funny? I've always been someone who finds humour in life's absurdities, rarely taking anything—least of all myself—too seriously. The daily spectacle of Indian politics, with its theatrical name-calling and endless allegations hurled across media platforms, initially entertained me. But my perspective shifted dramatically when I immersed myself in the harsh realities of drought-stricken villages, witnessing firsthand the devastation of farmer suicides and famine.

Now, when politically astute villagers corner me with pointed questions about Kejriwal's transformation—his newfound comfort with former adversaries, his convoy of cars, his first-class flights and private charters—I can only respond with a hollow laugh. What defence could I possibly offer?

I've taken to sharing a bitter joke with them. Imagine

a checklist of every promise we made publicly—each box now bears a damning cross. Remember PATDI? Those lofty ideals we promised our volunteers: Participation, Accountability, Transparency, Decentralised decision-making, and Integrity. Then there were our grand commitments to the nation: no VIP security, modest housing, simple transportation, zero tolerance for criminal candidates, term limits for party leadership, immediate implementation of the Jan Lokpal Bill, Swaraj, and Mohalla committees. Each promise systematically abandoned. Only one pledge remains uncrossed—the ban on relatives in the party. Though honestly, I suspect it's just a matter of time before that final domino falls.

The party's apologists—and there aren't many left—defend these betrayals with a tired refrain: 'This is the price of political survival.' But they fall tellingly silent when confronted with two glaring questions: How does one justify Kejriwal's alleged mind-boggling Rs 45 crore splurge on his Sheeshmahal's interiors? What catastrophe would have befallen him if his bathrooms had ordinary fixtures? I could go on, but why bother? No one dares answer these questions. This isn't about political necessity—it's about moral bankruptcy, about ethical collapse. Every time I think about this alleged flagrant abuse of public funds, my stomach turns. This isn't politics; this is decadence in its purest form.

Shah tweeted that there are eight other cases against the Kejriwal government and they will file the case one after the other. The central government and its agencies may not leave a single stone unearthed to find all the cases of corruption, if there is evidence. Life is going to be tough for the AAP government.

Kejriwal's ruthless pursuit of power defined his leadership. He showed utter disdain for those who no longer served his purpose, discarding them like spent tools. Those who dared voice dissenting opinions weren't merely sidelined—they were dealt with so harshly that it sent a chilling message throughout the party. Their public humiliation served as a stark warning, making potential dissenters think twice before challenging his authority. Of those who survived was Swati Maliwal.

I have known Maliwal for years. Back in the day, she was a fervent admirer of Arvind Kejriwal. Arvind, too, held her in high regard. He spoke highly of her, and it was clear he valued her not just as a colleague but also as a staunch supporter and a fan. I saw firsthand the respect he had for her. But something must have soured along the way, as often happens in these kinds of relationships. Still, what transpired later—her being allegedly assaulted by his people, and Arvind saying nothing in response—was nothing short of shocking.

The Arvind Kejriwal I once knew and admired is no longer the same.

In his place is a caricature of that man—a shadow of the leader who once inspired so many. The energy and vision that once moved people have all but disappeared. The acts that were once symbolic, meant to spark a revolution in the hearts and minds of the people, have degenerated into cheap theatrics. And now, they've become an outright farce. Look at the recent absurdities—Sunita Kejriwal's assertion in a press conference that Kejiwal's 'atma' (soul) was wandering the streets of Delhi while his body languished in jail, or Atishi, the new Marx-leaning Chief Minister, keeping one chair next to her empty, symbolising King Rama's presence while she played Raja Bharat. This would be very funny, if it wasn't so sad.

AAP, once a beacon of hope, is now a punchline, the subject of endless memes and jokes.

The spark has been extinguished.

When Arvind was granted bail ahead of the Lok Sabha elections, he begged voters to support him so he could stay out of jail. Very few did. AAP, along with Congress, lost every single seat in Delhi. Then, in Haryana, he again pleaded for votes, asking voters to show their anger over his imprisonment. The result? A dismal 1.79% (approximately) of the vote share. Now, he has abandoned his position as Chief Minister, telling the electorate that he won't return to power unless they send him a strong message through their votes.

Years ago, I made a conscious decision to step away from the distractions of the world and dedicate myself to a higher purpose—regaining the glory of our great nation. To that end, I quit my job, sold my house, and channelled everything into serving the poor. I had read somewhere that it takes 84 lakh lifetimes to be born as a human; I resolved not to waste a single minute of this precious opportunity.

For the last five years, my not-for-profit trust has been working in Beed district, Maharashtra—an area that suffers from the highest rates of suicides, droughts, poverty, and preventable misery. Our mission has been to build the nation from the ground up. To date, we have planted over 541 million trees across 4,600 villages in three states. We've helped increase farmers' incomes by more than ten times, according to an impact assessment by the Tata Institute of Social Sciences (TISS) ('Impact Assessment Study of

Agricultural Development Initiatives of Global Vikas Trust', January 2024), and we've established a world-class center in Beed to provide free training to farmers.

This recent political saga has actually clarified my path and shown the futility of reaching the lives of the needy through politics. It's shown me that I must focus directly on the poorest of the poor, the ones who truly need help. I can see the impact of my work with my own eyes, and it's been a blessing for both me and the country. Personally, I'm in a good place—working in a non-toxic environment, making a tangible difference in the lives of those who need it most, and doing so at a scale I never imagined.

When my publishers asked me to write a chapter for the new edition, my initial instinct was to decline. Writing on politics only invites toxicity, barbs, and endless trolling. I didn't want to go down that road again. But in the end, I decided that the larger purpose of my life—building a better, fairer world—was far more important than the pettiness that often surrounds political discourse.

While I have permanently stepped away from active electoral politics, my commitment to the betterment of this nation has not wavered. In fact, my entire life is now dedicated to serving the poor and working towards the welfare of India. It is in this spirit of service that I feel compelled to share my thoughts and frustrations, with the hope that future generations will understand why some movements succeed and others falter—and what we can learn from both.

This is not intended as an epitaph for Arvind Kejriwal or AAP. In fact, they may very well win the next elections, even in Punjab. History shows that unscrupulous politicians have flourished in this country before; we've seen politicians convicted of corruption while in jail still manage to secure electoral victories. As I've said before, winning elections is not my definition of success. What matters is the moral and ethical foundation that one brings into public life. The true measure of leadership is not power, but integrity.

India has weathered centuries of turmoil and hardship. It has endured the worst of times and always emerged stronger. These present-day setbacks, these fleeting blips on the radar, will not halt the country's inevitable progress. As for me, I take pride in the fact that I was an integral part of the revolution that helped change India forever.

1. How It All Began

'I request Mayank Gandhi to lead the India Against Corruption (IAC) movement in Maharashtra,' Arvind Kejriwal announced at the National Conference for the Forum for Fast Justice in January 2011.

He continued, 'Some of us have drafted a powerful Lokpal Bill that can root out corruption from the country. We discussed it with almost all political parties and asked them to take it up in Parliament, but no leader seems keen to even consider it. If implemented, this Bill can put many corrupt politicians in jail; therefore, we do not expect any political party to support it. To force the politicians to pass the anti-corruption bill, a mass movement, bigger than any this nation has seen, will have to be started.'

I was the moderator of a panel where Arvind was delivering a seventeen-minute-long powerful talk about the endemic corruption tearing into the nation and how the IAC movement could free people from the oppression of the corrupt. Arvind's passionate call stirred every patriotic fibre of my being.

Prior to announcing my name, Arvind had had a short discussion with me. 'Mayank, I really think you should take charge of the movement in Maharashtra. This is a decisive time. The country needs your full involvement.'

Arvind spoke in a manner I have come to associate with him—emphatic and persuasive. Before I could respond, he continued, 'However, since this requires your undivided attention, I request you to disengage from any civil society group or party that you are associated with.'

Arvind was referring to my earlier association with an Andhra Pradesh-based civil society initiative, Lok Satta (2003-2007); this was his way to urging me to disengage from them and work only for IAC. I had heard of some differences between Arvind and the founder of Lok Satta, a brilliant ex-Indian administrative service (IAS) officer, Dr Jayaprakash Narayan (JP; not to be confused with the erstwhile Janata Party leader).

In any case, Arvind had little reason to be concerned. I confessed to him, 'When I was a part of the Lok Satta movement in Maharashtra, there was a lot of petty and malicious politicking within the group. I quit a long time ago, disgusted with the bickering. I'm not a part of JP's team.'

It turned out that Arvind had heard a number of positive things regarding my work, my style of functioning and my passion for swaraj from a range of people, including Manish Sisodia—and now that my commitments were clear, he looked relieved.

Arvind put his arm around my shoulder and smiled, 'Mayank, Maharashtra—especially Mumbai—is really crucial. A lot will depend on you.'

*

I had known Arvind Kejriwal since 2003, when I worked closely with activist Anna Hazare for the passing of the Maharashtra Right to Information (RTI). Due to our common interest in activism, we remained in touch off and on. Arvind was doing some very interesting work in Delhi, and I was doing something similar in Mumbai.

While I had met Arvind only a few times, I had heard many inspiring stories about him. For instance, during his avatar as an Indian Revenue Service (IRS) officer, he'd regularly expose fellow officers who'd ask for bribes. While working with the Income Tax (IT) department, he was also operating as one of the founders of a grass-roots activism organization called Parivartan. He'd visit the Sundar Nagari slums of Delhi, attend to the grievances of citizens, and resolve their concerns, whether this had to do with getting a ration card or common income tax and electricity complaints. Arvind used RTI to help people get their work done in government offices without paying bribes, and he organized public hearings to hold government officials accountable.

There are two stories involving Arvind and Parivartan that are particularly motivating. As all of us know,

IT refunds can get held up for a variety of reasons, and the citizen gets severely inconvenienced. To resolve this, each time there was an impasse, a team of Parivartan volunteers would meet the concerned officer along with the assessee and ask for the date of refund. On the said date, they would reach the IT office with musical instruments. If the refund was refused, they'd sit on the floor of the office, sing songs, beat drums and clang cymbals, till the refunds were made.

Another story involved an individual who was asked for a bribe of Rs 25,000 by an IT officer to pass his refund order. Parivartan volunteers, along with select media entities, took a procession led by drums and cymbals, carrying a cheque of Rs 25,000 to pay the bribe. The officer, as expected, ran away from the back door.

I was bowled over by Arvind's approach and audacity. I became his admirer.

Swaraj was the common passion that I shared with Arvind. Swaraj means empowerment, and it seeks the participation of common people across all aspects of day-to-day decision-making in governance. Swaraj's foundation is transparency, as also holding people in power accountable to the collective will of the people. 'Take away power from the government and give it to the people,' I would say during my speeches.

Among other things, Arvind was a part of the Aruna Roy-led National Campaign for People's Right to Information (NCPRI), an umbrella body of various activists working for systemic reforms in the country. After the murder of some RTI activists and whistle-blowers, NCPRI members decided to work for an institutional solution. Arvind Kejriwal; eminent lawyer, Prashant Bhushan;

retired Supreme Court judge, Santosh Hegde; and former law minister, Shanti Bhushan were mandated to prepare a comprehensive Bill that would not only protect whistle-blowers but also deter corruption and redress the grievances of citizens. These four brilliant minds sat together and prepared a formidable draft Bill.

This draft Lokpal (later called Jan Lokpal and also the Citizen's Ombudsman Bill)[1] proposed an independent, autonomous body, along the lines of the Election Commission (EC) or the Comptroller and Auditor General (CAG) of India, that would neither be under the government control nor get influenced by it. Besides granting this autonomous body the right to investigate public servants in matters of corruption, the Bill sought to provide for the time-bound delivery of public services via citizen charters; encourage complete transparency in the issuance of contracts, leases and licences; and put an end to insidious forms of favour-mongering.

*

Back in January 2011, when Arvind said, 'Mayank, Maharashtra—especially Mumbai—is really crucial. A lot will depend on you,' I was compelled to reassess my life goals.

The fact was that, around that time, I was deeply immersed in spiritual practice and meditation. Arvind's passionate plea shook my conscience. 'What right do I have to indulge in my selfish desire for spiritual ecstasy and personal evolution, when the country needs my sacrifice?' I questioned.

Here was a country that was angry. People were growing increasingly agitated as corruption stories hit media headlines. One could hear the distant drums of a major 'dharma-yuddh' (a righteous war) against the inimical forces ravaging the country. The time had come to abandon my personal quest and join the battle.

I agreed to take on the responsibility of Maharashtra.

Behind the S.P. Jain Auditorium, seated on a stone ledge, buoyed by steaming cups of coffee, both Arvind and I spoke at great length of our resolve to transform politics in the country. Politics influences policies and decisions. To alter the destinies and lives of crores of our countrymen, we needed to make serious changes in the way politicians got elected and operated. I said, 'All the rot in politics begins with the way elections are fought and won. Our aim should be to bring in electoral reforms. We need to involve the entire country in this yajna, this purifying ritual.'

Arvind had a slightly different approach. 'Mayank, while I agree that electoral reforms are most crucial for the transformation of the country, it might be best to focus on corruption right now. Corruption is what provokes people—they're livid, what with so many scams unfolding. With corruption as our one-point agenda, we will create a massive movement. Once people come together, we can work on electoral reforms, too.'

It made sense. I consented. Then, I raised another important issue. 'I have seen many NGOs up-close. And I am wary of depending on the existing ones for support because many are compromised, corrupt or ineffective. I see real value in directly involving common people in the movement.'

Arvind nodded, then said, 'For our appeal to reach common people, it is important to have leaders these common people can identify with.' I was listening carefully even as evening fell. Arvind continued: 'We have brought together some very popular leaders in the movement already, including Baba Ramdev, Sri Sri Ravishankar and Swami Agnivesh.'

I raised an immediate concern: 'The presence of orange robes—these swamis—might make some segments of the country suspicious. What do you think?'

Arvind took some time and replied, 'That's a valid concern, but they have large followings, and right now we need dedicated numbers. We can see how best to deal with the saffron brigade later.'

As I later learnt, this was typical Arvind's style of functioning—use someone for the short term and start working on his exit parallelly.

I persisted, 'Instead of having multiple leaders, don't you think it will be better to have *one person* as the face of the movement? Collective leadership is good, but someone needs to be first among equals. In addition, such a leader should not be associated with any ideology and should have a reputation for battling dishonesty.'

Arvind looked at me knowingly. 'Who are you suggesting?'

'How about Anna Hazare?' I asked 'I've worked with him, and I know his strengths and limitations.'

Arvind seemed excited. He said, 'Anna is more than familiar with the Lokpal Bill . . . we have worked together a few times on it. But I want to know what your candid analysis is before making him *the* face of the movement.'

I could see that Arvind was seriously considering my suggestion. He was trying to understand my views more clearly, and sought cues not just in my statements and my voice but also in my expressions. Generally, I do not mince my words, but keenly aware that anything I said now would have huge consequences, I spoke in a measured way. Besides, Anna is a complex personality—so it was necessary to share a nuanced assessment, highlighting the good and the bad.

I started with his obvious qualities of great strength. 'For one, Anna is a role model for rural development. I have personally been to his village and have seen the extraordinary transformation he has brought about. Secondly, for a generation that has grown up with the stories of Gandhiji, Anna, with his Gandhian appearance and utterances, is a modern-day icon. Third, he is a very principled man. He has fought and won bitter battles against corrupt politicians, has fasted for the removal of dishonest ministers and officers and has ensured that the guilty get penalized. He is the tallest anti-corruption activist in the country. For IAC, we cannot get a more appropriate leader.'

Arvind concurred.

I continued, 'What I find most amazing is Anna's connect with the people—whether these are common men on the street or the politicians of parties. He has that indefinable quality called charisma, and when he says, "*Dil diya hai, jaan bhi denge, ae watan tere liye*" ("I have given my heart and will give my life for this nation"), I have seen the audience get emotional.'

Arvind smiled. 'This is great. Why did you stop working with him? Is there something that you are not telling me?' He looked at me questioningly.

This was going to be tough. Was I to tell all, or was it best to allow Arvind to discover some things for himself once he started working with Anna?

I hesitated, 'Well . . .'

2. Anna, the Enigmatic Leader

As I paused, Arvind's heart rate must have climbed.

Being honest was the best option. There was no point in hesitating. It was best to present the facts of my earlier interactions with Anna and his team, and let Arvind be the judge.

I started speaking slowly, choosing my words deliberately: 'There are four things that you will have to take into consideration while dealing with Anna. One is that his concepts of democracy, politics and nation-building are simplistic and vague. Second, he is a very stubborn man, and once he makes up his mind it is very difficult to change his views. Third, his style of working is very whimsical. Last, he is easily influenced by the people—many of them questionable—who surround him.'

Arvind likely had personal acquaintance with some of these aspects of Anna's personality, but he continued picking my brain anyway: 'So how do you think we can tackle this?'

After thinking for a while, I continued, 'Arvind, if you wish to get anything done from Anna, you will have to ensure that, at all times, there is one senior person from our side with him . . . this will reduce the influence of his team, and will also appeal to his ego and sense of self-importance. Even this won't be easy. Anna is a difficult man to work with, and has a record of not getting along with anyone over a long time.'

'What about his political affiliations?' Arvind inquired.

I responded, 'While Anna has contacts across the political spectrum, he does not belong to any ideological school.'

'That's good, isn't it?' Arvind asked.

'Yes,' I answered. 'Despite all that I have told you, the good in him outweighs the bad. By far, he is the best person to lead the anti-corruption movement.'

Arvind said, 'I think so, too. Let me go and meet Anna and see what he has to say. And thanks for speaking so candidly. I will keep everything you've said in mind.'

Thus ended our conversation.

On the way back home, I remembered my first meeting with Anna in 2003, much before the IAC movement.

Anna had planned to go on a fast unto death from 9 August 2003. His demand: the resignation of four Maharashtra Nationalist Congress Party (NCP) ministers accused of corruption.

I went to meet him and asked, 'Anna, how will the country benefit if four ministers resign?'

There was something magnetic about Anna even back then. He looked at me with his innocent eyes, and very politely asked, 'So what do you recommend?'

Excited that he was willing to listen to me—someone he was meeting for the first time—I suggested, 'Don't just demand resignations, ask for institutional reforms, too.' Anna was listening intently. I was encouraged to speak further: 'First, you should ask for the passage of Right to Information. Second, ask for an Act that regulates the transfer of government officers by giving them a fixed term. Third, demand reforms for empowering the gram sabha in villages. Finally, seek transparency and accountability in the administration.'

I continued, 'Anna, we all know of the existence of transfer lobbies that charge huge bribes in exchange for plum postings in various departments. The rot has spread wide and deep. Honest bureaucrats are terrified of corrupt politicians who have the power to arbitrarily transfer them. It is necessary to have fixed terms for A-class officials at the very least.'

Anna heard me with his eyes closed. This was his normal style of engaging with a conversation. After I finished speaking, he opened his eyes, grunted, nodded and went silent. I waited for some time for him to speak, but he seemed to be lost in his own thoughts. I left.

The next day, he announced to the press that in addition to the resignation of the four NCP ministers, he was going to demand the four institutional reforms I had discussed with him.

On hearing from the media that Anna had demanded institutional reforms, I was exhilarated. I rushed to meet him to thank him. That's when I was introduced to his small cohort of advisors. I asked them: 'What are Anna's views on the demands? Has he briefed you? Have you worked out the provisions in the Bill? How does Anna see this getting executed? Do you need any help from me?'

His team members seemed amused by my questions. 'Anna does not make Bills or give details. It is for the government to make the suggestions, and Anna will say yes or no,' one of them sniggered.

Now, it was my turn to be incredulous. 'We need to be clear about what we want, don't you think?' I asked.

But the entire lot seemed oblivious to the fact that Anna needed to prepare. The more I interacted with Anna's team, the more I was flabbergasted by their sloppy approach.

There was also the fear that Anna, by accusing ministers from the NCP, was exposing himself. In the corporate world, we were trained to consider all possible forms of retaliation, including defamation suits, and make plans to preempt them. So, I told Team Anna, 'I hope your leader has considered the possibility of repercussions when he makes such accusations.' The team dismissively laughed at my fears. No one had even considered the fallout. I was getting jittery. Were these people smug or plain foolish?

Being new to Anna and his team, I was not able to press beyond a point.

The stage was set for the 9 August fast at Azad Maidan. Anna came with a few hundred villagers and began his fast unto death. There was a lot of media attention, and people started visiting the activist-leader. His popularity was evident even among urban citizens and in the media.

I was fortunate to have learnt my concepts of democracy and reform while working with the highly organized and introspective JP. He was a brilliant IAS officer from Andhra Pradesh, who had worked in high position within the system. After many years of service, he realized that it was better to be outside the system and act as a pressure point for government reforms. I was heavily influenced by his deeply researched, rational solutions to improve the country.

Sometimes, I used to think: if only JP's understanding of governance could be downloaded and transferred to Anna's brain, the nation would really benefit! To make this fantasy a reality, I brought together Anna and JP. On my request, JP stayed back in Mumbai for many days to support Anna and his demands. For hours, the two would talk about the state of the nation, and I would listen to their fascinating conversations, feeling some proprietorial pride.

There was one particularly interesting conversation between Anna and JP that gave an insight into the way they thought.

JP said, 'Annaji, people like you are born but rarely. Instead of working in one village, if you were to take up 100 villages, would it not be better?'

Anna replied, 'I want to make one village 100 per cent, rather than spreading myself too thin and not doing complete justice to my work.'

'But, Annaji, if you contribute 100 per cent to one village, your net value is 100. While if you contribute even 60 per cent across 100 villages, your value is close 6,000—sixty times more,' JP reasoned.

These were captivating perspectives coming from two great leaders. Over time, I came to realize that there were two different schools of thought in civil society.

On one hand was the Anna school of thought which proposed that to change the nation, one had to change people. The belief was this: because systems are made and run by individuals, if people change, then the systems that run the country will change, too.

On the other hand, there was JP's school of thought—he (and others like him) suggested that systemic reforms were the only way to improve the nation. The system had to be designed such that there was an incentive for good behaviour and a strong disincentive to bad/corrupt behaviour. It wasn't civil society's role to change the character of people—that was best left to religion and parents. Civil society's role was to force the system to reform.

I found merit in JP's stance. In my view, India has some of the most wonderful individuals; offers excellent upbringing; and is spiritually inclined. If, in spite of this, our society as a whole is degenerating, perhaps it is because a solid system of checks and balances is not in place.

We have easy proof that this is the missing link. Consider Indians in the Western world: they have been very successful and ethical in nations that come with strong administrative and judicial systems. If Indians were fundamentally flawed, and/or if systems had no influence on behaviour, this stark difference in approach wouldn't emerge.

The fact is that robust systems make people behave in a moral and ethical manner. In any society, no matter the setup, 10 per cent of the population is generally honest, and 10 per cent is dishonest. The remaining 80 per cent behave as per the incentive and disincentive mechanism in place. If success is guaranteed when behaviour is upright, this 80 per cent segment will choose honesty. If the system offers an advantage to those who are unscrupulous, again, this 80 per cent segment will be immoral.

Thus it is my view that instead of changing players, it is important to change the rules of the game. It is a view that JP cherishes, too, and it is entirely possible that Anna's support for the Lokpal Bill, a form of institutional reform, became doubly emphatic after his discussions with JP. 'We are a first class nation with a third class government,' was a slogan Arvind picked up from one of my speeches during the IAC days.

By the sixth day of the fast for RTI (and other provisions), Anna's health started deteriorating. We were mounting pressure on the government to accede to Anna's demands at the earliest. Public pressure was building as well. On the seventh day of the fast, the government relented and its emissaries came to meet Anna. After they left, Anna called me. 'Mayank, the chief minister has asked me for a draft of my demands. Can a few of you start working on the demands that I have put forward?'

Anna's energy was fast depleting, so not a moment was to be lost. We moved promptly. We made a few minor changes to Madhav Godbole's excellent draft of RTI and presented it. We consulted various retired bureaucrats and experts for their thoughts on the other three demands. We submitted the details to the government for consideration as soon as we could.

I thought the government would hotly debate our proposals, but contrary to my expectations, everything was easily accepted—including setting up a one-man commission to look into the charges against the NCP politicians. While I had been prepared to punch a concrete wall, it turned out that we were taking a swing at a cardboard box.

The ease with which the demands were accepted could be linked to the moral authority of Anna and public pressure. But it got me thinking about how governments function. What made the government emissaries accept such tough provisions? Were they too busy to weigh the pros and cons, or did they agree simply because the demands came from Anna? Or did they believe that in the heat of the moment, it was safest to accept the terms, but these could easily be diluted later?

What did happen fairly soon, though, was exactly what I had tried warning Team Anna about. NCP emissaries filed cases against Anna in courts across various districts of Maharashtra, and Anna had to run from court to court, attending hearings. He was incapacitated for years.

During this time, I learnt something about Anna's style of activism. While, from afar, it seemed as though both the government and the band of activists arrived at decisions after deep thought, up close it was evident that the stances were instinctive and often superficial. It was a rude awakening.

The days spent with Anna made me observe him and the people around him closely. While I was very impressed with Anna's indomitable spirit and strength of character, I was equally concerned about the way he clamoured for media attention; his rather simplistic understanding of serious governance issues; and his single-minded focus on himself and his achievements.

The last concern, especially, asserted itself on more than one occasion. For instance, not long after his August 2003 fast, a series of public meetings in Andhra Pradesh were planned with Anna and JP. This was meant to be a precursor to several other joint collaborations among civil society movements. All preparations were done. The media was invited. Thousands of volunteers from the far corners of Andhra Pradesh came to Hyderabad. At the last minute, Anna casually cancelled the programme. His secretary, after multiple frantic calls, told me dryly, 'Anna is not well.' JP was devastated, and I was disappointed. Was Anna worried that JP would get more attention because the venue was Hyderabad? It wasn't an implausible conclusion.

Beyond all this, what also worried me about Anna was

his unpredictability. I recalled an episode involving Anna's desire to come to Mumbai to protest against a proposed amendment to RTI. He and his followers needed a place to stay in as soon as possible. After a lot of effort, I managed to find a large garden-cum-hall. The next day, Anna's secretary called, asking me to get together a large, young crowd, as Anna wanted to lead a youth protest rally. At a complete loss, I hurriedly called up some fellow activists, and we requested a few school principals to urge their students to participate in a rally. It was now time to wait for Anna to arrive. That's when a journalist informed me that Anna had changed the venue of his protest. *What?* I kept making repeated calls to Anna—and was finally told by his secretary that the protest venue had been shifted to Alandi, a town near Pune. No reasons were offered; no notice was given.

I also felt it was only correct to share these episodes with Arvind. Arvind listened, then had a hearty laugh. 'Let us see what happens in the future!' he said.

Well, in the immediate future, Anna and Arvind met in Nanded. They discussed the IAC movement at length, and finally, after many rounds of consultation, came to a decision. Arvind broke this news to me with great excitement. 'Mayank, Anna has agreed to lead the IAC movement. Now, you will have to play an important role—you'll be the bridge between IAC and Anna since both of you are in Maharashtra.'

I turned silent. While I did not want to dampen Arvind's spirits, I also wanted to clarify what I perceived my role as. 'Arvind, I am really happy to hear this. And I am sure that with his magnetism Anna will be able to attract the common people of this country. But I foresee some problems in Maharashtra if I am the "bridge". I know many members of Anna's organization Bhrastachar Virodhi Jan Andolan (BVJA) and have had altercations with them on serious issues of corruption. Also, BVJA considers Maharashtra its fiefdom and will see IAC Maharashtra as a threat to its pre-eminent position. To avoid any kind of conflict, it might best for our IAC Maharashtra team to keep a safe distance from Anna. You need a senior member from the central team to liaise with him.'

Arvind saw my point. And to his great credit, besides personally 'handling' Anna as much as was humanly possible, he gave Manish Sisodia the work of being Anna's shadow all the time.

Sometimes, though, managing Anna got especially challenging. Once, at the Mayur Vihar guest house in Delhi, Anna happened to be upset and locked himself up in his room. An hour passed; then two; then three. Finally, we began knocking at his door and begged him to come out. There was no response. We got increasingly worried. The accommodation was on a higher floor, and finally, one brave volunteer risked life and limb, clambered up some outdoor pipes and reached Anna's balcony. There, he saw Anna sleeping. Anna emerged the next day as though nothing had happened.

It was nerve-wracking.

I have to say this though. Despite all the trouble he gave us, Anna proved to be the appropriate choice. The nation was awakened, having found in Anna a mascot it could hold on to.

3. Who Am I?

As this book has been written in a style that is part-autobiographical, the events have to necessarily pass through the prism of my perspective. Thus it is important for you, the reader, to be acquainted with some of my values, beliefs and experiences.

Growing up in a middle class family in Mumbai—one where my mother Chitraben and father Ramesh both worked tirelessly to make ends meet and bring up three children—I learnt the importance of valuing the little we had. My mother worked as an accountant in a private firm for many years, while my father was involved with textiles and was later an estate broker. Due to some unfortunate setbacks to my father's business, we all had to start earning a living while in school and college. I tutored children and made some money, but it was Bharat, my elder brother, an architect, who took on the onerous responsibility of contributing to the family kitty while studying. My sister Hiran, an architect, too, chipped in by working while studying. This situation is not uncommon—it is representative of many middle class families.

People who have not faced penury sometimes romanticize it, but those who have experienced a dearth of resources know that there is no bigger disease than poverty. Honestly, beyond everyday inconveniences, if poverty is distressing it is because of the indignity and humiliation one is subjected to. I was sensitive to this even as child—and as I grew up, I came to have zero tolerance for arrogance and the assumption that a 'superior' could humiliate someone struggling. In fact, a few months ago, I got off my friend's car only because he was talking rudely to his driver.

I was a bright student, obsessed with reading. There were days when I'd forget to eat my lunch, so engrossed would I be with the stories I came across. My reading list was eclectic—ranging from science and politics to post-independence history and autobiographies, and most importantly, humour. Arun Shourie was a journalist I greatly admired. In fact, there were times when I'd rush to the railway station at the crack of dawn to collect the first copy of the day's paper and devour Shourie's forthright writing—I was such an admirer of his articles against the abuse of power that I could not bear to wait till 7 am, when the paper would get delivered home! Each book, every article opened my mind to possibilities, far from those battles of subsistence, and fuelled my desire to work with a large canvas. *Could I apply my intelligence and ability to transform my great country?* I used to muse.

This desire to propel national change was also shaped by the political leaders I looked up to. I used to enjoy listening to Madhu Limaye, George Fernandes and Atal Bihari Vajpayee, but, by far, the biggest influence in my life has been Mahatma Gandhi. I would spend hours in Mani Bhavan (Gandhiji's ashram in Mumbai, which also held—no surprises here—a library). The simple prose and authenticity of Gandhiji's *My Experiments with*

Truth—and his strength of character demonstrated by his openness, courage of conviction and willingness to accept his faults—touched me deeply.

If my commitment to work for the nation was strengthened, it was because of the events of the 1970s. I was seventeen when the Allahabad High Court disbarred Indira Gandhi as a member of Parliament (MP) and banned her from contesting the elections for the next six years on account of electoral malpractices; the case had been brilliantly argued by Shanti Bhushan. On 25 June 1975, less than a fortnight after the verdict, Mrs Gandhi declared the Emergency. With startling speed, opposition leaders were imprisoned, including Jayaprakash Narayan, Atal Bihari Vajpayee and L.K. Advani. Freedom of the press was muzzled, censorship was imposed and civic liberties were curtailed. As I watched a pall of fear envelope the country, my blood boiled. I had to do something! A young, idealistic student, I would slip away from college lectures and participate in protests, join street plays and liaise with activists. But it was all to no avail . . . the dark days dragged on.

Twenty-one months later, Mrs Gandhi, in a classic case of misplaced confidence, called for fresh elections, released all political prisoners and lifted the Emergency. Four opposition parties—the Congress (O), the Jan Sangh, the Bharatiya Lok Dal and the Socialist Party—decided to fight the elections (and her) under a single banner called the Janata Party.

I started campaigning for our local Janata Party candidate to the exclusion of all else, including my studies. Several ordinary people did. Finally, on 20 March 1977, it was announced that for the first time in independent

India's history, the Congress had been routed; the Janata Party had come to power. Democracy had been upheld. India had won.

It was a moment of ecstasy. But before any of us could bask in the joy of this victory, the Janata government started showings signs of instability. The leaders, unable to rise above their personal and political ambitions, fought like cats and dogs, which finally led to the collapse of the government. The Janata Party's betrayal and its representatives' naked lust for power shook the country—so much so that until the IAC movement roughly thirty-five years later, no one was willing to invest faith in a new set of leaders again.

On my part, I was in agony. As a young crusader, willing to lay his life for the nation, I felt cheated. I wanted to speak out—but I was too young and inconsequential to be heard. Disillusioned, I quit public life, got married, had children and started earning a living. I began my own little initiative.

As a small businessman, I had to get over thirty 'permissions'—some of them monthly, some quarterly and some annually—for conducting my business. Government clerks and officers would harass me for bribes. There were two options before me—fight them and, in turn, get slapped with so many penalties or notices that my business would stop; or succumb and pay them off. I admit, I took the more cowardly route, and justified this to myself by saying that I had a family and workers to support.

Over time, however, I also grew increasingly angry; I longed to fight the system and change it, so that the next set of Mayank Gandhis would not have to confront similar episodes of blackmail.

In the Mahabharata, Duryodhana, the conniving brother, and Bheema, one of the heroes, fought one another for a long period of time, without either coming any closer to a decisive victory. It was only when Lord Krishna showed Bheema Duryodhana's weak spot that the battle could be won by the hero.

Perhaps, all I needed to do was find that elusive 'weak spot' to transform the country. I kept searching . . .

And then, something started happening to me. I had lived in Mumbai all my life; I thought I had grown immune to images of squalor. Yet, suddenly, around the turn of the millennium, I started becoming increasingly sensitive to the scenes I witnessed—each time I'd pass the slums of Dharavi, I'd be moved to tears.

What was happening? I had never been this way. Was the fire within me—one that I had suppressed for many years—reasserting itself?

My growing unease made me start meditating. Every day, in silence, I'd try analyzing the inner workings of my mind.

And one day, maybe a fortnight after I had started meditating, I had a spontaneous spiritual experience—call it a moment of epiphany—that was to alter my life forever. The experience was so ecstatic, dramatic, overwhelming and transformative that words are inadequate to describe it—and this book, in any case, isn't the space to begin trying.

Among the many transformations that the experience spawned, the one that stands out is that I suddenly became absolutely calm—from a 'rajasic' (angry, passionate) personality, I became 'sattvic' (calm, unruffled). The vitriol dissipated, and instead, I was left with this realization—*who am I getting angry with? And for what? Everything is me.*

I have no doubt that spirituality is the source of all my strength and understanding. It also helped me gain clarity, so I now knew how I could serve the nation.

People hold a range of different views regarding how a country can transform. Some say, 'If you improve the judicial system, the nation will be rid of all corruption.' Others say, 'Education is the country's future.' Still others claim, 'Reform administrative systems, and India will become great again.' But I believe that, in a democracy, it is the political leadership that determines the nation's fate. And for the best possible set of leaders, one needs a strong electoral process.

There were two options before me in the path of nation-building. One was to create a people's movement to pressurize the political system to such an extent that it was forced to make changes—after all, if the legislative, executive and judicial branches steer the country, and media (the fourth estate) acts as the watchdog, the fifth pillar necessarily is civil society. It may not have legal power, but it can use advocacy, judicial intervention and mass mobilization to bring change.

The other option was to enter the political arena through elections, come to power and propel such changes from within. For this, a party with a foolproof electoral process was necessary, so that only the most worthy candidates would win, instead of those with dubious criminal records or communal inclinations, selected only because they happened to be 'winnable'. To begin with a clean slate—to ensure, in other words, that elections are won without money-power or a divisive agenda—creating a new party would become essential.

My foray into nation-building began by pushing for

change from the outside. In 2006—even while holding on to my business—I became a part of a group that drafted the Nagar Raj Bill, an urban parallel of the Panchayati Raj Bill, for empowering the common citizens of cities and towns.

Perhaps, a background is necessary. In 1993, guided by the vision of Rajiv Gandhi, the 73rd and 74th Amendment Acts were passed for the devolution of power in rural and urban areas respectively. With the 73rd Amendment Act, the Panchayati Raj system came into existence in rural India, and resulted in a substantial improvement in the governance of villages. However, there was an urgent need to create strong institutions of self-governance in urban India. That's where my group stepped in.

Based on this concept of Nagar Raj, some of us conducted a landmark swaraj experiment in the 2007 Mumbai municipal elections. We selected one activist from each of the thirty-seven polling booths of the Juhu constituency. These activists chose Adolf D'souza as the consensus candidate. With Adolf as our independent contender, we successfully defeated all the strong nominees from mainstream parties, without using money, muscle or a divisive agenda. In fact, for the entire campaign, we had spent just Rs 57,000—most of which had been collected from local residents by passing a plastic bag for contributions.

This was especially significant considering what one was up against. I remember, before Adolf's victory, when I was on the way to our campaign office, I saw a huge rally of cars and bikes, with around 800 people shouting slogans in favour of an independent candidate. I was surprised, as we had not expected him to be a serious contender. It finally turned out that he wasn't. When the results were declared all he got were around 200 votes. Apparently, there were separate rates for campaigning and a separate price for votes. The independent candidate had paid for volunteers to campaign and not for votes.

On another occasion, I tried spreading our campaign across the slums in the vicinity. My colleagues felt this effort was pointless—in their words, 'Most of the votes of the slum-dwellers are bought.' I, however, did not wish to be cynical; I wanted to involve the poor in our experiment. The day I visited the Irla slums near Vile Parle, what I saw startled me. There were hardly any able-bodied men or women at home. Almost everyone had gone campaigning. Those who were left behind were either the aged or children. When I tried announcing the name of our candidate, one well-built man emerged, who I later learnt was the local slumlord. He asked, 'How much are you willing to pay per vote?' I tried to tell him about the shining virtues of our candidate, how he planned to help the locality, and why we were committed to being honest. He laughed uproariously. I slunk away.

After Adolf's election victory in 2007, I quit working for civil society. I was bothered and irritated by petty nitpicking and ego fights. But in November 2008, when I saw Mumbai being attacked by terrorists, I decided that I could not stay away from working for the nation. I re-engaged with civil society.

During the 2009 Maharashtra assembly elections, my team and I tried to create one more demonstrable model of swaraj. Parivartan later worked on a similar prototype in Delhi, and a citizen group attempted it in Bengaluru. This model, in a small way, became the blueprint for

AAP's experiment in the 2013 Delhi elections.

Our candidate didn't win in the 2009 Maharashtra assembly elections—he could not, given the powerful influence of the 4Cs (corruption, communalization, criminalization and caste politics) on electoral results. Mainstream political parties had become experts in manipulating the vote bank by giving the four Cs primacy. The rest were bound to languish.

In the meantime, given my preoccupation with creating a workable model of swaraj, my business had been adversely impacted. My factory shut down due to a worker's strike, and I was in dire financial straits. That's when I got an unexpected call from an uncle who owned a large construction company. He spoke to me about the many dilapidated buildings in the island city of Mumbai, all of which were on the verge of collapsing. Indeed, over the years, many had, leading to the death of countless people. He offered me a job and—impelled by the desire to do something concrete at the grass-roots level, and equally, gain personal financial security—I accepted it. In the days to come, we created a strong and unique redevelopment model for Mumbai on a cluster basis—it was a model that offered a positive and practical solution to all stakeholders.

This was an exhilarating period of my life, as I helped the government frame vital urban laws and policies, even while liaising with the bureaucracy, media entities, non-governmental organizations (NGOs) and the judiciary. On the one hand, I engaged with global giants in the space of architecture and finance; on the other, I had to engage with the local populace and even gangsters.

After hearing a lecture in Shanghai about urban planning in Mumbai, I was offered a place on the advisory board of the Chicago-based Council of Tall Buildings and Urban Habitat (CTBUH), the world's largest not-for-profit body of global urban planners, architects and engineers, some of whom had been associated with such iconic buildings as the Burj Khalifa and Taipei 101. The irony was that I was neither a master planner nor an architect! But I was a fast learner, and soon, I was invited to speak and offer advice on master planning, and especially inner city redevelopment, in multiple countries. A world conference in Mumbai followed, attended by over a thousand top architects and planners from twenty-two countries, with seventy-seven of the world's great speakers. Things were going rather well for me, and I was growing financially stable.

That's when life took a complete U-turn, as it is wont to do. In mid-2010, my uncle expired. Around six months later, Arvind Kejriwal asked me to help him with IAC (and later AAP). For a while I juggled both responsibilities, until one took precedence over the other . . .

Now to go back to what would soon become one of the largest movements in the world . . .

4. Brick by Brick

WITH ANNA ENSCONCED AS OUR LEADER, IT WAS TIME TO start creating a base and a structure for an IAC movement.

Arvind called me and said: 'Mayank, let us start taking IAC to the people. We are planning a major public meeting in Delhi. Why don't you hold one in Mumbai, too? I'll ensure that Bengaluru, Chennai and other major cities follow suit. Gather activists and the media, and explain the need for the movement as well as the Lokpal Bill.'

Organizing a political event in Mumbai is easier said than done. Unlike Delhi which is the political capital of the country, Mumbai is the commercial hub, and it's rare for common Mumbaikars to gather together in large numbers for a political event. Also, while Delhi had large grounds for demonstrations like Jantar Mantar and the Ramlila Maidan, the Mumbai High Court has allowed just one major South Mumbai venue for protests—Azad Maidan. That would soon become our 'karma-bhoomi'.

I reached out to the usual set of activists representing middle class citizens and urged them to attend the meeting we were trying to organize. After hours of persuasion, there were 150-odd attendees. This was the state of Mumbai's civil society at that time—the turnout was inevitably low, and each time the crowd consisted of the same faces!

The challenge, then, was to build a strong and robust base brick by brick. A comprehensive list was prepared of NGOs; trade unions representing disparate interest groups; business cohorts; women's associations; taxi and auto driver groups; and agencies representing tiffin carriers, boot polish workers and coolies. We avoided any organization that was aligned with caste or communal interests. And we avoided political parties.

In addition, there were hundreds of small and medium civil society organizations in Mumbai. I personally called most of the leaders and invited them for a joint strategy meet at a hall in Colaba, Mumbai on 22 February 2011. We were pleasantly surprised when over 100 representatives attended. Even though each had a separate agenda, a common concern that bound them was corruption in the government. As Arvind explained the provisions of the anti-corruption Lokpal Bill, the response was enthusiastic, and a number of questions and points emerged which were systematically addressed. There was excitement all around.

It was my turn to convert the palpable excitement into a coherent action plan. I announced: 'Join us as we all come together to change the face of India. IAC is not an NGO but a platform that gives everyone a chance to participate while retaining our own identity and agenda. IAC has just one mandate: an anti-corruption Bill called Lokpal.'

I continued, 'Do not view this as a small meeting that you have chosen to attend . . . this is the start of a historic change. The few representatives that you see here will soon become thousands and lakhs. The spark will turn into a fire. Come, my friends, and own this new movement. Become its leaders.'

The clarity of our plans and the offer to grant leadership roles got the participants animated.

'In Mumbai,' I went on, 'we will not have a hierarchical structure but a form of collective leadership. Together, let us design a management structure in which each of those who are interested can be a part of the core strategic team, taking on various roles as per their capabilities and inclinations. One will have the freedom to make one's own teams, deliver goals and be accountable to the core strategic team.'

As someone who had worked in a senior position in the corporate sector, I had successfully managed groups consisting of a large number of people. But this was different. For one, as is obvious, there was no hierarchy, no sense of power, status and authority. For another, keeping corporate employees productive, engaged and motivated was not the same as enthusing volunteers. After all, in the corporate world, money, promotions and the fear of losing a job are motivators; what had to spur the IAC movement was passion, love and unbridled patriotism.

As a starting point, we decided the management structure had to:

- Give equal relevance to all
- Grant volunteers the freedom to work in a way they found comfortable (for, volunteers came from different backgrounds and spanned factory workers, homemakers, retired employees and managing directors)
- Offer space to those newly inducted as the momentum grew
- Keep alive the basic principles of accountability, non-violence, a non-political outlook and integrity

- Encourage the emergence of new leaders, especially among the young and women

The core strategic open circle followed the model I had proposed—comprising those who had the time, inclination and vision to deliberate and lead. As and when new volunteers joined, those who felt they could actively contribute could enter this circle, and those who could no longer give of their time could leave—all without too much disturbance.

Once this core circle (sometimes comprising up to thirty-five people) took a strategic decision via face-to-face meetings or conference calls, each member of this circle would volunteer to take up certain responsibilities (organizing events, media management, collecting donations, liaising with the police and the government, etc). Each member would then make his own team—with volunteers in charge of tactical and operational details—and deliver results, even while coordinating closely with the other teams, and keeping the rest of the core circle abreast.

As momentum surged, common people who had previously never shown any interest in the affairs of the nation seemed stimulated and wanted to take part in what appeared to be like a revolution. The organization structure that we had created was able to constructively engage with first-timers who came with a lot of enthusiasm but very little experience. Most significantly, we managed to keep the youth involved by choosing a medium that interested them—be it dance or music or street plays.

A strong, cohesive group in Mumbai had started coming together. The structure was stable, thanks largely to the involvement of an old colleague, ex-IITian Praful Vora, who remained by my side. Meanwhile, at the national level, a twenty-six-member core committee was formed. Unlike Mumbai, the IAC central team followed a hierarchical structure. Besides, most of the members were from Delhi and enjoyed the support of Arvind Kejriwal—except for a few like me who were from outside Delhi, given the responsibility of managing various states.

*

Admittedly, even as the IAC movement grew, there were upheavals and missteps.

For one, there was a growing perception that IAC was anti-minority and pro-upper class Hindus. The national core committee's composition was partly to blame—it was not representative of the country's multiplicity. I have always been against appeasement and tokenism, but if we want a truly national movement, the leadership should, in some way, broadly represent the diversity of the nation. The core committee, unfortunately, did not have any credible Muslim or backward class leader. The few prominent minority leaders who were involved in the early days left fairly soon and kept their distance for various reasons.

The perception that IAC was an upper caste Hindu movement only intensified during Anna's fast in April 2011, where a picture of Bharat Mata stood out as the backdrop of the stage. Given that this picture is often used during right-wing Rashtriya Swayamsevak Sangh (RSS) functions, it created the view that IAC was actually a covert RSS organization. As the movement started expanding, lakhs of Bharatiya Janata Party (BJP) and RSS members began to support IAC, some of whom believed in its anti-corruption principles and some of whom wanted to take advantage of the fast-growing discontent in the Congress-led United

Progressive Alliance (UPA). I was privy to information that the RSS headquarter in Nagpur, in fact, informally approved of their cadres extending such support. I welcomed their participation . . . but with a rider. While RSS members were as much a part of the country as anyone else and were well within their rights to support an anti-corruption movement, it was unacceptable if they attempted to support us as right-wing cardholders rather than as citizens. We made that amply clear.

Concerned that inimical forces could hijack the movement we had so carefully nurtured, we took a conscious decision not to allow political or religious leaders on to our stage. Also, no flag other than the national flag was to be permitted in any of the IAC functions. In spite of this diktat, Sadhvi Rithambara and a few other religious figures did address the public from the IAC stage—this was a mistake.

While I have often suspected that leaders representing minorities and backward classes choose their community's concerns over the nation's welfare, as part of IAC, I wished to reach out directly to those community representatives whose primary interest was the country's well-being. I called Swami Agnivesh and asked if he knew nationalist Muslim leaders from Maharashtra who could join us. He directed me to Javed Anand, an editor of a magazine. Promptly, I asked Javed if he could recommend a few good Muslim leaders. He told me that his primary concern wasn't corruption but communalism—nonetheless, he would try getting back with some names. Two days later, I saw an editorial in *The Indian Express* (dated 14 April 2011) by Javed Anand—he claimed that I was attempting to divide Muslims into categories such as good and bad! I was dumbfounded.

The second issue that kept plaguing IAC was this: while we portrayed a strong and cohesive core committee to the world, there were obvious strains and internal tensions in the meetings. Various leaders were trying to align decisions with their own agendas. There were those who wished to saffronize all pronouncements. Kiran Bedi resisted strongly when any resolution against the BJP had to be passed; the representative of the Art of Living was equally protective of the BJP. Then there were those who were trying to push through a far-left ideology; in their view, leftists were the natural allies of any agitation and Baba Ramdev, Sri Sri Ravishankar and the BJP were inimical to anything worthwhile. Fortunately, Anna, Arvind and I looked at issues subjectively, rather than viewing them through an ideological lens—and perhaps it was because of our concerted efforts that, eventually, no decision was taken based on religion or caste, and all conspiracy theories about IAC (and later, AAP) being in cahoots with the Congress/the BJP/American interests/the Central Intelligence Agency (CIA) dissipated.

The tensions within IAC often escalated as we inducted new members. There's one episode particularly that comes to mind. Medha Patkar was not a part of IAC in the early days, and I tried persuading her to join us given the tremendous grass-roots support she enjoyed. She, however, remained reluctant since she claimed to have reservations regarding IAC's leadership. It took Anna to convince her—he had come to Mumbai, and when I requested him to call her, he did. After an hour-long conversation, Medha Patkar agreed to participate in the IAC movement.

On my part, I talked to Medha about the work I had

been involved with and my desire to remake Mumbai and save the lives of the lakhs of people inhabiting dilapidated buildings. She seemed most appreciative, especially of the inclusive character of the proposal.

Therefore, Medha's response a few days later during a meeting in Delhi surprised me. Out there, someone objected to my participation in IAC because I happened to be a 'builder'. His description of my profession was only partially correct—while I wasn't a 'builder', I had been employed by my uncle who was one.

Arvind very cheekily looked at Medha and asked her, 'What do you think, Medhaji?'

Medha, who just days prior had been full of praise for me, said, 'I have also heard that Mayank is a builder, and we should avoid having builders, businessmen and industrialists in our group.'

Arvind was enjoying the duel. He now looked mischievously at me and asked, 'What do you have to say, Mayank?'

Bemused, I stood up, explained my position and offered to resign. At that juncture, everyone, except for Medha and a couple of others, petitioned me to stay. Arvind also conveyed a clear message of support by asking me to chair the next session.

That's where matters ended, but it brought home some facts. Many activists show a great antipathy towards wealth creators. What's odd is that after denouncing the 'evil rich'—after condemning 'those blood-sucking leeches waiting to deprive the poor'—these precise activists approach wealth creators for donations. It makes me wonder if their hostility is real or phony.

In my view, while it is essential to ensure that the wealth

of the nation reaches the poorest of the poor, there is an equal need for wealth creation. Undoubtedly, the resources in existence have to be distributed well, but the quantum of resources needs increase, too. For national prosperity, wealth creators are essential.

Today, when I work in destitute villages of drought-hit Marathwada, I depend on the support of philanthropic industrialists. Branding people as 'good' or 'bad', based on their class, is immature and, in some cases, diabolic.

Meanwhile, within IAC, the momentum was building. The structure of the organization was almost in place, the support among the people was growing, and the media was covering all things to do with it 24x7. It was time to take the next big step.

5. The First Fast

Every revolution comes with a distinct symbol—be it a logo, a song or a slogan. This symbol articulates the guiding principle of the movement, connects its leaders, and conveys an emotion that captivates the participants. IAC came to be associated with a number of emblems and phrases—including slogans like *Bharat Mata ki Jai* and *Vande Mataram*; the Indian flag; and catchy songs, some of them derivations of popular music. But the symbol of the movement was undoubtedly the 'I am Anna' cap.

The story behind the 'I am Anna' cap is rather interesting! One morning, while meditating, I recalled a scene from the movie *Nayakan* starring Kamal Haasan. In the film, policemen arrive to arrest a hero (modelled after Robin Hood) and ask, 'Who is Velu?' To protect the hero from the police, the entire crowd comes forward saying, 'I am Velu.'

That was my moment of revelation! I proposed we could all write 'I am Anna' on Gandhi caps, and from that day, we all became Anna. The symbol embodied the spirit of our leader Anna Hazare. On wearing the cap, we made the distinct statement that we identified with this Gandhian, with his principles.

An unfashionable, plain-looking cap suddenly became

a style statement! Young and stylish collegians would proudly wear the topi. Early in the morning, one could spot office-goers, boot polish workers in railway stations, the dabbawalas of Mumbai and even coolies wearing the cap. They were all making a proud statement—that they would not tolerate corruption and that it would be disastrous for anyone to seek bribes from them.

*

After the organization's structure was put in its place, the subsequent steps were carefully planned. Key members would speak to each other almost every day discussing the next stage of the agitation. Arvind was driving the protests nationally, taking all decisions after consulting with Anna who was stationed in Delhi. His colleagues from his existing NGO—Public Cause Research Foundation (PCRF)—were in charge of the agitation in Delhi, while I was handling Mumbai. The sober and balanced leader Prithvi Reddy was managing the protests in Bengaluru, and the firebrand Chandramohan (aka Chandru) was in-charge of Chennai. Prithvi, Chandru and I had the responsibility of converting the protests into a mass movement in our respective cities so that IAC, instead of being a Delhi-based movement, became a national one. Since Mumbai is the second-most important city in India (after Delhi) in terms of the support it can garner and the media it can attract, my team had a lot of additional duties.

In the evenings, all of those in-charge of key cities would have a conference call where Arvind would give directions. After that, we would hold a conference call with our strategy circle and deliberate over all the pros and cons of the discussion. The next morning, we would give our feedback to Arvind and finalize the action plan.

IAC was publicly demanding the immediate acceptance of Lokpal. The government was reluctant to accept any such demand from what it called the 'tyranny of the unelected'. Much to the government's surprise, the unelected gathered incredible support from the public; the masses loved the idea of Lokpal, simplistically viewing it as a weapon that would kill the demon of corruption. They perceived the Congress' resistance to Lokpal as an admission of the party's guilt. The daily confrontations between the government and the IAC leaders only helped the support of the general public multiply. For them, we were the heroes fighting a corrupt system.

This was a battle of perception, and we had to work a tightrope, so neither the public nor the government would pull away. The government was adamant. It kept resisting our pleas. So, to highlight the fact that we were reasonable, we eventually lowered the demands we had placed before it—instead of asking relentlessly for Lokpal, we went on to ask for a joint committee, comprising members of the government and civil society, that could draft tough anti-corruption laws. In response, the Manmohan Singh government selected some of its haughtiest spokespeople—Kapil Sibal, Manish Tewari, Salman Khurshid and P. Chidambaram—to publicly 'handle' Anna and IAC. The government couldn't have made a worse choice; all its emissaries sounded arrogant, dismissive and rude, and common people, who identified with us, were at once angered and hurt.

Upset with the approach of the government, Anna finally

decided to take matters into his own hands. He issued a warning that if Prime Minister Manmohan Singh did not constitute a joint Lokpal Committee by March-end, he would go on an indefinite fast from 5 April 2011. Some of the members of the core committee were concerned that we were using the weapon of a 'fast unto death' too soon—surely, a fast was the last resort. But Anna was in no mood to listen. I had seen the power of Anna's fast in 2003, so I supported his stand.

Manmohan Singh chose not to accede to Anna's demand, and the stage was set for a confrontation between the elected central government and its people. This was a serious miscalculation by the government and will continue to haunt it for years. Today, the Congress is only a skeleton of what it was in 2011—and the turning point that led to its downfall was its response to Anna. If only it had understood the mood of the nation!

*

The tiny window before Anna's fast unto death saw frantic preparation; we were at once excited and apprehensive. Volunteers started milling around, soaking in the tension and preparing for the battle ahead. When Anna spoke across TV networks, he proved to be a winner. He touched the hearts of all viewers with his simplicity, open communication and his willingness to lay down his life for the nation.

For the first time in history, we had another tool of communication besides the press and TV channels—one that was probably more powerful and personal—social media. And we had young experts on data management for Twitter, Facebook and online messaging platforms. In the days to come, we managed to trend across Twitter almost every night, with Arvind becoming one of the most followed people. Facebook was used to garner support. And mass messages were sent to the general public.

A door-to-door awareness campaign also began. Local volunteers would distribute 'I am Anna' caps and IAC badges at railway station and inside trains. Awareness rallies were held recurrently.

We also started a missed call service, so those who wanted to support us could simply give us a missed call. This missed call service gave us a huge database of supporters whom we messaged every day with action plans. Our supporters were increasing by the thousands. Feet-on-the-ground were assisted by fingers-on-the-keyboard. I mused that if there were social media during Gandhiji's time, India probably would have secured independence a decade earlier.

*

The month of April 2011 will be etched in the memory of Indians forever. Three days prior to Anna fasting, Mahendra Singh Dhoni had hit the ball out of the park to take India to a historic World Cup victory. Patriotic songs and slogans were heard everywhere. Crowds danced with jubilation, and youngsters painted their faces with the Indian tricolour. The young and old, the rich and poor, people of every caste, religion and gender soaked in the victory. Who could have thought that just a few days later the exact scenes would get repeated?

Come 5 April, and we were ready. Delhi was tumultuous. Jantar Mantar was overflowing with people wearing Anna caps. Everyone was under a spell. Emotional and delirious, strangers would hug strangers and smile as if something magical were unfolding. The media had seen nothing like this, and there was live coverage of the protest almost all day. People across the country were glued to the news.

In Mumbai, Azad Maidan, the designated protest venue in the city, was jam-packed. The atmosphere was unbelievably charged; the policemen stationed at Azad Maidan said that what they were witnessing was momentous. Generally, policemen are known to be at loggerheads with mass movements. But given that our approach was Gandhian, they had little reason to be harsh. We involved them with our protest plans, liaised with them regarding venues and timings, and they, in turn, helped us in every way they could. In fact, one of our slogans went: '*Yeh ander ki baat hai, police hamare saath hai*!' ('Let me tell you a secret, the police are by our side!')

The day Anna was to begin his fast, Azad Maidan played host to a number of passionate speakers . . . and then, it was my turn. 'The future is at stake here,' I said. 'This nation cannot and will not accept one more day of status quo. For far too long have we been used and thrown. For far too long have our voices not been heard. For far too long have we been taken for granted. Not any more. We will fight, and we will die fighting till the status quo is changed.'

I spoke my heart out on the stage. I could hear the audience shouting slogans. What I shared was precisely the feeling reverberating across the nation. The hundreds of thousands who were at Azad Maidan and elsewhere across the country were speaking in a unanimous voice. This voice had the unimaginable power to create history.

Ever since I had read about the independence struggle, I had a dream. I dreamt that the citizens of our nation would come together in huge numbers and drive change. I had lived that dream partially in 1977, and had seen quick glimpses of it when people gathered at the Gateway of India after the 26/11 Mumbai attacks. But, somehow, this instant seemed different, bigger and more focused. I was fortunate that I was in the middle of it as one of the key participants. The young and the old, men and women, the rich and the poor, businessmen and the unemployed, were all pursuing the common goal of transforming India.

Anna gave a rousing speech from Jantar Mantar to start the fast, and all of us who were seeing it on the big screen at Azad Maidan had tears in our eyes. After Anna's speech was relayed from Delhi and mine from the Azad Maidan stage, some members in the audience were so moved that they decided to join Anna in his fast unto death. Despite dissuading a number of those old and weak, or ailing, we were left with twenty-four committed citizens in Mumbai determined to join Anna's mission. This included Ratna Magotra, a heart surgeon; a young Naresh Thakur who had quit his job for the movement; the journalist Satish Mishra, among others. All twenty-four began an indefinite fast.

Many other volunteers stayed overnight, tending to those who were fasting. Celebrities we had previously only seen on screen came to show their support, singing and performing for a growing audience. It was like a still from the film *Rang de Basanti*. Here was a celebration of love and determination, compassion and enthusiasm. Here was a gathering to commemorate a new awakened India.

*

In the days to come, Anna lost weight, but continued his fast with dogged determination. Some of the Mumbai participants started showing signs of weakness, and by the fourth day, a few could not even muster the strength to get up. Doctors had to come twice a day to check on them. I asked all those ailing to consider abandoning their fast, but no one would even hear of it. These were ordinary people with extraordinary resolve. They became my heroes.

Also heroic were the large crowds from Delhi and Mumbai, coming together, pressing forward, their commitment never dimming. Within days, we had to expand our management team. From the stage, I would call for volunteers, and in a matter of seconds, there would be a queue willing to take on all kinds of work, including crowd- and media-management. To new entrants, I tried emphasizing the need for discipline and ethics; they responded with great restraint and care, and if ever the fame and attention impacted them adversely, more experienced volunteers would counsel them.

On a few occasions, though, managing this swell of humanity proved to be challenging. Once, we had a huge car and bike rally—it began in the suburbs and was to end at Azad Maidan. I was in the midst of delivering a speech from the stage in Azad Maidan when a senior police inspector came running to me and requested me to rush towards CST Station. Apparently, a group of volunteers had become undisciplined and were lying down on the road, blocking all traffic. I was concerned; it was against our grain to inconvenience the public. I ran to the site and literally saw hundreds of IAC volunteers sprawled across connecting roads, blocking all incoming and outgoing traffic. I had to think on my feet. I hopped on to a scooter parked on the road and started singing the national anthem through a megaphone. Instantly, all the volunteers stood up. They started singing together. Soon, we were able to clear the road.

Every day started and ended with soul-stirring volunteer stories. There was a Shailesh Saraf who took leave from his highly paid job in Hong Kong to join the fast. There was a thief who came to confess that he had stolen valuables from someone's purse and, inspired by Anna, wanted to make amends by donating some money. Stories of this kind kept us going.

During the fourth day of protests, an episode unfolded that I will never forget. We were driving towards Azad Maidan when I spotted a small rally, very orderly, with ordinary people shouting, '*Bharat Mata ki Jai*'. I was baffled. Who were these people? What were they protesting against? I stopped the car and approached one of the demonstrators. I was informed that the rally served as a token of support for the IAC movement. This wasn't a rally we had organized; we knew nothing of it. Perhaps this, above all else, was a sign that IAC had grown larger than its leaders; support for it was now spontaneous and self-driven. From 'our' movement—Arvind's, Anna's, mine—it had become the movement of the people.

*

One of the commonest complaints I've heard is that India's youth have stopped engaging with the affairs of the country, for they're only interested in Bollywood and cricket icons. However, I've always felt differently. I've said in my speeches, 'Why are we finding fault with those who are young? Has our generation given them any national icon they can follow? No. Instead, we have only been quick to blame one another and find fault; our generation has let down the youth of our nation. This is our collective failure. By standing here and working with boys and girls, I am making amends for the follies of my generation.'

The fact is that once young men and women found an icon they could hold on to—in this case, Anna Hazare—they began engaging with the country in full force. They were present throughout Anna's fast. Flash mobs, music, dances, poetry sessions, charged speeches, and mashaal and bike rallies became a part of their daily lives.

On my part, I kept trying to prepare the next generation of leaders by sending them for media bites, panel discussions and TV programmes. The stage *had* to belong to them. And they responded brilliantly. Boys and girls, some of them just teenagers, would hop from studio to studio, speak with rare verve, engage intelligently with TV debates and find the best possible idiom to convey their thoughts. The media appreciated their candour and openness, and viewers, tired of the platitudes coming from politicians, adored the new kids on the block. It was as if the youth were waiting to display their capabilities, and now that they had a chance, they were committed to showing what they were capable of. It was so heartening.

'There is no single leader for our movement in Mumbai . . . in fact, all of you are leaders,' I used to say from the stage. And the fact is, as more young people got involved with IAC, the movement became doubly energetic. Together, we danced, sang and hollered slogans. Together we learnt of the exhilaration that comes with nation-building.

*

As Anna continued with his fast, politicians from various parties became awestruck with the response that IAC was able to evoke. Prominent representatives of opposition parties, including the BJP, promised their support to the Gandhian and volunteered to demand government action. However, as per our internal policy, we could not allow politicians on stage. Thus it was: Anna turned away Uma Bharti and Om Prakash Chautala.

If we were wary of politicians, there was a reason. During a speech, I explained why: 'There was an Italian philosopher in the late nineteenth and early twentieth century named Gramsci, who spoke about "hegemony". When the thoughts of the elite—whether these are politicians or industrialists—willy-nilly become the thoughts of the general public, the rich and influential have hegemony over the poor. What one needs at such times is a counter-narrative.

'This happened during the freedom struggle. In the dark days of British hegemony, common Indians were made to believe that the English alone were capable of helping the nation develop. Then came Gandhiji who offered a counter-hegemonic narrative. He identified the British as looters and reminded Indians that they could be free. That's when the revolution for independence began.

'After independence, for the next six decades or more, the hegemony of Parliament and its politicians became supreme. Common people had one role, and one role alone—to vote the most influential of the lot to power every five years. Now, IAC has offered a counter-hegemonic narrative. It has reminded common Indians that they are more than just voters. They are powerful citizens who can and must get involved in matters of day-to-day governance. These citizens are supreme in a democracy, not politicians. Politicians are just representatives of the will of the people.'

This, more than anything else, was IAC's gift to the people. It reminded them that they had no reason to be submissive or fearful or servile. The roots of a counter-hegemonic narrative were growing deep.

Only six months prior, it would have been unthinkable to consider Anna Hazare, Arvind Kejriwal or me taking on the high and mighty with precision and ferocity—refusing to get cowed down, refusing to compromise, refusing to play footsie. Yet, here we were now, not only at the helm of a mass movement but also coming out of every government meeting to expose before the press the machinations of those in power. Slowly, the relationship between the rulers and the ruled was changing.

One day, I saw a fourteen-year-old child inform a group of policemen that their van was parked in the wrong lane. The policemen obviously did not pay much attention. Suddenly, that small child started shouting, 'Jan Lokpal, Jan Lokpal!' The senior constable looked at his boss, and the van was moved to a designated parking spot. The change in attitude was palpable. There was a complete absence of fear in the common citizen.

I have always loved this line from a poem: '*Sarfaroshi ki tamanna ab hamaare dil mein hai. Dekhna hai zor kitna baazu-e-qaatil mein hai.*' ('The revolution is stirring in our hearts; let's see if our opponents have the strength to confront this.') Probably, for the first time, as we voiced these words in unison, we appreciated its full meaning.

*

Needless to say, the government was taken aback by the tsunami of support for the movement. It deliberated for days over the best response. It offered to set up a committee headed by a government-appointed minister (and not a civil society member) to consider the Lokpal Bill, but we would have none of it. We wanted a *joint* committee. The government then pushed for the appointment of Sharad Pawar as the committee's chairman; Anna issued a strong statement, accusing Pawar of corruption. The government had to beat a quick retreat, and Pawar withdrew his nomination.

As days passed, and media pressure grew, the government found itself battling caught-in-the-headlight panic. The massive upsurge of support brought it to its knees. On 9 April, the government's resistance broke. It was finally forced to accept a joint drafting committee comprising five members from each side for preparing the new Lokpal Bill. Pranab Mukherjee and Shanti Bhushan were announced as this committee's joint chairmen. IAC was the clear winner in this round of the confrontation.

As Mahatma Gandhi's favourite hymn '*Raghupati Raghava Rajaram*' played in the background, Anna appeared on the dais, offered juice to a group of fasting women and then broke his own fast. He spoke about his next course of action to a cheering audience: 'This just the beginning of the fight against corruption. Our responsibility has now increased.'

I was more relieved than happy. As soon as Anna

drank some juice to break the fast, the twenty-four people I was worried for in Mumbai accepted refreshments, too. Each moment of this was covered extensively. History was being made.

As it happened, this was just the start. There would be many more twists and turns in the fascinating confrontation between the people and its elected representatives.

6. Eyeball to Eyeball

FROM OUR END, THE FIVE MEMBERS WHO WOULD BE A part of the joint committee for Lokpal were obvious. They were the four who had drafted the Bill in the first place—Arvind Kejriwal, Prashant Bhushan, Santosh Hegde and Shanti Bhushan. Anna, our leader, was the fifth. Unlike Anna, who only understood the broad principles of the anti-corruption Bill, the others had worked on the draft Bill and thus knew the tiniest of provisions in Lokpal; they recognized what was non-negotiable and what wasn't. There was little reason for them to prepare; they had done their research, were well-versed with every clause and were ready to confront the government.

However, I remained worried. Given that the government's emissaries included shrewd lawyers and politicians like Kapil Sibal, P. Chidambaram and Salman Khurshid, I feared that they would outwit our naïve activists. I was proven wrong—I overestimated the astuteness of the government's representatives and underestimated the street-smartness of Arvind and the legal acumen of Prashant Bhushan.

Soon enough, the government's men looked like amateurs before our team. They tried to browbeat the IAC members, but it was all in vain. We turned the tables on the government every single time—so much so that we even won the smaller clashes. For instance, we asked for video recording of the meeting, which the government shot down. But on coming under tremendous media and public pressure, it finally had to make its peace with an audio recording.

Battles are never fought on the streets or in boardrooms; they are always fought in the mind. And by our side, we had the master of mind games—Arvind Kejriwal. Here was an expert manipulator of opinion. I have never seen or heard anyone with such extraordinary skills.

For one, he ensured that the committee's debates remained combative. Rabble-rousing issues were raised by the activists such as the inclusion of the prime minister, the higher judiciary and the lower bureaucracy within the ambit of Lokpal. If the government hesitated or refused a suggestion outright, the implication was that it had something to hide.

Concurrently, Arvind ensured that the debates were covered by the media. Kapil Sibal would constantly ask IAC members not to disclose the goings-on within the draft committee meetings. But Arvind refused to pay heed—he'd address the nation and give the IAC version of what had transpired inside. When asked why he'd broadcast closed group meetings, he'd assert that he was a representative of the people and it was his duty to keep them informed. Back then, I was inspired by what I thought highlighted his genuine commitment to transparency. However, when I tried adopting the same principles of transparency and accountability in my later dealings with him during the 2015 National Executive meeting, the results were disastrous. But I'm getting ahead of myself.

Arvind's media strategy not only ensured that the ruling government seemed inept but also consolidated the support coming from the people. To further strengthen his base, he'd make sure that each evening all of us were in various media studios explaining the technicalities of our proposals and the government's stance. Viewers loved this, identifying themselves with us, and cheering each time we won a point against a seasoned politician. If it ever became obvious that a politician was resisting Lokpal because he was terrified of getting imprisoned, the average citizen's anger would make itself evident.

Our working style had a definite routine. After internal meetings, the leaders of key Indian cities would listen to the press statements coming from both sides, then speak to either Arvind or Prashant Bhushan for clarifications, quick briefings and cues on how to engage with media debates. Then, each leader would brief his team. At night, the TV debates would begin. *Times Now* was one of my favourite platforms. Arnab Goswami, the anchor, would direct pointed questions at Congress spokespeople—the poor Sanjay Jha, in most cases—then gesticulate to me off-camera to attack them. Almost always, I, and other representatives like me, would emerge triumphant.

Arvind also knew how to use maxims to his advantage—one of them being, 'Politics is the last refuge for scoundrels.' He made allegations against the most powerful leaders in the nation, sometimes flashing the flimsiest of documents as evidence. The media would cover this, having secured its headlines for the day; the public, willing to believe the worst about politicians, accepted the news as fact. The anger only sky-rocketed. Since the wheels of the judiciary move slowly, IAC had a convenient fig leaf. Whenever accused of shooting-and-scooting (making wild allegations and vanishing), Arvind would say that he could not even consider filing a case against a minister or a politician given how time-intensive the process was; he asserted that his aim was to place corruption cases before the court of the people—thus creating more anger. This is how the seeds of a revolution are sown.

Arvind also recognized the importance of Anna. While Anna did not understand the intricacies of the Lokpal Bill, his political sense remained extraordinary. He knew the mood of the nation, and like an expert musician he pulled the right strings. Every speech of Anna's entered straight into the hearts of the people.

Internally, some of us guessed that nothing substantial was going to come out of the deliberations of the joint draft committee. After all, we had made demands that no government would be able to accept. On my part, I suspected that Arvind wanted a much bigger change in the country. For him, the Lokpal movement was a launch pad for revolutionary reforms in the country. Neither Anna nor most of the key IAC leaders nor the politicians and the public realized this aspect of the movement. I, however, did see this pattern in every move that Arvind was making. Each gesture was rooted in the moment, but its impact was also meant to be long-term.

Just as we had anticipated, the joint committee collapsed, given the intractable differences between the government and the activists. We had a quick chat on the phone with the core committee, and Anna declared that 16 August would be the beginning of the next phase of his protest. He'd start another fast unto death.

*

I am convinced that above and beyond the strategies we built, it was the foolish manner in which the government handled the movement that made it so successful. In one of my speeches, I said: 'Let me reveal the names of those who have contributed to the tremendous growth of the movement.' The crowd was all ears, expecting a mention of Anna or Arvind or Kiran Bedi. Instead, the first name I dropped was 'Kapil Sibal'. I followed that with 'Manish Tewari', the Congress MP who had once insulted Anna.[2] Then came 'Salman Khurshid'. By now, the audience was rolling with laughter.

The way the Congress responded to this popular movement was a lesson in how NOT to tackle popular uprisings. Some Congress leaders on national television would mock Anna or the movement as a whole. At such times, I'd be compelled to say, 'Every time Kapil Sibal, Manish Tewari or Salman Khurshid open their mouths, the membership of IAC increases by the thousands. We need to thank them for their support.'

I sometimes used to wonder, if Rahul Gandhi had visited Anna and said, 'Annaji, I agree with you, corruption has become a menace. We are willing to listen and consider the steps you propose to help the nation. Please guide us'—what would have happened then? History would have changed. The movement would have fizzled out, and Rahul Gandhi's stature would have spiralled skywards. But since the young Gandhi has lived in an ivory tower, surrounded by sycophants, the idea likely did not even occur to him or his acolytes.

*

Swami Agnivesh had wished to become a member of the draft committee from our side, but many of us were not comfortable with him. While he certainly had an impressive résumé—he had worked for the downtrodden in Haryana; he had flirted with politics as a member of the legislative assembly (MLA)—my personal meetings with him left me feeling wary.

One day, a senior volunteer called me and said, 'Mayankbhai, I had gone to the Taj Hotel in Delhi. There, I saw Swami Agnivesh enter a room to meet Kapil Sibal. I kept vigil, and after over two-and-a-half hours, both emerged with wide smiles. Why is Swami Agnivesh meeting Kapil Sibal while the joint drafting committee meetings are on?'

I did not have an answer. It could well be that they had a personal association . . . but in the midst of such a major political battle, it was only right for Swami Agnivesh to keep his distance from those trying to discredit the IAC movement.

The next day, I went to Delhi for a core committee meeting. I travelled with Arvind in his car, shared the information I had received, and asked if Agnivesh had informed IAC about his encounters with Sibal. Arvind informed me that while Agnivesh hadn't come forward with any information, he had also heard similar rumours from other quarters. In fact, a few days prior, when Swami Agnivesh had left his phone unattended, a clever volunteer had checked his call history; he spotted multiple calls to Sibal.

I was asked to confront Swami Agnivesh in the core committee meeting held at Prashant Bhushan's house. As soon as the meeting started, I innocently asked, 'Swamiji, we know that you are in close touch with some senior leaders of the Congress. As a key member of the IAC movement, have you informed the core committee about the purpose of these meetings?'

Swami Agnivesh seemed flustered. Then, he began yelling, trying to defend himself. His body language was like that of a child caught with his hand in the cookie jar. He claimed he had personal work with Sibal.

'What sort of personal work?' I persisted. 'You should have avoided meeting him at this crucial juncture. And if you had to have such meetings, it was your duty to inform us.'

Arvind Kejriwal, Manish Sisodia and others joined the row and challenged Swami Agnivesh. They asked him to quit the core committee.

Anna was silent. He seemed lost in thought. Finally, when the commotion began dying, Anna raised his hand. Everyone turned silent. Anna said, 'Swamiji, what you have done is not right. However, because you have been our colleague for a while, we will give you one more chance.' It was a Gandhian gesture. I appreciated the fact that he chose the path of forgiveness. Unfortunately, Anna's offer proved to be far too generous.

Towards the end of August 2011, during Anna's Ramleela Maidan fast, Swami Agnivesh was caught on tape talking on the phone to Kapil Sibal. He was saying (and I translate): 'They've become mad like rampaging elephants. The more the government concedes, the more adamant they become. No more ground should be conceded. What they're doing to the government is not correct. I'm ashamed.'[3]

The stakes on both sides were very high. The Congress

was able to find a mole within our movement, and we were able to identify and remove him . . . but not before feeding him a fair amount of false information. Ever since we had grown suspicious of Swami Agnivesh's leanings, we had started throwing the spotlight on irrelevant subjects, granting them more prominence than they deserved. Swami Agnivesh would listen carefully. The next day, inevitably, we'd find the representatives of the drafting committee with copious notes on the immaterial issues we had leaked. The government representatives would tie themselves up in knots arguing over these petty points, while much to their chagrin, Arvind would gloss over them. Strike and counter-strike.

*

I have to say, of all the core committee members, Arvind was the most unaffected. Once, past midnight, when I reached Prashant Bhushan's Mayur Vihar house—a house that was used frequently by our volunteers—I saw Arvind sleeping on the floor on a thin bed sheet. He woke up and welcomed me in. I asked, 'Arvind, where do I sleep?' He patted the bed sheet by his side and said, 'Come, sleep here.' The whole night, I tossed and turned; I was unused to sleeping without a mattress. Arvind, on the other hand, slept peacefully.

On another occasion, when Arvind came to stay in my small house, his approach was similar. When the toilet ran out of water, Arvind filled buckets from the adjoining bathroom and carried them across. Not once did he complain or expect others to come to his assistance. It was as though he was beyond the small inconveniences of everyday living.

Not surprisingly, logistics did not preoccupy him. Once, when IAC was in the midst of planning a major protest in Delhi, I told Arvind, 'You're asking thousands of people to come to Delhi from all over the country . . . that's all very well, but how will we arrange for their stay and food?'

Arvind dismissed my concerns. 'Arrey, what is the big deal? We will sleep on the road outside Ramlila Maidan. Let everyone buy food from vendors. This is not somebody's wedding . . . these are people coming together for the country.'

*

In the early days of the movement, I especially cherished my conversations with Arvind. He had very strong views—most palatable and some not. For instance, when I hinted at the fact that our movement had to create and nurture a new generation of leaders, he vehemently disagreed: 'Don't waste time cultivating leadership . . . leaders are born, not made.'

On another occasion, when we were discussing the need for reforms, I intervened: 'How do we get reforms accepted? In my view, there are three routes: judicial intervention, advocacy and mass mobilization. And the last is especially effective. When all five pillars of democracy—the legislature, the executive, the judiciary, the media and civil society—are ineffective or corrupt, the only answer is awakening and empowering the people of the country . . . especially the youth.'

Arvind interrupted, 'Mayank, I appreciate your thoughts. But it isn't easy to mobilize people. More often than not, they are plain apathetic.'

'Well, there is our target audience,' I said. 'Our duty is to shake off their apathy. It may not be easy . . . but nothing worthwhile is.'

These were the moments—pure and unsullied by power—that kept motivating me. What also helped was that, during the IAC days, Arvind and I were in sync; our views and strategies were aligned.

That said, it was interesting to watch how the leadership team operated. Our core committee meetings in Delhi came without agendas; a plan of action was almost never circulated, and if it was, it was never followed.

These meetings were fast becoming an 'Arvind show'. Since he had no patience for processes, he would ask some of his loyal foot-soldiers to raise those issues that needed resolution. While the overt aim was to have a discussion, the underlying purpose of the core committee meeting was to secure a stamp of approval on whatever Arvind wanted. To ensure this happened, he'd very cleverly lead the subject to the outcome he wanted and then throw a loaded question at Anna. Anna was generally lost in his thoughts while the meetings were on. He'd shake himself out of his reverie when he'd hear his name being called, and after thinking for a while, give his approval. In light of this, a press note would be drafted inside the meeting, read out aloud and approved. A few members would then go outside to meet throngs of journalists and present the resolution before the nation.

Generally, Kiran Bedi, Prashant and (in the rare case) I were the only ones trying to counter a point Arvind wished to push through. Admittedly, as I've already mentioned, Kiran Bedi viewed all things from the perspective of the BJP, trying to scuttle or postpone anything that could hurt the party's interest. But Prashant Bhushan had no personal agenda. His observations were always sharp and thought through, and his opposition would be on technical grounds.

Arvind, on his part, had a very loyal supporter in the core committee named Naveen Jaihind. He came with bull-like aggression. He attacked or shouted down anyone who came in the way of his leader's view. Later, Jaihind's services would be used by Arvind to corner Yogendra Yadav in Haryana.

The fact is that Arvind had started creating a small coterie. These inner circle members came with one agenda alone: proclaiming their loyalty to their leader. Arvind used them skillfully to outmanoeuvre his adversaries. In return, they were allowed to remain close to the power center. Be it Manish Sisodia or Sanjay Singh or Durgesh Pathak or Dilip Pandey or (more recently) Ashutosh—none of them would say anything that was not engineered by Arvind. He was the puppeteer.

*

During core committee meetings, something rather strange came to our notice. Even while meetings were in session, news headlines would flash revealing the details of the discussions. Clearly, someone within the room was leaking information!

On one occasion, we submitted our mobiles for inspection . . . but to no avail. Shazia Ilmi teased that news leaked to such an extent that we could ask *The Indian Express* to draft the minutes of the meeting. I jokingly suggested getting a plumber to stop the seepage.

After a few meetings, I decided to solve the mystery myself. I started observing the behaviour of those present in the room and began developing a hypothesis. The proof to support it came much later . . . and this will be explored in another chapter.

Meanwhile, 16 August was fast approaching, and we knew that it would be a defining moment in the history of our country.

7. 16 August 2011

AUGUST 2011: IT SEEMED LIKE WE WERE AT THE CUSP OF something momentous. All of a sudden, the work I was involved with to earn a living seemed superfluous. My heart wished to involve itself with the cause of the nation. I had to choose; I could no longer balance both worlds.

One day, Arvind was in Mumbai, and both of us were travelling together by an auto-rickshaw through Aarey Colony in Goregaon. I shared my thoughts with him. 'I'm finding it hard to juggle work and IAC. I think I should quit my job. What do you say?'

Arvind simply concurred, 'Quit your job.'

An important life-changing decision . . . and yet it happened so naturally, as if someone up there was choosing for me. There was little analysis guiding the decision; there was no attempt at chalking out the pros and the cons. I did not have a bank balance, my children were studying, but none of these practical concerns deterred me. When my family learnt of my decision, it stood by me like a rock. My wife Minal told me, 'You do what you think is right. We are all with you. Maybe this is God's signal, it is *He* who will look after us.'

I dispatched my resignation letter to my company on 12 August. It was four days before Anna's fast. I was free.

Unlike the hundreds who quit their jobs, moved as they were by their emotions, I remained absolutely unemotional. I was convinced that a force beyond me was determining the flow of my life, and I just surrendered to it. I have always held that while the trigger for a decision can be the heart, the bullet should be guided by the head. In other words, while emotions can motivate certain decisions, the action should be objective and thought through. Now, this approach would hold me in good stead.

*

A special core committee meeting was convened to prepare for the now-or-never fast. An elaborate and detailed plan was prepared as a run-up to 16 August, and all major IAC centres were requested to follow this to the T.

In Mumbai, we undertook a series of padyatras to talk to people, distribute pamphlets and screen films on the Jan Lokpal Bill. Soon, we made our big move—we organized the mass burning of a weak and diluted Lokpal Bill that the government had introduced in Parliament. Along with Ralegan Siddhi and Ghaziabad where Anna and Arvind were protesting, Mumbai saw smoke and fire. Thousands of us burnt the Bill, ably supported by sloganeering volunteers and flags-waving demonstrators. When Arvind, then Anna, called, and asked after the mood in Mumbai, I was on the stage. I exhorted the people in front of me: 'Anna and Arvind want to know if Mumbai is ready. Scream your support such that it reaches Delhi!' I held the phone towards the audience, and thousands roared. Mumbai was ready.

On witnessing a people's frenzy, and the growing inferno of Bills, Kapil Sibal—like a supporting actor in a two-person act whose role was to set the stage for the hero's punch lines—said, 'This Bill is Parliament's property. This is an affront to Parliament. Burning copies is bad for democracy.' That offered Arvind the opening he needed. He thundered, 'Kapil Sibal says burning copies of the Bill is an insult to Parliament. We say bringing a sham Bill into Parliament is an insult . . . not burning the Bill.' The crowd hooted with joy.

After our bonfire-protest, we started prabhat pheris or morning walks across Mumbai, waving the national flag and singing patriotic songs. At night, we'd have candlelight and mashaal rallies.

Since the railways are the lifeline of Mumbai—at least eight million people in this city travel by train every day—we would position ourselves outside stations, and people would join us, repeating slogans. One day, with the tacit support of some railway employees, we entered a packed bogey and put up banners inside a train temporarily named 'The Jan Lokpal Express'. The driver used the internal public address system to talk about the Lokpal Bill and its benefits. The idea was adventurous, and it was led by our youth.

During this time, we also started a referendum across all stations asking the general public about their preferences: did they support the government's Lokpal or the Lokpal drafted by us, Jan Lokpal? To my surprise, people not only had a ready answer but also knew about the distinctions between the two Bills. It was a proud moment for me. Thousands of Bills are passed in democracies, without the engagement of the public; what was happening now was unprecedented. Not only did the common man know of the Bill but he was also debating each and every provision.

As for the result of the referendum, it was a foregone conclusion: 98 per cent of those interviewed favoured Jan Lokpal. Soon enough, Delhi, Bengaluru and other cities followed our example, started a referendum, and came back with similar heart-warming results.

The next plan of action was to begin a 'Week for the nation'. Key members announced: 'If the whole country takes to the streets for a week, beginning 16 August, we, the people of India, can force the government to enact a strong Jan Lokpal Bill!' Prashant Bhushan in the meantime appeared across TV screens, explaining the minutiae of the Bill and how it could deter the corrupt. I told the crowd, tongue-in-cheek, 'We are paving a shortcut road from Parliament to Tihar Jail. We might have to conduct the next cabinet meeting in a prison cell if Jan Lokpal is passed.'

*

The government was growing jittery. Just a couple of months prior, it had used force to disrupt Baba Ramdev's huge protest; tear gas shells had been lobbed, and lathi charge had been resorted to. The common man had been outraged, and the Supreme Court came down heavily against the strong-arm tactics of the government.

Now, the government was perplexed and didn't know what to do. It could neither accept the movement's terms nor ignore the anger of the masses. Pushed to the wall, it imposed Section 144 (which prohibits the assembly of more than four people) in Delhi and threatened to arrest anyone breaking the law.

This played right into our hands. Arvind roared, 'The government can crush one Anna, but it won't be able to crush 120 crore Annas. The government can impose Section 144 in one place. But will it impose curfew across the whole country?'

Finally, Anna set the tone for the future: 'A *jail bharo andolan* is going to be the next step after the fast. We will flood the jails in the country.'

On 15 August, through a well-wisher in the Mumbai police force, we learnt that there was an order to arrest some of us to foil the 16 August protests in Mumbai. We scheduled an emergency conference call and informed the core group that it was only a matter of time before Ruben Mascarenhas, Praful Vora, Naga Srinivas and I were picked up.

For the moment, the four of us decided to go underground. We lived with friends. We changed our cell phone numbers and adopted code names so as to continue interacting amongst ourselves and with select fellow supporters. Chandra, Bhagat Singh, Sardar and Mukesh Insurance now stood for Vora, Srinivas, Ruben and me respectively. We made provisions. Late in the night, I sent a message to everyone on my list: 'If Anna gets arrested in the morning, everybody should come to Azad Maidan for a peaceful protest.' To ensure that the demonstrations would not collapse for want of mentoring, I selected a standby team of leaders.

I'm given to understand that attempts were made to track us, but since we could not be found, the idea of getting us arrested was dropped. In the meantime, I warned Arvind that Anna might get detained and that it was best if they prepared a video message from Anna to the media. This was followed through.

16 August dawned. Close to 7.50 am, when Anna

Hazare was about to step out of his Mayur Vihar accommodation, he was detained, along with Arvind, Kiran Bedi and Manish Sisodia. From Chhatrasal Stadium, Anna and Arvind were sent to Tihar Jail. 'This is the second fight for freedom, and this movement will not halt now,' said Anna as he was taken away. The news came in fast and thick.

To make any public movement successful, one of the key requirements is an intransigent and arrogant opponent. Luckily for us, the Congress government was all of this, and foolish, too. This made our task relatively simpler.

As news of Anna's arrest spread, there was an uproar in both houses of Parliament—the opposition supported the IAC movement and was quick to castigate the government for the harsh steps it had taken to curb peaceful dissent. On the streets of the country, protests broke out. Thousands started courting arrest.

IAC released the pre-recorded message of Anna Hazare. 'This is a fight for change,' he said. 'Unless there is change, there is no freedom, there is no actual democracy, there is no true republic, there is no true people's rule. The protests should not stop. The time has come for no jail in the country to have a free space.'

Within hours of this 'second freedom struggle', Anna was released. He, however, refused to leave prison. He chose to remain in Tihar Jail, where he began his fast. For the next three days, television crew and vans gathered outside, while his core team scrambled in, recorded video messages, and circulated these for live broadcast.

In Mumbai, the public began bristling with anger. Slogans rent the air—among them '*Bharat Mata ki Jai*', '*Anna tum aage badho, hum tumhare saath hai*' ('Anna, forge forward, we are with you') and '*Vande Mataram*'. Azad Maidan was packed; sixty-eight people decided they'd begin a fast unto death in solidarity with Anna. A few hundred members of the BJP came to the grounds with their party flags to support the movement; we had to request them to back us as ordinary citizens rather than as members of a political party. As the crowds surged, live TV feed of the fast at Jantar Mantar was cut off at Azad Maidan. The police feared a riot.

The crowds got inflamed, and it was my primary task to keep them disciplined. A lot of people came forward to court arrest. I spoke to the cops and arranged for around forty police vans to take us to jail. I instructed everyone to stand in a queue and enter the vans in peace.

That is when I made a major tactical error. Instead of staying put at Azad Maidan to the end like a captain of a storm-tossed ship, I told the volunteers that I wished to get arrested first. I clambered down from the stage and walked to the police van. The crowd grew tense and began rushing behind my wife and me. All order broke loose; mobs jostled, pushed and shouted. Hundreds of volunteers tried elbowing their way in with me. Some climbed on top of the police van with flags in their hands, screaming. The policemen were on edge; mild lathi charge followed. I saw the crowds bristling; they were turning against the police. I was terrified that things would take a violent turn. To deflect anger away from the cops, I started shouting, '*Yeh andar ki baat hai, police hamare saath hai*'—the slogan we used to voice in calmer times, conveying the fact that the police supports us. This acted as a trigger; the crowds relaxed. Volunteers and policemen recalled that they were compatriots not adversaries. I followed this slogan with the national anthem. Things cooled down.

That day, countless Mumbaikars were jailed. Many of the volunteers, who were released after a few hours in detention, rushed back to Azad Maidan to get arrested. Some got detained as many as four times in a single day. Mercifully, the police destroyed the contact details of most of the arrested citizens—several were young students who would have struggled to get through college or find jobs if Indian penal code sections had been attached to their names. As for me, I was released only late in the evening, perhaps because it was obvious that I would rush back to Azad Maidan and intensify the agitation.

Shortly before I courted arrest, there was an episode that moved me deeply. While I was walking towards the police van, a young constable caught me by my hand. With tears in his eyes, he said, 'Sir, I want to quit my job right now and get arrested with you.' I hugged him and said, 'You are also serving your country in your own way. Do not quit your job, be honest, and serve the nation as a policeman.' The moment epitomized the patriotic zest consuming all those gathered at Azad Maidan.

On the night of 16 August, as I tried to sleep, the scenes of the day kept flashing before my eyes, particularly when the protesters grew furious with the police. We had come very close to mob violence; this went against the essence of the movement. I had not fulfilled my role as a leader, and I needed to make amends.

The next day, my chief aim was to reduce the intensity of the fury. I started a fast to cleanse myself, made a substantially less fiery speech, and tried to focus on the spiritual core of the movement. Bhajans and songs like '*Vaishnav jan to tene re kahiye*' and '*Allah tero naam*' set the tone. Almost miraculously, the atmosphere became less charged with frantic energy. Uncontrolled anger made way for controlled determination. This would be the mood defining Mumbai till the end of this phase of dissent.

*

In the days to come, the movement spread far and wide, inside the country and outside. Millions of 'I am Anna' caps were sold or distributed at no cost; T-shirts reading IAC or Anna were worn to offices; and Anna masks were flashed by young and old.

We had a dedicated team at the central office processing all information regarding rallies, protests and fasts. Each morning, we'd send out messages conveying the day's programme to our eleven lakh strong database of phone numbers. At all times, there was a whiteboard at Azad Maidan which carried details of the events for the next couple of days—this was looked up extensively by the public and the media.

Most significantly, every hour, the media—whether this was the Indian press which was harvesting huge TRPs or the foreign media that remained camped at the capital, keenly aware that history was in the making—got updates and messages about events across the nation. We were told by multiple journalists that this was the most structured and well-managed movement they had ever seen. If the media wanted stories, we had a bouquet of over a hundred to offer at any given time. Channels came to be packed with footage, panel discussions and debates involving young emerging leaders from our organization.

Viewers were enthralled. I personally knew of people who watched news channels for thirty-six hours at a stretch.

Suddenly, saas-bahu serials were passé; the unfolding protest against the political class was far more engaging. It is anyone's guess if the media fared better because of the movement or the movement gained because of incessant coverage. What we do know is this: there was an 80 to 90 per cent increase in the number of news viewers; a 30 per cent increase in the time spent following a news network; and India TV, when it ran *Aap ki Adalat* with Anna and Arvind, had the highest viewership it had ever recorded.

The hunger for high TRPs occasionally led to episodes of fake news. Once, while I happened to be in the middle of a debate at the NDTV studio, my wife (who had accompanied me) started gesturing frantically. After the debate, she told me that one channel (that shall remain unnamed) had a half-hour programme dedicated to a huge fight between Arvind and me. This was odd—since we hadn't fought! I called Arvind up immediately. Apparently, the channel in question had showed Arvind and me standing with our backs to one another, a flash of lightning separating us (a la *Deewar*). Later, I learnt that the channel had orders to show scenes of in-fighting amongst core committee members for extra TRPs, and the channel, at its wits' end, decided to spin a story around the one picture it had of Arvind and me facing in two different directions.

*

It must be said that even in this time of gravitas, there were moments of hilarity. A lot of these moments sprung from the desire of strangers to offer 'advice'—often, advice without any kind of backing. Today, I realize that this must have been the predicament of our cricketers, too; they must have been flooded with messages on how to confront Shane Warne and Shoaib Akhtar.

In the thick of the agitation, we had more calls than I can recount regarding how Arvind, Anna and I could deal with the government or uplift the nation, or why this was a no-win situation. I eventually began asking a volunteer to handle my phone, take calls, and politely ask all those dispensing advice to help with the movement.

This soon became my favourite joke:

Q: How many Indians does it take to change a light bulb?

A: 500. One to change the bulb, forty-nine to just stand and watch, fifty to make suggestions, and 400 to tell him that it cannot be done.

One day, a gentleman who used to work with Air India told me on telephone that he wished to meet me. Since he was persistent, despite everything I needed to look into, I took time off to see him at a coffee shop. He said, 'Mayank, the only reason our nation is poor and weak is because we eat paani-puri.' This was unexpected; surely I had heard him wrong. Innocently, I asked, 'What did you just say?' He continued, 'I've lived in America for a while, and people there are happy and healthy because there are no paani-puri stalls. If our country bans such vendors, we could become the greatest nation in the world.' I had tears in my eyes.

On another hectic day, I got a phone call from a new Ghatkopar-based volunteer. He wanted my help. I asked him what the problem was, anticipating a crisis in the suburb. He said, 'The problem is that I have a *batak ki aatma* (the soul of a duck) trapped in my body.' Amused, I asked him what I could do besides offering bread crumbs. He missed the joke.

*

Azad Maidan is in South Mumbai where the city's main businesses are located. When the protests erupted, several office-goers began visiting during lunchtime and post-work. Students and homemakers, on the other hand, didn't always make their way there—after all, they lived a long way off, in the suburbs. In order to reach out to them, we would, on alternate days, hold rallies outside the fringes of 'town'.

By now, our ambition had grown; we wished to take the agitation to the far corners of Mumbai. Images from Tahrir Square, where 50,000 people had gathered, flashed before my eyes.

To make that scene from Egypt a reality in Mumbai, a group of young volunteers and I met for a cup of tea at Kyani's. We discussed the fact that Delhi was the epicenter of IAC—almost everyone popular in the core team was stationed in the capital, including such charismatic leaders as Anna, Arvind, Prashant Bhushan, Kiran Bedi, Medha Patkar and Kumar Vishwas. 'The young leaders of Mumbai are equally capable,' I told the group. 'Why don't we prove that the support of the average Mumbaikar is second to none?' The challenge was accepted.

Our aim was to bring Mumbaikars, whether they were in the suburbs or elsewhere, out of their homes—this was not going to be easy since we would soon be in the middle of a festival. However, we persisted. To the large database of eleven lakh people, we sent out emotionally charged messages, urging Mumbaikars to match Anna's (now) six-day fast with a six-hour rally. Volunteers also met the heads of churches, temples and mosques, and requested them to spread the word.

I was confident of my team and my delegation skills as I flew to Delhi for a meeting with the core committee. I told the leaders in Delhi that in my city, we anticipated a gathering of one lakh citizens. Everyone was sceptical. At 4.30 pm on 21 August, 20,000 Mumbaikars gathered at Bandra station, chanting anti-graft slogans. In the next one hour, the trickle turned into a deluge . . . over 1.5 lakh citizens began marching towards Juhu Circle, in what was perhaps the city's biggest ever apolitical public rally. The Western suburbs were brought to a grinding halt for nearly five hours.

I reached Mumbai at 5.30 that evening, and I joined the huge march at Santacruz. Protesters were blowing conch shells, singing and chanting slogans. Despite the rains, the crowds swelled. Now, over two lakh Mumbaikars marched towards Juhu Circle. Cops tried to divert the protestors at Juhu Beach, but nothing could stop these citizens. Disciplined and dogged, they took over the city's suburbs.

At 7.35 pm, the rally reached its destination, and over the next couple of hours, that junction was completely clogged. Juhu Circle turned into a Tahrir Square, just as we had visualized.

I was atop a truck and about to start speaking, when a junior cop asked me to leave. I requested him to give me fifteen minutes to address the huge, expectant crowd, but he arrogantly threatened us with water cannons. I was surprised; perhaps he was unaware of the mood of the nation. I asked the truck driver to hand me the keys of the truck and leave. From there, I told the people that policemen were planning to disrupt a peaceful demonstration. Lakhs of voices roared at once in disapproval, and before I could complete my speech, the DCP rushed to me and apologized for the behaviour of his junior cop. I was reminded once more: the police force was never an adversary.

Buoyed by Sunday's unprecedented turnout, the next day, we gheraoed the houses of eight MPs across Mumbai, Thane and Navi Mumbai. We asked them to tender a response to the Lokpal Bill. 'They owe us an answer . . . after all, they are our representatives,' we said to journalists. 'Our volunteers will camp outside the houses of MPs till they get answers.' Some MPs managed to run away, while others professed their support for our cause, even though this went against their party line.

Back at Azad Maidan, two senior members of IAC had begun carrying a tin container with a slot, into which people could donate both by cheque and cash. Every evening, we would count the money in public and announce the sum. After two-and-a-half days, we had enough to pay for the stage and other miscellaneous expenses that go with organizing an event of this scale. We subsequently hoisted a banner announcing that we needed no further money.

The fact is that a public movement and financial propriety go hand in hand. Such care alone builds faith. As leaders of a large movement, we viewed ourselves as trustees of the donations being collected, and every rupee had to not only be accounted for but also spent with great care. Our inspiration remained Mahatma Gandhi, who used to meticulously write his expenses every evening in his diary.

IAC and AAP remained credible as long as they were transparent about the collection and utilization of public funds—going so far as to display the entire donation list on the website. The downward spiral began when the website removed the list.

*

Anna was shifted from Tihar Jail to the Ramlila Maidan in New Delhi on 19 August. Arvind had been released as well.

As Anna's fast slipped into its seventh day, his health started failing. The government grew increasingly concerned because if anything untoward happened to Anna, it would be disastrous. They started negotiating the terms and conditions for the Jan Lokpal Bill. Arvind and most others, including me, did not wish to make compromises, at least vis-à-vis the key deliverables, because we knew that if we held our nerve, the country would get a foolproof anti-corruption law.

By the tenth day, Kapil Sibal and Chidambaram started accepting some of our key conditions, but it was not enough. While we put on a show of extreme bravado, internally we were tense. In a tent behind the Ramlila stage, we would discuss all developments, sometimes up to ten times a day, and debate whether it was best to continue the protest or stop it. It was a tough call. If we accepted anything less than what we were demanding, we would never ever get another opportunity of this kind, and the nation would lose out. And if we held on, Anna's health could collapse. It was like walking on a razor's edge.

We knew we had to take a decision, and no matter what it happened to be, it would have a huge impact.

Most of our leaders had never had so much responsibility. Every meeting proved to be tumultuous with participants shouting, wanting to put across a point. There was so much at stake.

Each leader responded differently to stress. Arvind was like a yo-yo, with huge mood swings—angry one moment and emotional the next. True to his style of leadership, he started making plans to trim the existing core committee and bring in more loyalists. Kiran Bedi, on her part, hovered around Anna, a keen devotee. She was quick to praise his thoughts, sometimes even before he enunciated them. Others were oscillating between differing options, unsure and on tenterhooks.

In the meantime, Anna's BVJA colleagues began expressing strong worries about Anna's health. They conveyed to him that his IAC colleagues were just not concerned about his well-being—our one-point agenda, they claimed, was getting an unaltered Jan Lokpal Bill passed. A wedge started developing between Anna and IAC.

Vilasrao Deshmukh, a minister in the union cabinet from Maharashtra, was an old friend of Anna's. He was contacted by BVJA to arrive at a settlement, so Anna could break his fast. That is how he emerged as the link between the fasting Gandhian and the Prime Minister's Office (PMO). Deshmukh was informed of Anna's three key demands: a citizens' charter for the redressal of grievances, a move to bring the lower bureaucracy under Lokpal, and the setting up of Lokayuktas. (If Lokpal is a central governing body that has jurisdiction over all MPs and central government employees for corruption cases, Lokayuktas are meant to function similarly at the state level.) Deshmukh was informed that if these conditions were accepted, Anna was prepared to end the fast. He took on the task of communicating with the prime minister.

Twelve days into Anna's fast, Union Minister Vilasrao Deshmukh handed over a letter from Prime Minister Manmohan Singh conveying Parliament's acceptance of the demands. Anna could finally end his fast. On 28 August, he accepted a glass of tender coconut water mixed with honey from two girls, one Dalit and one Muslim, Simran and Ikrah. Vilasrao Deshmukh—one of the fifteen ministers listed by IAC as corrupt[4]—stood next to him and sang the national anthem. There was tremendous heartburn in the IAC camp.

As an insider, I could see that things were not going well within the organization. The distance between Anna and the rest of the IAC leadership was widening. Things were soon to go further downhill.

8. The Aftermath

AFTER A 288-HOUR FAST, IT SEEMED AS THOUGH THE people's Parliament had emerged stronger than the Indian Parliament. We were confident that we had won the Lokpal Bill issue; what remained to be done was merely a matter of procedure.

Anna set the tone for the future. Taking his eyes off Lokpal, he raised the twin issues of the decentralization of power and electoral reforms. 'Corruption has increased today because of centralization of power,' he said. 'True democracy will come only from decentralization of power, which will in turn come from power reaching the hands of the people.' He added, 'Corruption will reduce only when the election system changes . . . tomorrow, even if the government agrees to the entire Jan Lokpal Bill, we are not going to keep quiet; we will continue to agitate till a change comes . . .'

*

Anna is a leader with great tenacity. In fact, Dr Naresh Trehan, who examined Anna after the fast, confirmed that Anna, as a seventy-four-year-old man, had remarkable control over his body. 'Medical science may not be able to fully understand this,' he said, 'but truly he has managed to live on his reserves.'

Therefore, when a determined Anna commented on the possibility of electoral reforms—a cause I am passionate about—I was convinced that we were on the right path. Besides, I was aware that even if the Lokpal Bill was passed in its totality, it would resolve very few of the issues confronting the country.

My belief remains that incremental or cosmetic alterations in the system of elections are insufficient; there has to be a significant shift. While 'none of the above' (NOTA) or the right to recall could have some impact, transformative reforms need to be addressed. For instance, there must be a serious debate about whether the existing model of first past the post (FPTP) can be replaced by proportional representation (PR). Let's understand these terms: PR is the idea that seats in Parliament should be allocated so that they are in proportion to the votes cast; FPTP, on the other hand, aligns itself with the rather simple principle that the candidate with the maximum number of votes wins.

Clearly, FPTP comes with its share of problems. For one, it disregards a sizeable number of votes. Think about it: if one candidate wins 3,50,000 votes and the other gets 3,50,001 votes, then there is little regard for 3,50,000 votes and voters.

Second, it encourages candidate-centred voting. The politician who gets just *one more* vote wields disproportionate power. Consequently, FPTP brings with it a desperation to win elections, using all means, fair or foul.

Last, parties win a disproportionate number of seats under FPTP, which is detrimental to the interests of a democracy. In 2014, the BJP swept to power with 282 seats (out of 543), i.e., 52 per cent of seats with only

31.3 per cent of the votes. In 2004, the Congress came to power with just 26.5 per cent of the votes; and most ironically in 1999, the BJP came to power despite getting a vote share five percentage points lower than that of the Congress. This is an insult to the Indian voter and detrimental to a democracy.

Now, unlike FPTP, PR recognizes every vote. In multilingual, multi-religious countries like India, it is sensitive to diversity, ensuring that all sections are fairly represented in the election. It has the potential to reduce the impact of money, caste and communal politics, as candidates cease having constituencies where they can purchase votes. Last, parties gain seats in proportion to the number of votes cast for them. Let's consider this through a hypothetical example. Let us assume that the Congress, the BJP, the Bahujan Samaj Party (BSP), and the Trinamool Congress stand for elections. Depending on the number of seats they contest, they make a list of their own candidates, all selected democratically by the party members. Voters will vote for a party, and based on the percentage of votes gathered, candidates are selected on a priority basis for Parliament.

In the 16th Lok Sabha elections, let's compare how parties were represented under the FPTP model, and how Parliament would have looked if PR had been adopted. The results are startling!

16th LOK SABHA AS PER FIRST PAST THE POST

Name of the Party	*% of Votes Received*	*Seats*
Bharatiya Janata Party	31.3	282
Indian National Congress	19.5	44
All India Anna Dravida Munnetra Kazhagam	3.3	37
All India Trinamool Congress	3.8	34
Biju Janata Dal	1.7	20
Shiv Sena	1.9	18
Telugu Desam Party	2.5	16
Telangana Rashtra Samithi	1.6	11
Communist Party of India (Marxist)	3.2	9
Others	31.2	63

16th LOK SABHA AS PER PROPORTIONAL REPRESENTATION

Name of the Party	*% of Votes Received*	*Seats*
Bharatiya Janata Party	31.3	169
Indian National Congress	19.5	105
Bahujan Samaj Party	4.3	23
All India Trinamool Congress	3.8	21
Samajwadi Party	3.4	19
Communist Party of India (Marxist)	3.2	18
Telugu Desam Party	2.5	14
All India Anna Dravida Munnetra Kazhagam	3.3	13
Aam Aadmi Party	2	12
Others	26.7	135

This is not to say that PR does not come with its

complications and limitations. But a debate regarding its merits and demerits will ensure that we, as a nation, will arrive at the best possible set of electoral practices. Similar debates need to be had about the advantages of having a presidential form of government as against the Westminster model, and the direct election of the chief minister by the general public rather than by the elected MLAs.

But the most important reform that has to be undertaken is the democratization of all political parties. Internal elections supervised by the Election Commission should be compulsory. The account details and the sources of funds should be made available. I wanted IAC to push for this.

*

While the success of Anna's fast elated the people of the country, the mood within the IAC camp remained somber. For one, fighting the centre was taking its toll. The government has gone all out to divide us. Allegations and counter-allegations were telecast live, and an attempt was made to erode the reputation of several members. Kiran Bedi, Prashant Bhushan and Arvind Kejriwal were served with breach of privilege notice for 'derogatory remarks against Parliamentarians'.[5] Financial impropriety allegations were made against Kiran Bedi. And Prashant Bhushan was physically assaulted for his comments on Kashmir.

In the instance of Kiran Bedi, it was alleged that she either flew economy class or availed of a massive concession in tariff—even while accepting reimbursements for full, non-discounted business class fares from sundry organizations inviting her. Kiran Bedi argued that the money she saved did not benefit her personally but went towards an NGO. While most found this a specious argument, the episode was glossed over since her intent seemed altruistic.

Then, there was Prashant Bhushan who believed that Kashmir was not a piece of land, but represented the people and their aspirations, and that Kashmiris had to have a say in how they wanted to be ruled. In a press conference on 26 September 2011, he said, 'It is my personal opinion that no country or part of its territory can be governed without the wishes of the people with the help of army. This is not in the interest of the country and the people [. . .] I want that the situation be normalized, army be withdrawn, the Armed Forces Special Powers Act be also withdrawn and then try to persuade the people of Kashmir to stay with India. And yet, if the people want, then there could be a plebiscite, and if the people of the Valley want separation, they be allowed to separate.'[6]

I strongly disagreed with his position. But on 12 October, when angry right-wingers assaulted Prashant in his chamber, I felt things had gone too far. I was upset that politics had degenerated into violence.

We called an emergency core committee meeting to discuss Prashant's statement. Prashant explained that he had only aired his personal views on the subject. He was, in turn, advised to watch his comments and only articulate the stances of the movement as long as he remained a senior leader. Deftly, IAC distanced itself from Prashant's view.

*

In truth, we did not need our adversary to wreck us. We

were doing it ourselves. Unbeknownst to outsiders, the core committee team was under great stress. What was to be a moment of great joy was now turning into a battle of personal egos. Instead of consolidating our victory, we were trying to salvage the unity of the group.

Fissures between Anna and the IAC movement were only expanding. Anna's team had been working assiduously on the leader's mind, waylaying him with false stories. Every passing day, Arvind would receive unpleasant news from the Anna camp—this would rattle him to such an extent that he'd call me as late as 2 am. He'd need someone to discuss developments with or simply vent.

Then, there were fissures within the core group itself. Now that the members thought that the single-point agenda of Lokpal had been achieved, they wished to exploit the mood of the nation to serve their own agendas. Each was marking allies and adversaries in the group. The air was charged with mistrust.

Until now, IAC core committee meetings had been 'Arvind shows'. However, soon after Anna ended his fast, in one of the first internal meetings, things were different. Arvind sat silently, interrupting but rarely. Each of us could sense the gloom. India may have been optimistic, but the room was ominous. Anna refuted almost any suggestion that Arvind or his team made, while Arvind grew increasingly sullen. Kiran Bedi remained adamant regarding several points. Anna grew judgmental. As the meeting progressed, stray allegations about the misuse of funds were heard. There were also references to core committee changes. Finally a truce was called, but it was uneasy.

With Anna staying back at Ralegan Siddhi, Arvind told

his confidants, 'Can we get Anna back to Delhi? Because the more he stays in Ralegan, the more likely it is that his people will turn him against us.'

From Delhi, Arvind kept calling Anna regularly to ensure that he had some control over his thoughts. After all, in the village, surrounded by his cohort, Anna was inclined to believe that he was being used; that the four-member team of Arvind, Prashant Bhushan, Kiran Bedi and Manish Sisodia was superfluous; and the entire IAC movement was going strong only because of him. This is the same mistake that Arvind would make much later.

Anna, tiring of Arvind's calls, began avoiding him, as also a probing media. He swore a vow of silence. Anna's blogger Raju Parulekar began expressing Anna's views through a series of blogs; he claimed Anna wanted to remove the 'undemocratic and fascist' Arvind Kejriwal, Kiran Bedi, Prashant Bhushan, and 'their pawns' from his core group.[7] An informant in Ralegan Siddhi informed Arvind of these developments. Team Arvind was shaken.

Distrust, malice and slander became the hallmarks of both ends. Arvind, Kiran Bedi and Manish finally decided to meet Anna, settle the issues and clear all allegations. The meeting was somewhat successful. For a while, all differences were papered over. Promptly, Anna disowned Raju Parulekar and the blog—just days after aligning himself with his posts.

The turn of events reaffirmed my fears about Anna's eccentric and unreliable disposition. In all honesty, I was losing respect for him.

*

The Lokpal Bill was to be taken up for discussion in the winter session of Parliament. There were clear indications that the centre planned to water down the provisions it had accepted. In the past, when the government had tried to outsmart us, it had failed. This was because we had been together. Now, internal disputes had sucked away our energy and focus; we were easy targets.

Betrayed and fatigued by daily squabbles, we were not thinking straight. Something needed to be done to bring the movement back on the rails. In desperation, we decided to undertake a limited fast during the winter session of Parliament. We thought that we could exert pressure on the government and make it accept the Jan Lokpal Bill in its entirety, as had been agreed.

In December, Delhi is known to be forbiddingly cold, with low visibility. We needed another city to act as the headquarters.

'Mayank, will you be able to manage the protests from Mumbai?' the core committee asked.

'What would that entail?' I asked.

'Organizing all the logistics.'

I was ready; I had full confidence in my team. I came out of the meeting, and the next day we announced that the fast would begin in Mumbai on 27 December and stretch across three days.

The burden to prove that the entire nation was with IAC shifted from the political capital to the financial capital, Mumbai.

9. BKC: A House Divided

The battle lines were once again drawn between the government and civil society. Parliament was to debate the provisions of the Lokpal Bill between 22 and 29 December 2011. Anna decided to begin a three-day hunger strike from 27 December 2011 to put pressure on Parliamentarians. The onus to organize this successfully fell squarely on me.

Some days before Anna's fast in Mumbai, I got a message from Sri Sri Ravishankar's disciple: 'Guruji is in Mumbai and wants to meet.' I expressed my inability to see him as the agitation was around the corner. But the disciple insisted: 'Come for 10 minutes.' So, I went to Ghatkopar, a suburb of Mumbai, where he was staying. There were hundreds of followers in the building compound enjoying music and food. I was escorted to the presence of Sri Sri. With great courtesy and love, he made me sit next to him and have dinner.

After the meal, along with Sri Sri and a few of his key followers, I went to one of his rooms. Sri Sri complained gently, 'Baba Ramdev and I are being sidelined, our pictures have been removed from the website. We aren't even called for consultations by the IAC leadership. Ramdevji feels that IAC is doing this as we are perceived as religious leaders . . . and we suspect the complete leadership team is against us.'

I nodded, 'You are right, but only partially. Prashant Bhushan, Medha Patkar and many others feel that having religious leaders will compromise the non-religious nature of the movement. But, simultaneously, many of us feel that you and Baba Ramdev add great value to the movement. Can I request you to postpone your trip to Germany and join Anna for the forthcoming protests?'

I was taking a risk by inviting him; I knew that I could well face the ire of some of those in the core committee. But I genuinely felt that Sri Sri Ravishankar and his followers would grant the movement great momentum.

Smiling, Sri Sri took my hand and said, 'Mayank, I certainly can cancel the trip to Germany. But I am not sure if the other members of IAC will appreciate my joining the demonstrations. Rest assured you have my complete support.'

Now, I pressed: 'Guruji, you say that you completely support the movement. In that case, in my presence, why don't you instruct your senior members to bring your supporters to the venue in large numbers?'

Sri Sri smiled, and I smiled back knowingly. Both of us understood that it was not going to happen.

Back to preparing for the fast.

*

A fast should be the final weapon. Using it for small battles defeats its efficacy. After the successful fast unto deaths in April and August, one more fast—that too, for just three days—did not evoke any passion from a fatigued nation. Whereas a fast unto death comes with a degree of urgency, a three-day fast generates neither sympathy nor commitment.

Public opinion, for the first time, was indifferent to IAC. It was felt that the movement was arrogant and was trying to blackmail the political system by demanding 'my way or the highway'. People asked, 'If the goal was really to pressurize the government to pass an effective Lokpal Bill, why did the agitation not coincide with the start of the winter session of Parliament? This would have given IAC enough time to build mass support. Why has it been timed with the end of a Parliament session?' These were valid questions and there were no convincing answers.

People were also unclear about the purpose of the agitation, and we were fighting an uphill battle to win their support. However, since the core committee—including me—had taken the decision to forge forward, it was my role to make a success of this ill thought through protest.

Sometimes self-assured, sometimes nervous, our team began working with full vigour. The headlines, the incessant press coverage—even if largely negative—and the constant feedback being received from the media and other allied groups made us believe that the dharna would attract huge crowds. That was the first mistake I made, and it led to more errors of judgement.

Based on the assumption that we'd have a huge number of participants, we thought that the pocket of Azad Maidan we generally used for demonstrations would prove to be inadequate. Therefore, we requested senior police authorities to open the gates along the western end of the grounds. We didn't get the permission we needed. Therefore, we decided to shift the venue to the MMRDA, Bandra Kurla Complex (BKC), which could hold up to 60,000 people. The cost of renting this space was prohibitively high. A volunteer, who also happened to be a senior lawyer, suggested that we file a public interest litigation (PIL) in the High Court to waive off the rent or subsidize it. He opined that we would get a ruling in our favour very easily since we were organizing a democratic protest for public welfare. Unfortunately, the High Court dismissed our petition. My confidence in the lawyer's assessment was another error in judgement.

On 24 December, I explained the entire episode to the core committee members via an email. I then told them that, after the court debacle, we had finalized things with MMRDA. We changed the name of the applicant to PCRF and got discounted rates applicable to social organizations. I concluded: 'I still believe that we did the right thing. [. . .] It was a decision that our team in Mumbai took for the betterment of the movement, and if there is any negative fallout, I take the blame.'

With the venue in place, the third mistake we made was not to barricade the open land so as to create a compact congregation area. There is a dictum in public life: *always ensure that hall/ground you have booked is tinier than the crowd you expect.* I made the cardinal mistake of not following this dictum.

We constructed an elaborate stage for the fast, following instructions from the central IAC office. Arvind arrived on 26 December, looked at the stage under construction and felt that it ought to have been much smaller and simpler. But it was too late to rectify this.

*

The day of the fast started with a car and bike rally that led Anna and other leaders from Juhu to the venue.

People lined along both sides of the 10 kilometre stretch. The response was reassuring. An NGO arranged for free food; the police provided excellent security and had senior officers in a special tent at the site.

Then, our senior karyakarta (volunteer) got phone calls from the Intelligence Bureau (IB) in Delhi; the bureau asked for the quick closure of the event and the dispersal of people. We opposed this. To our dismay, we found the traffic police stopping the entry of vehicles into the BKC area; buses, cars and auto-rickshaws were being turned back. The authorities cited security issues. Given that BKC is over five kilometres away from the railway station, and the only way to navigate the distance is by taking public or private transport, thousands of protestors failed to reach the destination. When we confronted a senior police official, he claimed helplessness.

For this reason, apart from a number of others—including protest weariness—there were far fewer people at the dharna than we had anticipated. Worse, there wasn't even a remote possibility of the crowds gathering as days progressed—this typically happens as the fast enters a critical stage during a fast unto death protest, but with a three-day window, this turning point just does not emerge. Given the expanse of the venue, the crowd of 10,000 looked sparse. The images flashing across newspapers and TV channels pointed towards a demonstration that had barely taken off.

Parallel IAC protests in other cities met with a similar fate, with just 1,000 people congregating in Ramlila Maidan, Delhi and 200 in Bengaluru. IAC had faltered. The timing, the location, the strategy—all of this was wrong.

Ever swift to take advantage of the turn of events,

Anna's Ralegan cohort began discrediting the IAC Mumbai team. Matters reached a boil when one of the volunteers at IAC did not recognize Anna's sister and stopped her from using the special entrance to enter the venue; the Ralegan team touted this minor incident as a personal affront to the Gandhian. The volunteer, on his part, apologized profusely to Anna, but Anna was angry and threatened to walk away. In any case, displeased as he was about the strength of the crowd and the poor press coverage, he chose to spend most of his time backstage.

On day two, we got a message from Baba Ramdev that he would come to meet Anna at the venue with a large number of supporters in the evening. This worried Anna and Arvind. After all, the media would notice that Baba Ramdev had more supporters than IAC! 'Avoid Ramdev's visit' was the unsaid demand.

Day two also saw Anna growing increasingly unwell; the doctors warned of complications. We called off the strike and announced its end before evening fell.

Anna delivered the concluding speech, thanking everyone including the performers—everyone *except* the hundreds of volunteers of IAC Mumbai. He had neither the time nor the inclination to meet those who had worked tirelessly behind the scenes and the many who fasted in solidarity with the movement.

Incidentally, while Anna was lying backstage and discussing the possibility of a premature end to his fast, I saw a close confidante of Arvind Kejriwal—IAC's media manager—take pictures of him. I was standing next to the media manager and could see the images being captured. In half an hour, media headlines declared the end of the fast—even before Team Anna could make a formal announcement—with precisely the same photographs.

Already, if you recall, I suspected someone was leaking stories from internal meetings; my belief was it was the media manager. Now, my hunch was confirmed. I shared my concerns with Arvind, but he dismissed my misgivings.

*

Anna went back to Ralegan Siddhi. I counselled my inconsolable team and began a postmortem of the event. The injustice of all that had happened over the past two days was galling. I absolved the volunteers of all blame and took responsibility.

Among other things, we tallied accounts. We had received all payments from the Delhi IAC team. Our chartered accountants audited each transaction, checking even the minutest of bills. We sent these details to Delhi, and their audit team did another round of verification.

Yet Anna was convinced that there had been some kind of financial impropriety—possibly because that is what his cohorts made him believe. Anna asked Arvind to furnish proof of financial scrupulousness, and Arvind explained each transaction. Despite this, Anna maintained that there was something amiss. He had decided so. The explanations we offered were irrelevant.

During the next core committee meeting in Delhi, Anna raised the issue of financial misconduct, making an accusation that some money had been misappropriated; he, then, vaguely suggested that I was involved. I was annoyed. Looking straight at Anna, I stood up and said, 'There are two ways to deal with this allegation. The first is to set up a committee to study each of Anna's contentions. The second is for Annaji to apologize to me.' I continued, 'Till the time an inquiry committee is set up or an apology is tendered, I will not attend core committee meetings.'

In the weeks to come, I was overwhelmed by calls from core committee members regarding Anna's allegations. Most of them expressed support and advised me to lie low. That was not my way. I wanted to clear things.

I wrote to my fellow members:

Dear Friends,

I think the last few weeks must have been stressful for IAC because of issues raised by me and about me.

I am also feeling the discomfort of having to explain my intentions over and over again and pacifying other people's suspicion. Errors of judgement have been coloured to look like a ploy, there is fear of upsetting status quo [. . .]

I accept that I am naïve and unlike you not a big fighter and activist. But I was a high net individual who was inspired by a cause, left a well paying job to listen to his heart. To be accused of petty pilferage, not by outsiders, but the very people who inspired me, the ones I am continuously publically [sic] defending is becoming unacceptable. I cannot be made to feel apologetic for fighting for my country or doing the right thing.

Also there have been some serious inconsistencies with who we are and what we stand for. Whether it's our anti-high command stand, our flag of transparency, our view of internal democracy. These are becoming irreconcilable to my conscience.

It makes sense for me to spare this unnecessary stress to all of us and for me to leave the Core Committee.

Whilst leaving, I would like to state that we have a very powerful group in Mumbai with a duly elected 17 member IAC representative team, supported by 15 zonal teams, advisory body and support team of around 60 people. They are all dedicated to the nation, IAC and Anna.

> [. . .] Why am I being continuously bombarded with accusations of financial irregularities? Audited accounts are being questioned. But these are just accusations in the air. No one is really trying to verify anything. It is become [sic] ridiculous and insulting.
>
> With my resignation I request you to grace me by leveling an inquiry against me. This includes all the financial irregularities I have been accused of. (The last I heard was that Anna believed that I was amassing wealth in Gujarat in the name of IAC.) I would not like to go under a cloud of ambiguity.
>
> Wishing this group all the best. Rest assured I will leave gracefully without any media attention.
>
> Regards,
>
> Mayank Gandhi

While my resignation was not accepted, I stayed firm that I'd keep away from the core committee till Anna apologized.

Soon after, I'm told, Arvind confessed to Prithvi, 'I know that Mayank is right, but if Anna demands that Mayank be removed from the movement, I will. Mayank might have a few supporters in Mumbai, but he cannot damage us, while Anna is followed by lakhs.'

When Prithvi related this to me, I told him Arvind was correct. 'Compared to Anna,' I said, 'I am nobody, and for the good of the movement I am willing to step back. But I will not bow before a lie.'

Deep within, I knew that I could be the latest victim of Arvind's use-and-throw policy. That didn't worry me deeply—the nation and this uprising that could steer it in the right direction came first. I told Arvind, 'If Anna insists, please do not protest . . . remove me from the movement, and I will go without any fuss.'

Finally, a few well-wishers and senior members from the Mumbai chapter went to meet Anna with every single expense detail. They wished to present the facts. Anna didn't engage with them—he simply kept the papers and said that he would investigate matters himself. That was the last anyone heard about the issue.

*

As 2011 drew to a close, we could assess the highs and lows. Undoubtedly, this had been one of the most exciting years since India's independence. Beginning with the conception of the IAC movement in January, to the many moments in April and August when the entire nation stood as one, 2011 had ignited a people's idealism. Common citizens had found a voice, a conscience and a rare kind of audaciousness. The hegemony of the political class had been destroyed. The most notable winner was India.

Yet the year ended with the failure of the BKC dharna, more in-fighting between core committee members, and a chasm between Anna and IAC.

Politically, here's where we were: On 20 December 2011, the cabinet approved its own version of the Bill. On 23 December, the government introduced the legislation in Parliament, in the midst of protests from opposition parties and our own volunteers. Four days later, the Lokpal and Lokayukta Bills were passed by the Lok Sabha. However, the Rajya Sabha opposed the Bill.

Now, more than ever, it was important for the movement to regroup, but some of us sensed that we were broken from within. The stage was set for a series of self-defeating decisions and reactions.

10. Welcome to the Party

When the protest at BKC proved to be a damp squib, Anna responded rather poorly. He went back to his village, sulking and angry. After a few months, he decided to demonstrate his strength in Maharashtra. He planned a Lokayukta tour across his home state without IAC, under the banner of the BVJA. The momentum of IAC and the cause of Lokpal were being hijacked by Team Anna.

However, in keeping with the mood of the nation, Anna's rally began failing wherever he went. Crowds were absent and the media lost interest.

Suddenly, Anna left his tour midway. He chose to participate in a protest dharna on 3 June 2012 organized by Baba Ramdev in Delhi. Anna was sharing the stage with Ramdev after a year. Arvind, Manish and Kiran Bedi also attended the rally—but there was some obvious ill will between Arvind and Baba Ramdev. Arvind, in his speech, went on the offensive: 'There are serious allegations against fifteen ministers out of thirty-four. That is why they are not passing Lokpal Bill. Manmohan Singh is the leader of those thirty-four ministers.' Taking umbrage against these personal attacks, Swami Ramdev publicly castigated Arvind's stance: 'Today, we thought that we would not take anybody's name. But Arvind took names. We don't want any controversies. The names have been taken in some context. We are against personal criticism.' Arvind and his team left the venue in anger, and Anna did not utter a single word to protect his protégé.

Given his strained association with Arvind and IAC, was Anna trying to explore the possibility of another platform, or was he trying to send a message to Arvind? We'd find out eventually.

Back in Maharashtra, the lack of support for the Lokayukta rallies was making the BVJA team nervous. They desperately wanted to demonstrate their strength in Mumbai to IAC. The Mumbai BVJA head gave an ultimatum to IAC volunteers: 'Choose between Anna and Mayank.' The volunteers felt it was unfair to have to make a choice. They wanted to support both of us. Equally, they felt that all the work they had done over the past year, to make IAC Mumbai strong, decentralized and an internally democratic force to fight corruption, was being squandered by unhealthy bickering.

The BVJA failed to gather the resources it needed. In desperation, the BVJA team decided to approach me for funds, so as to organize a venue and gather crowds. I arranged a conference call at night amongst our IAC team members. Everyone was agitated. 'Let's teach these BVJA guys a lesson' was the common refrain. I had to mediate and calm the entire lot. Finally, we decided not to allow messy internal politics to vitiate the mood of the nation. I urged the volunteers to put aside all differences and ensure that Anna's rally would not be a fiasco.

On the day of Anna's rally, we marched with flags from Lower Parel Station to Nare Park. Out there, just a handful of people were seated. We joined them. I had obviously not been invited to share the dais with Anna and his team, so I sat with the audience, listening to the proceedings. The moment journalists saw me, they rushed towards me. They sensed the simmering differences between IAC and Anna and, expectedly, sought clarity. I told the media, 'There is no difference between us, this is a BVJA programme, and we all have just come to support them.' Anna noticed that the media's attention had shifted towards me. He was left with no option but to ask me to come and sit by his side. The entire episode was unfortunate.

This petty tussle for supremacy was exactly the kind of politics that we had wished to counter. Now, to see us caught in the middle of a power wrangle left me pained.

*

The dwindling support of the people was evident not just at Anna's rally or in Maharashtra but all across India. Everywhere, people seemed tired of the protests and the countless reports emerging regarding differences between factions.

When our volunteers would go door to door, they would get questioned. I began counselling those who had difficulty facing criticism from the public. In weekly meetings in Nanavati School, I cited examples from the Independence struggle. After Gandhiji came back to India in 1915, it took him thirty-two years—a time marked with huge ups and downs—to achieve his goal of freedom from the colonists. 'At least the English had a country to go back to. Our corrupt rulers are much worse. They're deeply entrenched in the system. Dislodging them from power will be a much tougher task,' I'd say. 'After the Chauri Chaura incident of 1922, where policemen were killed by violent protesters, most of the volunteers thought that the independence struggle was finished. But the movement continued. Similarly, we need to have patience and maturity to succeed.'

However, I knew, the morale was low. When there's optimism, all censure can be glossed over. But once events start going downhill, everyone is on edge. Core committee members, volunteers and the general public were quick to attack one another and get hurt.

In internal meetings, too, things were proceeding dismally. Inconsequential matters were hotly debated, with both factions (Anna's and Arvind's) trying to outwit each other and claim supremacy.

Anna publicly contradicted everything Arvind said. He was deeply upset that Arvind had called Pranab Mukherjee—who was to take oath as president soon—corrupt.[8] Arvind, on his part, was still smarting over the presence of Vilasrao Deshmukh on 28 August. And now that Anna was supporting Pranab Mukherjee—a man the Arvind camp wished to run a campaign against—Arvind read Anna's politics as one that backed the corrupt when convenient. The entire atmosphere was toxic. It was evident that sooner or later the factions would split. For now, the camps were biding time since public opinion was staunchly against both sides.

Some of us started thinking about the way forward. I came to the conclusion that there was no option but to create a political party and harness the support of the people. In February 2012, Arvind had already shared his desire to go down the political route with Prithvi and me, and I agreed with him. When decision-makers start ignoring the will of the people, the best strategy is to make one's way into politics and become a decision-maker oneself.

Emails on this subject were exchanged among Prithvi, Arvind and me. In a letter dated 14 March 2012, I told both of them that while we had to 'think things through' before venturing into the electoral turf, there were three compelling factors recommending a move in this direction:

1. We couldn't depend on movements alone since they were known to be mercurial. The national movement had granted us leverage, and we had to encash this. A people's anger could translate into electoral gains were we to enter politics.
2. There happens to be a wide gap between how participatory democracy should be and how it operates today. If our movement spurred small incremental gains, and little else, it was hard to see it creating sufficient pressure within systems of governance. Entering electoral politics and making large-scale changes seemed like a more effective route.
3. Systemic reforms are vital, and if we could enter the political set-up electorally and attain decision-making status, we'd be in a position to set the agenda, which would then be hard to reverse.

I continued in my email:

> Status quo is unacceptable. I am sure that our group will soon start imploding with dissension, opposing viewpoints, pressure from hardened and skilled opponents and [the] media. But it is more than likely we might have the window of opportunity to make some serious changes in the culture, agenda and working of our democracy and start a serious debate on certain issues [such as

> the] decentralization of power, [and the] role of [the] legislature, executive, judiciary and civil society in the next year or two. It is very possible that our group [will] get discredited and people might get cynical about civil society—but the 'Amrit Manthan' or churning will be good for the nation. It's a risk worth taking. The Greenpeace movement in Canada had a progressive agenda and in its first election it got 14% votes—now it gets less than 1% votes, but its agenda has been picked up by the mainstream political parties. [. . .]
>
> Note: Assam Gana Parishad [AGP], Lech Walesa's Solidarity Party are some examples of movements converting successfully in the electoral arena.
>
> AGP imploded with many breakaway factions and was not really able to demonstrate that [it was] different from other political parties, with [. . .] issues of corruption and nepotism. But it had a few years, [when] it could have done much—but [the] lack of clarity in thinking and poor leadership has led to [the] AGP being one of [. . .] many parties.
>
> Lech Walesa entered politics with the slogan 'I don't want to, but I've got no choice'. After becoming the president of Poland, his confrontational style broke the party into multiple parts, and after 5 years, he lost the elections, and the party [has] been relegated into oblivion. But he achieved a lot during his reign.

Prithvi generally agreed with the sentiments expressed in the mail and added some of his views to the exchange. Finally on 17 March 2012 Arvind sent back a reply:

> Hey guys, extremely good ideas. Really excellent [sic]. Can't we meet and discuss? First put down all such issues on paper and then discuss. Come to delhi. Anna

> is quite free here. Come tomo. Anna is free whole day. Let's discuss all this with him too. He is quite open.

We met Anna in Delhi. He was willing to consider the idea of forming a political party, but he went on to make suggestions that were impractical. We realized that perhaps the time wasn't ripe for such an endeavour.

It's possible that Arvind and Anna discussed the issue once more—because in April, Arvind travelled to Himachal Pradesh to explore the possibility of supporting candidates or fielding fresh ones himself. Some of us were surprised that Arvind had made such a move without taking his core committee into confidence. When confronted, Arvind explained, 'Anna told me to go on an exploratory trip. I still have high regard for his political acumen, and therefore I went with Sanjay Singh . . . just to explore.' While nothing came of the Himachal Pradesh trip, I had an uneasy feeling that we were being manipulated—but by whom?—Anna or Arvind?

*

While the idea of creating a political party was being explored, there was a simultaneous need to quickly win back public favour.

The hope was to create a climate conducive to forming a political party. A strategy was devised by Arvind's team to use one stone to kill many birds:

- Win back the sympathy and affection of the common people for the movement
- Recharge disheartened volunteers
- Slowly take away the leadership baton from Anna, portraying him as inconsistent and unreliable
- Project Arvind as the leader of the movement

- Distract attention from Baba Ramdev's fast that was to begin on 9 August

With this end in view, Arvind decided to go on a fast unto death along with Manish Sisodia and Gopal Rai. IAC made the following set of demands from the government: constituting a special investigation team (SIT) comprising honest retired judges who could look into serious corruption charges against fifteen cabinet ministers including the prime minister; passing all pending cases against party chiefs like Mayawati, Mulayam Singh Yadav, Lalu Prasad Yadav from the CBI to the SIT; and setting up fast track courts which could pass judgements regarding the allegations against MPs.

On my part, I had decided to stay away from the core committee meetings; so, I was not privy to the discussions preceding the event. While I personally was not in favour of yet another fast unto death, as obedient soldiers, my team and I put all our might behind the decision.

Anna was invited to join the protest. He sensed that it would be disastrous to decline our offer as the perception would then go out that he had derailed the movement. Ever sensitive to public opinion, Anna reluctantly agreed to involve himself. But, as was now becoming typical, he allowed the terms of his commitment to remain vague and kept the IAC core team in a state of suspense. Then, suddenly, one day, he went incommunicado. There was panic.

On 22 July 2012 (three days before the fast), I received a call. It was Arvind's voice. 'Mayank, this is it. Pranab Mukhejree's election as president is all but final. The fast becomes doubly significant. Any news from Anna?' I told him I had received no updates. Arvind needed some kind of assurance that Anna was joining the fast. He wanted this to be the final showdown with the government. We all knew that public patience had run dry, and whatever remained to be achieved had to be realized by way of this agitation alone. It was a last chance.

Volunteers from Mumbai as well as Delhi went to Ralegan Siddhi to assess Anna's stance, but he remained non-committal. I volunteered to contact Anna myself and determine whether he was going to join the fast—but no one in Ralegan Siddhi picked up the phone. Finally, I received a call from Delhi. 'Anna has decided to join us,' I was told.

I remained doubtful. I told Arvind, 'I am pretty sure Anna's team will bring up trivial issues and create hurdles. Even though he has agreed, Anna is capable of doing a complete somersault.'

'Mayank,' Arvind replied, 'we are tired of Anna's sulking. We are going ahead with the fast whether Anna comes or not.' Arvind's voice was steely.

Late at night, on the 24th, there was still no guarantee about Anna's presence. Then, out of the blue, I received a message from Anna's camp: 'Anna will not be attending the fast and will disown IAC unless and until Delhi concedes to his demands and stops attacking Pranab Mukherjee and others. In Delhi, no one seems in a mood to budge. Please intervene.' Anna had placed several demands before the IAC team, a key one being that posters plastered across Jantar Mantar, showcasing Pranab Mukherjee in the list of the most corrupt, had to be removed.

I called up Arvind. 'We need to accommodate Anna. Losing Anna at this juncture will be catastrophic. A lot of credibility will be lost if he does not participate.

Besides, the nation looks at IAC as Anna's movement. I understand that managing Anna is tiring, but we need to have him on board.'

Arvind replied, 'Mayank, I agree with you. But it is just unbearable to deal with them. Anna doesn't answer my calls. I have to get through to at least three people before I can reach him. As soon as I accept one of his demands, he makes another. When we reach consensus regarding that demand, his mind changes. All this is just getting out of hand.'

I could empathize with Arvind's situation. But personal comfort had to be sacrificed in the interest of the larger good. Finally, after an intense discussion, Arvind accepted Anna's key demands. Posters of Pranab Mukherjee were covered with white cloth.

Now, Anna again backtracked. After promising to join Arvind on 25 July for the fast, he announced that he would grant the government a window of a few days to take action. Team Arvind felt devastated and cheated.

In Anna's presence, Arvind and the rest began their fast. By the fourth day, it became obvious that the protest was failing to have an impact on people. Meetings supporting the fast, held elsewhere in the country, were facing an equally poor response. When I'd speak to strangers for feedback, they'd tell me, 'You all are good people, but you will not be able to achieve anything substantial.' They were right. What had our achievements been so far? No Lokpal had been passed. Few demands had been met.

If people were disillusioned, it was also because the internal differences between Anna and Arvind were now evident. Arvind, despite bowing to Anna's demand to remove Pranab Mukherjee's posters, decided to criticize

India's soon-to-be president severely from the stage, thus indirectly sending a strong message to Team Anna. He went a step further and called for 'sampoorna kranti'—a revolution that engaged with more than just Lokpal—to plant the idea of a political alternative in people's minds. All at once, volunteers and supporters started veering away from Anna and towards Arvind. Anna saw this change in mood; he was upset that Arvind was outshining him. To maintain his position in the movement, he decided to join the fast after the fourth day. Arvind, in response, released his book *Swaraj* and instructed all volunteers to distribute copies. This was a game of one-upmanship between a master and his protégé.

To make things worse, Anna threatened to leave the venue if the strength of the crowd did not increase. Arvind, too, was worried. Frantic calls were made throughout the country asking every IAC coordinator to send more volunteers—but this was not going to be enough.

Incidentally, fairly early on, a panic-stricken, Kiran Bedi had invited Baba Ramdev for help. The yoga guru had thousands of committed supporters. I can almost picture him rubbing his hands in glee when he received Kiran Bedi's call—at last, he could prove that *he* was the man with the ability to draw people—that too, days before his own fast. Baba Ramdev arrived with an immense crowd; for now, he seemed to have a clear edge over the IAC movement. Arvind had no option but to smile and welcome him, but in his heart, he was seething.

Later, Arvind, Prashant Bhushan, Medha Patkar and many of the core members of IAC conveyed their annoyance to Kiran Bedi for having invited Baba Ramdev.

The battle for one-upmanship grew increasingly

complex—with Anna, Arvind, Swami Ramdev and Kiran Bedi all jostling for power. These were games within games. Interestingly, when Baba Ramdev later shared the stage with the then Gujarat chief minister, Narendra Modi, Arvind hit out at Kiran Bedi, criticizing her for jeopardizing the principles guiding the movement. Sanjay Singh and others, on their part, lashed out at the Baba, while Kiran Bedi and Kumar Vishwas came out in complete support of him.

As the fast continued, the government—now familiar with our strategy—wisened up. It decided to completely ignore us. Earlier, there'd be ministers and senior politicians who would rush to meet the IAC team for a discussion. This time, no MP or senior government functionary sent word to us. There were no 'negotiations'. This indifference was unexpected, and the team huddled together looking for ways to respond.

By the eighth day of the fast, Arvind's health started deteriorating and the government doctors advised hospitalization. Arvind, unwilling to give up, announced that if the doctors tried force feeding him, he would remove all intravenous tubes and end his life. The announcement was dramatic, and it filled my eyes (and the eyes of everyone around us) with tears. We couldn't let anything untoward happen—but in the face of government apathy, what could we do?

Suddenly, it seemed like we had no option but to start a political party. After all, if the just demands of civil society movements were not heard, what alternative was there? Crores of people had supported the demand for Lokpal, but this had fallen on deaf ears. The most popular leaders had been trying to pressurize the government from the outside, but this, too, wasn't working. The power to make laws and policies in a democracy seemed to lie squarely in the hands of the political class. So, perhaps it was time to 'get into the gutter to clean it'.

In my own instance, my original reason for joining the movement had been to lead it towards electoral reforms. My first choice had been to be part of a pressure group that would clean the political system and destroy its indebtedness to dishonest money and vote bank politics. But with the people's movement petering out and the government turning cold, I came to the conclusion that we had to take on the task of forming a political party that could win elections honestly. We could not give up.

As this realization hit me, I delivered a speech in Mumbai: 'We are "crazy" people. Having decided to transform the country, there is no question of stopping till we achieve this end. We had begun this movement without the intention of becoming activists or politicians. We came to change the country and are willing to do whatever it takes. So, now we are left with two options. Either we allow our leaders to die and forget the idea to which crores have lent their support. Or we enter the system and take on the corrupt. We have given the government opportunities to reform. But it has treated the will of the people of the country with disdain and contempt. It is time to go into its den and challenge the status quo.'

'Should IAC become a political party?' I asked from the stage. There was a roar of approval from Mumbai that must have reached the ears of Delhi. The people of India's business capital were overwhelmingly in favour of forming a political party. When we tested ground in other parts of the country, a similar response was received.

While I was in Mumbai, a lot continued unfolding in

Delhi; this was related to me by Arvind and I relay it here. On 1 August, Yogendra Yadav, arguably India's greatest psephologist and one of the most brilliant thinkers on politics and economics, decided to break the deadlock. Along with twenty-four eminent people in the country, he drafted a letter asking Anna, Arvind and others to end the fast. 'Instead of giving up your life by fasting, you must use your life to fight for a better India. I beseech you to abandon the fast and form a political alternative,' the signatories said. Anna agreed with the proposal, and the next day, he let Arvind know that he wished to proceed with Yogendra's recommendation. Arvind told me he was reluctant and wanted a three-day referendum across the entire country before taking such a major step. But he was overruled.

On the evening of 3 August, from the stage, all leaders spoke in favour of forming a political party, except for Anna Hazare who wanted to create a political *alternative*, not a party.

Prashant Bhushan said, 'We had no intention to enter into politics, but we make this announcement out of compulsion. We have a government which will not do anything even if people come out and protest.'

Arvind thundered, 'This party will not be a party but a movement. A movement outside Parliament as well as inside.' And then, he added, 'There will be no high command and candidates will not be selected by the leadership but by the people themselves.' Who knew that in the future, these words would seem ironical?

Anna announced that while he would not join any political party, he would support the party of his aides and travel across the country seeking the backing of the public.

The response of millions of supporters was emotional and, in some cases, heartbreaking. Most die-hard volunteers were upset that a people's movement had transformed into a political party. Several donors were aghast. These were people who hated politics and had joined a non-political group to fight villainous politicians. To suddenly find themselves as part of the villain's gang shocked them. It took a while to get them to accept a new identity, but once they did, they displayed the same passion for change.

Politicians were equally quick to criticize us. They tried to discredit the agitation, claiming that our civil society movement had been just a front; we had harboured political ambitions all along. We refuted the allegation.

Meanwhile, the talking heads of television asserted that we'd never reach a place of political power because we had lost credibility.

There was a divide within the IAC leadership team as well. Kiran Bedi opposed the formation of a political party as this would compete with the BJP. Santosh Hegde wanted to stay away from politics in general. General V.K. Singh, a known BJP sympathizer, distanced himself, too. The group which stayed together during the tumultuous IAC days was now disintegrating.

The necessary plunge into politics had been propelled by numerous compulsions. But was the drama of the fast real or staged? At the back of my mind, there were multiple stray memories and comments that kept coming back.

*

After the fast, Anna returned to Ralegan Siddhi. About a month later, when Kumar Vishwas visited him, Anna made a series of constructive suggestions regarding the creation and the administration of a new political party. So, superficially, things remained fine.

It was when Anna went to Jindal Farms near Bengaluru for treatment that everything changed. Arvind tells me that Sitaram Jindal of Jindal Farms, purportedly an RSS sympathizer, influenced Anna's thoughts and asked him to stop Arvind from forging forward. Anna, taking advantage of one of Arvind's emotional outbursts on TV—Arvind had claimed that if Anna ordered him to stop, he would pay heed—told the media that Arvind should not form a political party.

I saw Anna's comments on TV and immediately called Arvind, asking him to rush to Ralegan Siddhi. Arvind and Prashant went to meet Anna. What followed was relayed to me. Anna brusquely asked Arvind and Prashant, 'What do you want?' Arvind replied, 'Annaji, we have come all the way from Delhi, at least offer us some water.' Anna was hostile, and there was tension in the air. Arvind put forward some key questions: 'Annaji, you say that good people should be elected from other political parties . . . even if they are, tell me, how will you ensure that those who are elected will listen to you and not to their own party bosses? Also, you have always maintained we should listen to the voice of the people. All polls, including TV opinion polls, are overwhelmingly in favour of the formation of a political party.'

Anna scoffed at Arvind and said, 'What is the value of TV channels? If you want to know the real opinion of the people, you should conduct a proper opinion poll.' Taking a cue from this discussion, Arvind started a nationwide online opinion poll using Facebook, Twitter and SMS services. An overwhelming 76 per cent of the 7,00,000 people surveyed supported the formation of a political party. IAC Mumbai members also met Anna at Ralegan Siddhi on 16 September and handed over a memorandum signed by hundreds of volunteers expressing their strong approval of a political option.

But Anna's mind was made up. When, after these overwhelmingly positive opinion polls, Arvind went back to his mentor, the latter pooh-poohed the idea of a political party again. 'What is the value of these opinion polls by uninformed people? Let us seek the opinion of some eminent people who will give a studied reply as to whether a party should be formed.' So, Arvind's team, in conjunction with Anna, made a list of forty-two prominent opinion makers and had a meeting with them on 19 September in Delhi. Some of those present were General V.K. Singh, Santosh Hegde, Kiran Bedi and Yogendra Yadav, as also, of course, Anna and Arvind. Everyone was allowed five minutes to comment, after which they had to offer their assessment of whether a political party could be formed. Six out of the forty-two members—including Kiran Bedi, Santosh Hedge and V.K. Singh—did not favour the formation of a political party, while the remaining were in support of the creation of one.

A resolution in support of a political party's creation was drafted and read out in the meeting in the presence of all. To the astonishment of those gathered inside, Anna—ignoring the accepted resolution altogether—stepped outside the hall and announced that not only was he against the formation of a political party but he was also against his name or picture being used if such a party were to emerge.

Late in the evening, Anna met Baba Ramdev and had a surreptitious closed door discussion; this led to endless speculation. The media got wind of the episode and several news channels began commenting on the rendezvous. This infuriated Anna to no end.

I remember Arvind telling me that, over this period, he had lost nine kilos and had to take sleeping pills … all because of the stress of having to deal with Anna's changing moods and stands.

*

In the midst of such drama, some of us focused on building a charter for a principled party. We decided that the political party we created would abide by the five key principles—PATDI—no matter what.

1. Participation (Bhagidari): Our movement was built on the philosophy of participation. The true stakeholders in the party were our volunteers, and in matters of governance, the chief participants had to be common people—whether this was for the preparation of a manifesto, for crucial decision-making or for a referendum. For elections, volunteers were to play a key role; candidates had to be selected by volunteers and scrutinized by the committee.
2. Accountability (Jabab Dehi): Anyone holding a position of responsibility had to be accountable to the volunteers and the general public.
3. Transparency (Pardarshi): Meetings had to be open for all volunteers to observe. We had to be transparent with all our dealings, the minutes of meeting, and the processes guiding decision-making. We also had to be transparent about all expenses and collections, which had to be uploaded on to our website; this would make us unlike other

political parties.

4. Decentralization (Vikendrikaran): The aim, at all times, had to be strengthening gram sabhas or mohalla sabhas, so people from the smallest of communities could decide policies best suited to their needs. Internal party elections had to be held every three years, from polling booth level right up to the post of the convener of the party, with volunteers voting across board.
5. Integrity (Sachai): The principles of truth and accountability had to be foregrounded. No corruption, no nepotism, no questionable candidates—these had to be our guiding tenets. We would not tolerate compromises with other political parties.

Some of our other principles were:

- We would fight the elections without resorting to corruption, communalism, caste politics and criminalization.
- We would not align with any other party.
- There will be an internal Lokpal headed by retired judges to investigate complaints against elected candidates.
- We had to work unlike other political entities by remaining simple, humble and attuned to the needs of our people.

In essence, we sought a political revolution. We had not come here to replace one dubious leader with another but to change the rules of the game altogether. History was waiting to get created.

11. Picking Up Pace

We were at the cusp of change. From a civil society movement that was supposed to be unselfish, we had metamorphosed into a species called 'politicians'—supposedly selfish, spending their lives fighting for power and position.

Our chief leader had changed from the revered Anna to a brash, angry and impatient Arvind. People were wary of his new avatar; we had to battle allegations that Arvind had betrayed Anna to secure power. The media remained on guard, keenly listening to every statement coming from us.

The first National Council (NC) was organized in Delhi on 24 November 2012. Around thirty-five of us from Maharashtra reached there and joined another 300-odd highly excited members from all over the nation. I was given the honour of moving the resolution for the formation of the party; this was approved by the enthusiastic founder members. In that historical meeting, it was decided that the twenty-three-member National Executive (NE) would draft the Constitution of the party, work out other details regarding its functioning, and constitute a Political Affairs Committee (PAC) comprising a few members who would handle day-to-day affairs.

Arvind Kejriwal was unanimously selected as the national convener, amidst loud cheering.

I was one of the few who transited from being a core committee member of IAC to an NE member of AAP. Some of the other key members of the NE were:

Manish Sisodia: Manish had been working with Kejriwal on RTI for many years. He was hardworking, sincere, and completely in tune with the views of Arvind.

Prashant Bhushan: As we know, Prashant Bhushan, is a brilliant Supreme Court lawyer, and the son of former union law minister, Shanti Bhushan. He was also instrumental in exposing several of the major corruption cases within the government, including the 2G and coal scams.

Yogendra Yadav: A renowned psephologist and a former senior fellow at the Centre for the Study of Developing Societies (CSDS) in Delhi, Yogendra Yadav had been (and still is) working on the ground across the nation, mentoring various movements.

Gopal Rai: Closely associated with students' politics in Uttar Pradesh, Gopal Rai was shot at and badly injured during his campaign for the decriminalization of students' politics in Lucknow University.

Sanjay Singh: Here was the political face of the movement. His keen understanding of politicking could not be questioned. Some of his values though were questionable.

Kumar Vishwas: Here's the poet politician. He had made a career of lampooning the government during most of his speeches and TV discussions. He is a brilliant speaker.

Pankaj Gupta and Krishna Kant (Sanjubhai): They were, respectively, the national secretary and national treasurer. Both were sincere, working diligently behind the scenes.

Naveen Jaihind: In two words, 'Arvind loyalist'.

Shazia Ilmi: Shazia was the prominent Muslim face in Team Kejriwal and a spokesperson for many a television debate. She was both ambitious and combative.

There were other key members, too, like Dinesh Vaghela, Prof Ajit Jha, Christina Samy, Prof Anand Kumar, Iliyas Azmi, Habung Payeng and Yogesh Dahiya. Our vision was simple and clear: to help the people of this country believe in themselves, and to create a benchmark by proving that it was possible to contest and win elections without the use of traditional political techniques. Ours could not be just another party. Ours was a movement, an andolan—an andolan that would have inner-party democracy, an andolan that would not follow the concept of a high command, an andolan that would be accountable to its volunteers, an andolan that was responsible and completely transparent about funding, an andolan based on the principles of PATDI, an andolan that dared to break all political barriers. All of us remained hopeful that the shackles of corruption and political status quo, that had corroded the country for ages, would be smashed. It was time for a massive change.

I have always believed that all those that say, 'Politics is the last refuge of scoundrels,' have done a major disservice to the world. 'Politics should be the place for the best', for the brightest and most capable servants of mankind. We had to prove that.

The workings of the NE were slightly different from

those of the IAC Core Committee. Within IAC, Anna was the titular head and Arvind had to get his decisions passed through Anna; this offered an opportunity for those who differed from Arvind to shoot from Anna's shoulder. But with no Anna, it was Arvind's show all the way. Later, there'd be confrontations with Yogendra Yadav and Prashant Bhushan, but, even then, Arvind controlled the flow of the meetings completely through his surrogates.

The NE pushed for a three-point broad-based action plan for the party. For one, it said that the primary focus of the party had to be contesting the 2013 Delhi elections. Second, it suggested tapping into those states (especially in the North and the West of India) where the party had considerable support. Third, it petitioned the use of the media, especially social media, to garner maximum publicity, innovate and develop the party.

Names and symbols become the identity of any party, and we were fortunate to chance upon three very powerful props (and, unfortunately, one terrible one). First came the name: we called our outfit the Aam Aadmi Party (AAP)—the common man's party—since it was driven by the ordinary citizens of the nation. A masterly stroke.

Then came the matter of a symbol—what could we use? The Election Commission, it turned out, had some symbols that were not yet chosen, and we asked the NE to select one of them. While some chose the torch and some, the candle, to me it was clear—there was nothing more powerful than the broom. This symbol conveyed the fact that AAP was not a party of the elite, for the elite, by the elite. The broom spoke to common people, to the poor and the illiterate, who recognized a party by nothing more than a pictograph—they'd instantly know whom to vote for. The symbol made it clear that the 'jhaduwallas' would release the nation from the grip of high prices and corrupt officials and clean the system; all they had to do was go to the polling booth and press the 'jhadu' button. The broom became our mascot.

Then came the question of the famous Anna cap. We chose to retain it but change what was written across. It would now read: 'Aam Aadmi Party' and 'We Want Swaraj'.

The only symbol that didn't quite work for me was the flag with Arvind Kejriwal's photograph. This was probably the first party flag in the democratic world with the leader's big picture plastered bang in the middle! And this decision was made secretively, without any discussion in any party forum. It emerged as an edict from the top. Was this the start of the megalomania the media would later discuss?

*

In Maharashtra, since the days of the IAC movement, we had nurtured a wonderful and diverse team of youth leaders. I was confident that AAP would grow systematically throughout the state. Brick by brick, the IAC had been built. Similarly, brick by brick, AAP would be developed in the state. Maharashtra and Mumbai had a distinct working style, and we had a great team that would help us go the distance. While none of us had imagined that the ride would be smooth, we were convinced that, with laser-like focus, we would prosper.

Given that the sudden transition from activists to politicians had shaken many young, idealistic and inexperienced volunteers, the time was ripe for a heart to heart talk and for some counseling.

I called a meeting of all our volunteers, I said, 'Life

gives an opportunity to some of us to be a part of history, of the future . . . to direct change. We are amongst those fortunate ones. We can boast to our grandchildren that when history was being written, we were part of it. This country, for the first time in many decades, is ready for a change. We can steer it in the direction we choose.'

A young colleague wanted to know how things would shift for each of us now that we were a part of a party. I smiled, understanding his concern: 'There are more than 1,500 parties in the country. Do not look at any one of these as role models, we are different. We are an andolan. Earlier, we used to operate from outside the system, now we will work from within as well as without. But our carefree, revolutionary attitude will have to be curbed, and we'll have to adopt, instead, a responsible, organized manner of working.'

I continued: 'Instead of getting attached to positions, posts, fame and the adulation, we have to learn to be "nirlep"—unattached. Do not take yourself too seriously or get stressed. Avoid playing power games. We have not come here to become ministers. We want to set the agenda for the country, and make our party a platform for the aspirations of those who are sick of corruption and troubled by a rise in prices. If, tomorrow, other parties mend their ways, we don't even need to be in politics!'

Two hours passed in such talk, after which each of us renewed our commitment to stick to our founding principles and work ceaselessly for the people.

*

In the background, an unpleasant development had been gaining ground. After the last round of accusations by Anna, where he indirectly suggested that I had been involved with the misappropriation of funds, there surfaced a similar allegation, via mail, that I had been involved in a corruption case while helping my uncle, the builder.

I was hurt—the accuser knew me but did not feel it worthwhile to clarify matters. Equally, I was puzzled. If I were corrupt, would I be foolish enough to join an anti-corruption movement? The absurd allegations looked like a smear campaign. Worse, based on this malicious letter, a newspaper article alleged that I had misappropriated funds from my NGO to help a construction company. Other newspapers and TV channels tried to dig deep into the allegation, but they failed to find any evidence to back the claims.

I wasn't the only victim of such slurs. In August 2012, when Anjali Damania, a fearless activist and, later, the convener of the party in Maharashtra, exposed an irrigation scandal, accusatory articles surfaced against her. Like me, she was disturbed. Together, we had a talk with Arvind; we told him that these allegations had to be responded to with clarity and facts. If these complaints were not dealt with, we'd have to live under a cloud of accusations. Arvind saw what we meant. He informed us that, to begin with, he'd create an Internal Lokpal that would investigate us.

I was relieved. This was exactly what I had pushed for when Anna had made covert statements about my dealings. Now, with an Internal Lokpal, I was optimistic that all spurious accusations would be disproved.

The Internal Lokpal of AAP consisting of Admiral Ramdas and Ileana Sen dealt with my case. The ombudsmen were handed over each of the complaints against me in the form of newspaper articles. They, in turn, refused to view articles as proper complaints, arguing (justifiably) that there were thousands of articles every day and if cognizance was taken of each one, work would never cease. Instead, a formal complaint with an affidavit was called for. In addition, it was clarified that only complaints against NE members would be considered—so, unfortunately, the allegations against Anjali were never formally refuted.

A formal complaint against me was lodged on 25 January 2013, and detailed allegations were presented on 28 February 2013. I was asked to explain my stand by 11 March 2013—which I did a day before my deadline. My answer was sent to the complainant for his rebuttal.

I had the highest respect for the Lokpal bench—it included those with honourable reputations—and I had every intention of respecting the judgement. If the Hon'ble Lokpal had reason to find fault with me on moral or technical grounds, I was happy to leave the NE, AAP and public life.

The Lokpal met and interrogated me, going through all the allegations. Finally, after a great deal of deliberation, it gave a speaking order, concluding with this judgement: 'In accordance with procedure laid down by AAP for enquiry by Lokpal, following is our unanimous opinion: There is no substance in the Complaint and the respondent stands exonerated of all charges.'

An immediate casualty of entering public life is that one becomes vulnerable to (sometimes unsubstantiated) attacks. My first instinct was to quit, as allegations disturbed my peace of my mind—but then I thought: 'If I quit now, I will let down lakhs of people who have trusted me with their love and respect. There are a handful of disruptive entities . . . and we will only be strengthening them by giving importance to their accusations.'

This was the thought that kept me within AAP in its early days.

12. The 2013 Verdict: A Foot in the Door

IN DELHI, THE 2013 ELECTIONS WERE APPROACHING.

A plan had been made to make Arvind the face of the movement. We had to build his image as an angry young man, willing to do whatever it took to defeat 'evil'. Posters were designed of Arvind, eyes smouldering, hair damp, fighting police water cannons and exhorting, '*Niklo bahar makano se, jung lado beimano se.*' Get out of your houses, he urged, and fight the corrupt.

The core issues guiding the election battle had to be those that directly affected the life of each person. While corruption was a theoretical subject, the high cost of electricity and water was an everyday reality. A team was set up to study what the party could promise in terms of reducing the electricity rates and, also, how much water could be disbursed free. Once the team gave a clear go-ahead that the government could afford reducing electricity rates by 50 per cent in the lower bracket, we were ready. Sheila Dixit had managed the finances of her government well, and Delhi was one of the few budget surplus states in the country. The new government could afford the concessions we wished to push for.

Arvind seldom brought up issues in isolation, but

connected them to industrialists and politicians, to underscore the existence of crony capitalism. To foreground his concerns about the cost of electricity, he accused the Delhi government and private power distribution companies of being hand and glove.[9] This got him eyeballs.

Now, he raised the battle pitch. He decided to go on an indefinite fast in the Sundar Nagari slums on the issue of the reduction of electricity rates. He also pushed for a civil disobedience movement called the 'bijli-paani satyagraha', asking people to pay only 50 per cent of their electricity bills.

There was a clear strategy guiding this move. Arvind knew that it was impossible to win elections in India without the support of the poorer sections of society. Generally, a large part of the poor's votes are dictated by money, caste or religion. Arvind had decided not to use any of the conventional election winning tools, and hence a mass civil disobedience movement, was the best bet. This, above all else, would project him as the messiah of the poor.

Already, he was gaining some notoriety since he had confronted the government head on. He kick-started this 'bijli-paani' campaign by restoring the power connection of a labourer, after his power supply was snapped for the non-payment of a bill amounting to Rs 15,166. In a speech, Arvind announced, 'Bijli-paani satyagraha has started in Delhi. Stop paying electricity and water bills till the Delhi government withdraws the tariff hike. Let's unite and fight corruption. If they disconnect power, people will reach in large numbers to reconnect it.'[10]

Even as Arvind began his satyagraha, our volunteers distributed leaflets all over the city, gathering signatures in support of a reduction in electricity rates. They traversed the length and breadth of urban centres, going to slum pockets where residents did not know anything about Kejriwal or AAP. They confronted numerous questions, several skeptical. But as soon as they told residents about AAP's mission, or that Arvind had put his life on line for them, they earned people's trust.

One evening, I told Arvind: 'We have over 300,000 signatures objecting to inflated electricity bills. I think it's time to break your fast.' But Arvind remained firm. Eye clearly on his goal, he said, 'Let the number rise.' It was only after receiving 10,00,000 signatures that he agreed to break his fast. He had survived without food for fifteen days.

*

The biggest challenge in this country is to win elections honestly. Consider this: in a Lok Sabha election, every constituency has around three serious contenders from different parties. Each of these candidates spends nothing less than Rs 10 crore for campaigning, so in every Lok Sabha constituency, there is an expenditure of Rs 30 crore. As the Election Commission has mandated a spending limit of Rs 70 lakh per candidate, the largest chunk of expenditure is inevitably in cash. And to get so much cash, a candidate has to necessarily indulge in corrupt practices. Parties must buy the media, pay slum dwellers or slum lords or villagers or opinion makers, release exorbitant advertisements, and incur the cost of vehicles and paid workers—in short, they have to throw large sums of money in the last few weeks of campaigning to buy votes.

But corruption is rarely restricted to an airtight bubble. The politician has to seek the help of others like bureaucrats, industrialists, builders, etc, all of whom seek substantial dividends. So, in the process of fighting one Lok Sabha seat, as much as sixty crore of corruption money can get generated, assuming that the partners-in-corruption make an equal amount. As there are over 500 constituencies, we're looking at corruption touching a figure of Rs 30,000 crore. And this is the just for the general elections! State and local elections generate an equal amount of, if not more, corruption.

Worse, this is a never-ending cycle, with those getting elected having to make more money for the next election.

Nowadays, money is only one of many factors that drives votes—after all, all candidates pay. Religion and caste are the new trump cards. Since winning is the ultimate goal, communal leaders, who know exactly how to exploit caste or religious sentiments, are granted seats. Reservations and riots are direct fallout of such vote bank politics.

In this scenario, an honest politician becomes an oxymoron. You can either be honest or a politician. Sometimes, I am convinced that even politicians have become victims of a vicious cycle—as much as they may want to be principled, they know that it is impossible for the idealistic to survive. Consequently, definitions shift. An honest politician in today's India is one who takes money from industrialists or builders or businessmen and gives all of it to the party, while a dishonest politician takes the money but keeps a part of it for himself. Either way, there's a trail of illicit cash.

Therefore, in 2013, in Delhi, what we were attempting

was unusual. We wished to demonstrate that elections could be won through good old honesty.

*

The transformation of our andolan from activism to politics was enthralling. Our rawness worked for us. We kept looking for newer and more creative ways of campaigning, collecting donations and garnering support. Arvind, in one of his speeches, aptly summed up our position: 'We have come not to do politics, but to teach politics.'

To ensure that elections were won without corruption, we had to create systems that would reward fair practice. Elected politicians had to be assured that they wouldn't need to worry about making money for the next round of elections. Ordinary citizens had to be encouraged to contribute clean money to the party, and the party, in turn, had to fund its candidates.

We made a few decisions that would pave the way for honest politics, and equally, help us win the 2013 elections.

For one, we decided to make concrete promises. All sorts of vows had been made over time by politicians, few of which had translated into reality. The credibility of party politics was at an all-time low, and voters had grown cynical, convinced that no matter which party won, they would lose. Indeed, voters believed that it was far better to take what they got—money or incentives—rather than expect parties to deliver on their promises. It was to convince voters that we were committed to their cause that we promised a 50 per cent reduction in electricity bills and free water supply to the poorest, after doing our due diligence. Arvind's fast unto death further underscored AAP's seriousness and willingness to do everything it could to keep its pledge.

Second, we decided to leverage the power of social media. We had some of the most dedicated citizens in the party, many of whom were computer wizards. Our exceptional social media campaign let us engage directly with literate sections of society in India and outside.

Third, we charted out a detailed map for the upcoming elections, pinning down the minutest detail. A comprehensive selection procedure for candidates was spelt out. A candidate securing the signatures of over 100 local supporters could submit his name. This candidate had to fill a form disclosing his criminal history, political background, wealth, knowledge of swaraj and participation in social movements. The form was to be studied by the Screening Committee; it would then shortlist and announce five names for a particular constituency. These names would be advertised on AAP's website, along with the details that had been submitted, and public opinion would be sought. If there was an allegation against a candidate, common people could make all disclosures with evidence. After this, the opinion of volunteers was to be sought. Finally, after considering all the facts, AAP's PAC had to take the decision about the candidates who would be fielded. That the system was strong was proven when, at the last minute, a Rajouri Garden candidate was removed because allegations had surfaced against him.

Fourth, we were clear that there would be zero tolerance for dishonesty or criminality. Strict instructions were issued that neither the party nor the candidate would make communal or caste appeals. Winning was not the sole priority. The priority was setting a benchmark for contesting elections.

Fifth, AAP had to have completely transparent funding.

Each donation received had to be displayed on the official website in a matter of minutes. Once the funding target of Rs 18 crore was achieved, the party stopped collecting money. Every rupee was properly accounted for. Any discrepancy in funding was to be dealt with severely.

Our manifesto, too, was noteworthy. The public was consulted, and an able team comprising Yogendra Yadav and Manish Sisodia drafted it. A reduction in electricity rates, auditing electricity companies, offering free water up to 20,000 liters per family—these were some of our promises. Along with this, we vowed to fight for Jan Lokpal and prioritize education and health. A pro-poor budget was proposed. Additionally, each of the seventy constituencies was asked to prepare its own manifesto.

However, everything was not as it had to be. After Yogendra Yadav, Prof Anand Kumar, and Atishi Marlena (a young and brilliant thinker and activist), among others, worked for months to create a comprehensive, detailed national policy on key issues facing the nation—across the economy, environment, industry, foreign policy, labour—Arvind rubbished the idea of policy-making. 'Let us not make complicated policies which can create controversies. A simple, populist manifesto—that is enough to win an election,' he said. While I was not in favour of policy vagueness, it was impossible to make Arvind think differently.

*

What grabbed headlines for AAP was Arvind's announcement that he would stand against Sheila Dixit in the elections.

On my part, when I got wind of this move, I was most

enthused. What audacity! And what complete disregard for power and personal victory! Arvind had chosen not to play it safe; rather, he had volunteered to lead from the front. This was independent India's biggest dharma yudh—a veritable war where a small band of honest, daring patriots dared to take on the Hydra-headed corrupt—and Arvind and our merry band were charging forward.

When news of Arvind's decision to fight Sheila Dixit went public, I sent a message to him late at night. 'Arvind, you don't worry about Sheila, I will fight the battle on your behalf. You take on Delhi.' My conscience wouldn't let me live a normal life in Mumbai when the battlefield was in Delhi. By 5 am, Arvind excitedly replied, asking me to come as soon as I could. The next morning, I talked to my family, seeking their permission to remain stationed in Delhi. While I was actively involved with party affairs from Mumbai, the battleground was now Delhi, and I had to be there.

Soon after, I reached the capital and went to stay in a hotel. The waiter working there saw my AAP badge and asked me if he could have it. When I told him that I was part of AAP's NE, his eyes shone and he asked: 'Can I just come with you and see Arvind Kejriwal?' Later, I learnt that the cleaner of the room, too, was an ardent AAP supporter. When I made my way to the hotel's entrance, all the auto-rickshaw drivers waiting outside asked me for AAP badges. The support coming from all quarters energized me. Over the next few days in Delhi, I talked to over a hundred workers and drivers, all of them were in favour of our young party. I felt as though I were in the epicenter of a revolution.

*

Since we were leveraging all channels to get our message across, I told Arvind, 'We need a revamped website and a party newsletter which can be distributed to the people of Delhi.' Arvind connected me with his architect-friend Satyendra Jain and his website designer.

I met Satyendra Jain in a restaurant, and he immediately offered to fund the newsletter every month. However, when he suggested giving me cash, I grew uncomfortable. I spoke to Arvind, and he suggested that Satyendra Jain could directly pay the printer of the newsletter every month. That is how *AAP Ki Kranti*, the party's newsletter, was born. Simultaneously, I worked on restructuring the website, so as to make it easy to navigate, and so it would become attractive and effective.

During this time, Arvind also asked me to take charge of training and monitoring seven of AAP's candidates, including Somnath Bharti, Saurabh Bhardwaj and Shazia Ilmi. Working with both Somnath and Saurabh proved to be an enriching experience.

Somnath was a lawyer and was passionate about the movement. He had a huge sofachair in his office on which he'd sit like a king, surrounded by his small team. As soon as we were introduced to each other, Somnath said, 'Mayankji, I have a wonderful strategy for the election.'

'What is that?'

Somnath continued, highly excited, 'I want to make a computer game!'

I was taken aback.

He continued, 'In this game, AAP volunteers will be wearing caps and hiding behind trees . . . and when the time is right, they'll come out and shoot the Congress and the BJP.'

I grew anxious.

'I will give this game free of charge to the students, and after they play it, people will be certain to vote for us.'

I sat in stunned silence.

Thankfully, the idea died a natural death.

My brief interaction with Somanth made it clear that we were still novices making sense of mainstream politics. But what we did have was enthusiasm. Somnath was hardworking, sincere, popular in his constituency, and willing to fight for the party's core principles—this would hold him, and us, in good stead.

While Somnath was flamboyant, Saurabh was entirely the opposite. He was a soft-spoken engineer who had quit his job. To me, he was the ideal candidate, and I was glad that after his victory he became a minister in the Delhi Government. We used to interact every day, and I enjoyed guiding him.

As for Shazia, she was one of the most aggressive and combative candidates. She sought attention and resources for herself—possibly because she was in a tough constituency. It was unfortunate that she lost by few votes.

*

During the Delhi elections, I also had the opportunity of interacting with Yogendra Yadav. I must confess, to begin with, I had an uneasy feeling about Yogendra. This wasn't for any logical reason; I was simply wary because he spoke very sweetly. I felt that there was a gap between what he thought and how he presented himself. Fortunately, when he invited me to stay at his house for a few days, I was able to see that I had been harbouring a misconception.

A key giveaway of a man's character is the way he

behaves with his family. Yogendra used to cook and clean dishes, and was more than an equal partner while running his house with his wife. When I discussed politics and social issues with him, I found that he was a virtual mine of information and had balanced opinions. The doubts I had about him vanished, and I came to realize he was genuine.

Yogendra Yadav and I were given the task of designing the campaign plan. A Delhi Campaign Group (DCG) was created for guiding the overall strategy of the party, for the implementation of plans, for firefighting and emergency decision-making, and to ensure smooth coordination between various sub-groups. We would either meet or schedule a conference call each day, and would periodically report to the PAC or NE. The DCG members included:

- Arvind Kejriwal, chair: He was in charge of the DCG as a whole, and looked into communication strategy and content, and the budget.
- Manish Sisodia: He handled media management, helped with communication strategy and was a spokesperson.
- Yogendra Yadav: He was to oversee data collection and research, and was also to steer our communication strategy. (Later on, his role was enhanced, and he became chief spokesperson of the party.)
- Pankaj Gupta: He looked into funds and donations.
- Mayank Gandhi: I was in charge of volunteer management.
- Sanjay Singh, Gopal Rai, Durgesh Pathak, Dilip Pandey: They were to supervise campaign management.

In addition, Kumar Vishwas was to oversee communication strategy as well as social media.

Once our roles were assigned, I took on the task of gathering volunteers from all over the country for campaigning closer to the time of the elections. I made multiple calls, sent messages, updated blogs and participated in Google Hangouts. Thousands of volunteers from the far corners of India flooded the streets of Delhi for campaigning. What was even more extraordinary was that we had NRIs trooping in from across the world, hoping to contribute to this people's party. I received hundreds of inquiry calls from the United States, Australia, the United Kingdom, Canada; each wished to assist AAP. Unknown faces became friends, stayed at the homes of volunteers, and assisted in every way they could. Together we created a tsunami of a campaign. We were everywhere—in public spaces, in shops distributing caps, in maidans shouting slogans, singing and dancing. Maharashtra led with the highest number of volunteers and the largest donations. But the rest weren't far behind.

Other parties, long used to dealing with each other, were caught unawares with the support that AAP was getting. Their response? Denial and accusations. Sheila Dixit told the media, 'The Congress is in a direct fight with the BJP. AAP doesn't even qualify as her opponent.' In another interview, she commented, 'I would like to ask AAP what's your policy, what's your ideology? What are you going to work for? And what is your record?' Elsewhere, in a magazine interview, she went on to assert, 'Kejriwal is not even on our radar!'

Digvijay Singh, a senior Congress leader, wrote a letter to Arvind Kejriwal, where he described him as 'a self-serving ambitious megalomaniac with scant regard for democracy'.[11] On another occasion, he tweeted, 'Arvind Kejriwal is like Rakhi Sawant. They both try and expose but with no substance.' A senior leader went on to challenge Arvind: 'Let Mr Kejriwal first get elected as an MP or MLA or even a municipal corporator.'

While some of our volunteers and leaders grew angry, I was glad. I wanted the opposition to underestimate our strengths. Arvind, on his part, said, 'The Congress seems completely rattled and baffled. That is apparent from Digvijay's letter.'

Yet, perhaps, deep down, Arvind was anxious. I recall, when I spoke to him about a friend who conducted opinion polls, and suggested that we conduct an internal opinion poll of our own to gauge the real mood in Delhi, Arvind replied, 'Sure, but will the polls display a positive result and favour us?' I was surprised. Did perceptions matter or did the truth? I did not appreciate the suggestion that a poll that favoured us alone was worthy of attention. I let the idea die.

But what remained alive was my desire to see an honest movement gain ground. This was a do or die battle for our future. India could wait no more.

*

Soon, it was election day. And then, it was time for the results to be announced. In Mumbai, confident that the Delhi elections would not disappoint, we arranged a public meeting where we kept announcing news updates as they trickled in. The crowd grew increasingly euphoric.

Despite the Congress' dismissal of us (or perhaps because of it), and despite Arvind's own nervousness, the final results were entirely in favour of truth and justice. India won. Delhi overwhelmingly declared that change had arrived. AAP, a one-year-old party, secured 28 seats, completely decimating the Congress and preventing the BJP from getting an absolute majority. Equally, in a mega political shocker, Arvind Kejriwal defeated three-time chief minister, Sheila Dikshit, in her constituency by roughly 22,000 votes.

TV channels that had predicted a handful of seats for AAP were left red-faced. The cynics, who had said that this day would never arrive, were dumbstruck. The TV pundits, who believed that the target set by AAP was too high, now conceded that we had pulled a miracle through sheer hard work and idealism.

While AAP had not secured a majority, it had certainly fared far better than anyone had anticipated.

*

As news of Delhi's election results trickled in, in our office at Mumbai we had a queue, winding up the staircase and across two floors, of people who wanted to meet me and join the party. We had put up a banner with Arvind's picture saying, 'If you want to join the party for a position or a post, you are not welcome. If you want to join to serve the nation, you are at the right place.'

There were several entities from rival political groups who wished to jump ship and volunteer with AAP, but we remained wary of them. This was a crucial period for us; here was an opportunity, but also a threat. We wished to scale up our party and make it national, but we also knew that there was a danger of inducting those who were power hungry. We had to remain balanced, sober and cautious, without getting swayed by national hype.

AAM AADMI PARTY

आम आदमी पार्टी

यह देश के लिए तन मन और धन न्यौछावर करने का अवसर है।

"आम आदमी पार्टी कोई पार्टी नही है, इस देश की राजनिति को पारदर्शक और स्वच्छ करने के लिए एक राजनैतिक क्रांति है। यह आजादी की दूसरी लड़ाई है। यह भ्रष्टाचार, घरानेशाही और अपराधिक जैसे बातों से राजनीति को आजाद करने की लड़ाई है। इसलिए इसमें किसीभी प्रकार का निजी स्वार्थ बहुत बड़ी बाधा बन सकता है। इसलिए अपने मन को अच्छी तरह से टटोलकर देख ले की मन में किसी कोने में कोई पद पाने की लालसा या किसी कमिटी का सदस्य बनने की या चुनाव में टिकट पाने की तमन्ना तो नहीं है? ऐसे में आप देशभक्ति का काम नहीं कर पाएंगे और कल आपकी इच्छापूर्ति नहीं हुई तो आप दुखी होंगे। दुखी होकर आप पार्टी में तनाव निर्माण करोगे जो देशद्रोह जैसे ही होगा। क्या आप निस्वार्थ भाव से देश के लिए सर्वस्व न्योछावर करने के लिए तैयार है? यदि हाँ, तभी संकल्प पत्र भरे।

अरविंद केजरीवाल

/AAPMumbai /AAPMumbai www.AAPMaharashtra.org 7303150500 Mumbai@AAPMaharashtra.org

By temperament, I am composed and calm. I needed to ensure that our volunteers had a similar attitude. I had to keep them in check if they displayed sign of rudeness of arrogance. I spent long hours counselling our members and only admitting newcomers who genuinely saw AAP as a tool to serve. In Mumbai, we went so far as to ensure that no new member would get any position in the party until he served the nation well for eight months. We were not looking for short-term gains. We had a long-term goal—establishing a government of integrity.

Personally, I felt vindicated. My goal of creating a model of fair electoral success had been achieved. For probably the first time since independence, we were seeing that honesty and winning elections were compatible. Delhi's election results proved that the future of India could be sculptured by good and honest people who had no desire to use dishonest means.

13. 'I Quit!'

THE VERDICT IN DELHI PRESENTED BEFORE US VERY interesting permutations and combinations.

Out of 70 seats, 32 were won by the BJP, 28 by new entrant AAP, and 8 by the Congress (the remaining 2 seats were won by others). As no party had won a majority in the assembly, if a coalition government wasn't formed, Delhi would be put under president's rule until a fresh election six months later.

The BJP, sensing that the mood favoured AAP, took a principled stand; it chose not to indulge in horse-trading or seek the support of the Congress to gain a majority. The BJP had another sly motive guiding its decision—it wanted to put AAP in a spot.

We now had one of three options:

1. To be in opposition
2. To call for fresh polls
3. To take support of the Congress party to form government

A 28-seat conquest, while clearly not the majority, was seen as a major victory for a new party, and the perception in Delhi and outside was that AAP had won. The onus, therefore, was on us to form a government. Shirking that duty would disappoint the public. Yet . . . taking support from the Congress seemed completely unethical to us. We were in a quandary.

It was then that the Congress decided to offer outside support to AAP to honour the verdict and avoid a re-election. The Congress knew that if there were a re-election, its traditional voters, many of them already lost to AAP, would abandon the party entirely, and it would have no presence in the Delhi assembly. By offering support, even though from the outside, it would remain in the game.

How were we to respond to the Congress' offer? We mulled, and after lengthy discussions, we decided to go back to our principles of transparency and participation. We had already been espousing the model of a referendum to involve people with urgent decision-making. This was the model we now had to embrace.

We framed a (rather smart) question for the citizens of Delhi: *Should AAP form the government?* 272 Mohalla Sabha meetings were called, and around three lakh responses were received. We sought people's opinion online, too; we got 6,97,310 responses through our website, phone calls and text messages. A huge majority was overwhelmingly in support of AAP forming the government.

We had to respect the common people's decision. Despite our reservations about the Congress' support, we decided to form the government. Thus ended the political impasse brought about by the 8 December verdict.

*

In keeping with the spirit of his party—one that favoured the common people—Arvind's swearing-in ceremony was in the Ramlila Maidan. For the first time, this was not a site of protest, but one of opportunity. When I reached the venue, I saw thousands waving the flags, crying, shouting slogans and dreaming of a better India.

From a huge stage, Arvind spoke, his voice constricted by far too many overwhelming emotions: 'Friends, today is a historic day. This oath is not taken by Arvind Kejriwal and the six ministers. The people of Delhi have taken the oath as chief minister and ministers. This movement was to give power into the hands of the people. Today is a victory for the common people. People have done a great work at the elections. People of the country had lost hope. But this time, in the Delhi polls, people showed that elections can be fought with honesty, elections can be won with honesty. I want to thank Ishwar, Allah and Wahe Guru. The victory looks like a miracle. Two years ago, we never thought people will be able to uproot corrupt politics and establish a people's government. This is just the beginning. The real fight is a long one. But six-seven ministers cannot fight it alone. If 1.5 crore people of Delhi come together, we can uproot corruption.'

And then, in his earthy voice, he sang, along with thousands of others, a song that asked for peace and brotherhood:

Insaan ka insaan se ho bhaichara, yehi paigham hamara.
Har ek mahal se kaho ki jhopriyon main diye jalaye.
Choto aur badon main ab koi phark nahi rah jaye.
Is dharti par ho pyar ka ghar-ghar ujiyara.
Yehi paigham hamara.
Insaan ka insaan se ho bhaichara, yehi paigham hamara.

I felt lucky to be a part of that moment.

When Arvind ended his speech with '*Jai Hind, Inquilab*

Zindabad and *Vande Mataram*', the energy all around was electrifying. Some became emotional, many wept, strangers clung to strangers.

As Arvind was leaving, I met him. He looked at me and gave a spontaneous warm hug. It had been an emotional ride, and we had come a long way.

*

From the outset, we sensed that our government, with tenuous Congress support, would not last very long. We had to use every minute to build support for the party for the next phase. Hence, the AAP government started functioning dizzyingly fast, ticking off each item on the agenda. Exemplary governance was shown, and the media supported us. In a matter of a few weeks, AAP sharply reduced the price of public utilities, moved hundreds of officials who were suspected of corruption out of key jobs, and ordered his own ministers to shun red beacon cars.

Arvind is a brilliant manager, and he micro-managed every decision. His cabinet was capable and driven. While it had almost zero experience in matters of governance, it displayed zeal.

It is not vital for politicians to have experience in governance. It is the intent that matters. Many a times, if experience is married to corruption—if liquor contractors control excise, and criminals control home ministries—there's need for those who are unsullied, untested. AAP came with the right intent, and in Arvind, it had a leader who was qualified.

That being said, AAP consisted of a bunch of activists; these were system-breakers and not system-makers. Our task was to push for development, but we were masters of confrontation.

For instance, on the night of 15/16 January 2014, Law Minister Somnath Bharti, in a vigilante-type operation, raided some houses where women of African descent were living, accusing them of running a prostitution and drugs racket. His high-handed behaviour was caught on camera; he spat and made racist remarks. The country was shocked by his behaviour, and was doubly shocked with AAP justifying his conduct.

In a similar vein, on 20 January, less than one month after coming to power, AAP decided to begin a protest, demanding executive control of the Delhi police. The police force, as per the Constitution, is under the control of the central government; AAP, however, pointed out that, under such a situation, it could not deliver good governance. It also began an indefinite protest seeking statehood for Delhi.

In the biting cold and rain of the capital, Arvind and many volunteers spent a night sleeping on the city's roads. Their protests could come in the way of India's Republic Day celebrations on 26 January—and their lack of respect for this seminal day upset many. An angry Arvind said his party was not responsible for any disruption to the annual parade (which was meant to pass just metres away from the protest site).

Expectedly, AAP came to be labelled as a party of anarchists. The more often we slipped into situations of conflict, the more annoyed voters got. They wanted governance, not everyday protests. AAP's tussle with the police and the central government only irked them.

Arvind, in less than a week, shattered his own image, doing all the things the average politician—the creature he so despised and derided—was known for: neglecting the law; bullying, browbeating and threatening all detractors, including the media; throwing the capital of India into chaos; and even threatening to interrupt the most visible national event that projected India as a united, powerful nation. AAP, rather than governing well, was being disruptive.

It was time for us to understand that our role had changed. We were no longer the adversaries of the system, we *were* the system. Since I was concerned about the direction the government was taking—and was also overwhelmed by calls from supporters condemning the party's negative behaviour—I decided to write to Arvind. My email read:

> Dear Arvind,
> Please reconsider the blatant aggression. I specially did not appreciate Somnath's language (BTW, it's looking terrible on TV). Please find a[n] honorable way to pass [a] strong resolution in the Assembly [for statehood].
>
> Also, after having made the point [about] police inaction, every incident, rape or corruption [scandal] will bring in more support to our cause. Many of our supporters, specially outside Delhi, are getting worried and jittery.

Fortunately, the very evening my email was delivered, the protest that was derailing the capital was called off.

Around this time, I began to notice certain changes in Arvind's behaviour. After shunning pomp and show, he now seemed to seek all the frills that go with key positions. Government employees are often perceived as extracting all the perks they can get from the system; maybe Arvind, as an ex-revenue officer, saw value in going down the beaten path.

The first indication that there was a gap between what Arvind said and did came when he decided to move into two adjacent, sprawling five-bedroom duplex houses. When confronted, Arvind remained brazen. He refused to pay heed to the media or to public opinion. As an onlooker, I was at once shocked and puzzled since the Arvind I knew would sleep on the floor and lead a most Spartan lifestyle.

Around that time, there was an NE meeting. Arvind was on his way. While we were waiting for him, I sent him a text message: '*You are damaging the positive image of AAP for such a small thing and if you continue to insist on the houses, I will have no option but to register my public protest.*' Ten minutes later, Arvind arrived and told the press that he had decided to forego the houses; he wished to look for a smaller residence. Whether it was because of my message, I will never know. But I was happy that he relinquished what seemed like a dangerous pursuit.

*

Early on, we faced a huge question. The Lok Sabha 2014 elections were around the corner. Did it make sense for us to contest? If so, how many seats could we stand from? Did we have the resources required? Did we have the bandwidth for this mammoth project?

Arvind's view was that of an activist. 'Let us fight a symbolic battle, by standing in a few constituencies with notoriously corrupt ministers and challenging them. Take on the most visible emblems of corruption!'

Yogendra Yadav had a different proposition. He suggested that because AAP had a relatively firm presence in urban areas, the party had to fight across the metro cities, while focusing specifically on some states. His calculation showed that in Delhi, Punjab, Haryana and Maharashtra, the party could get more than 10 per cent of the votes, and if it managed to win over 6 per cent of the votes in four states, it would become a nationally recognized party. On hearing this, Arvind mocked him: 'Yogenji, are we here to get 6 per cent? You all talk like losers . . . we are here to win.' Chastened with this admonition, Yogendra withdrew his suggestion.

A National Executive meeting was called on 4 January 2014 to strategize and arrive at tactics to win the general elections. It was a packed meeting, and as speaker after speaker stood up to give his views, Arvind entered. He listened to various opinions, and then he put forth his thoughts. He wished to fight across those constituencies where there were corrupt MPs. As soon as he sat down, Shanti Bhushan came in. The mood in the room had been ambivalent until then. 'Today, the Congress is in shambles, and the BJP is discredited. AAP is the rising force, and people are looking at it with great hope. We will be doing a major disservice to the country if we do not offer it honest and good candidates. We must field the maximum number of candidates across the country—as many as 400—and give a voice to those who want honest politics.' Raising his pitch, he said, 'I ask you, my friends—must we starve the nation of honest politics simply because our party lacks audacity?' The atmosphere got charged, and Arvind and the rest of us started clapping. Arvind took the mic and, against thunderous applause, said, 'Let's go for broke.' The cheering did not stop for five whole minutes.

Various strategic decisions followed. I vividly remember a meeting where we had to decide whether Yogendra Yadav would focus on Haryana or take on a national role in the party. Manish Sisodia and some others were keen that Yogendra be stationed in Haryana, while Prashant and a few of us felt that he should contribute to the national campaign. While the proposal was being put on the table, Yogendra walked out of the room saying, 'As I am the interested party in this decision, it would be improper for me to stay in the room . . . the members will find it difficult to frankly give their views.' Finally, it was decided that Yogendra Yadav would be the spokesperson of the party and play a national role.

In the run-up to the elections, there were some things that were already aligned in our favour. In a short period, we had been able to garner a disproportionate amount of attention. Social media, TV and the print outlets kept flashing news from AAP. Despite all the early hiccups, the honeymoon period was still alive and well. We could leverage this to have a solid chance in the general elections.

However, we still had work to do. Fighting elections in India is both an art and a science. It comes with two major components: the environment and the ground force. While we had been able to reach the hearts and minds of most people—we had nurtured a conducive environment—our presence on the ground was negligible (except in a few states).

To fight elections across the nation, we needed ground force. We also needed to project our leader as a genuine claimant for the highest post; sustain a mood that favoured the party; and, in a fight against Goliath, appeal to voters to support David.

How were we to achieve all of this? There seemed to be only one answer: we had to resign from the Delhi government in a blaze of glory.

There were a number of factors that motivated this decision. For one, Arvind needed to be freed from his responsibilities as chief minister to campaign nationally for the party.

For another, cracks had already begun between AAP and the Congress in the Delhi government; it was only a matter of time before the alliance fell. Besides, even if the alliance were to survive, it would be impossible to fight the general elections across the country saddled with allegations of colluding with a corrupt Congress. If we had to paint the BJP and Congress as villains and gain the sympathy of the voters, we had to be free of both of them.

Equally, the Lokpal Bill, which we had promised in our manifesto, was still on our minds. As a national force, there was a far stronger chance that we'd be able to pass it in its original form.

An exit strategy was planned. To create a wave of sympathy for the party and its leader, Arvind had to be projected as a 'martyr'—as someone willing to give up everything for a cause célèbre—in this case, the Lokpal Bill. We decided to push for the original Lokpal Bill—which no opposition party would accept—place this before the assembly, offer the BJP and Congress a wide berth to object, and allow Arvind to become a hero by resigning.

Yogendra Yadav and some of us, including me, felt that this move was hasty. We suggested organizing a referendum across Delhi before resigning . . . but we were in too much of a hurry.

On 8 February 2014, Arvind spoke to the press. 'If the Jan Lokpal Bill is not passed, then I have no right to stay on as the Delhi chief minister. I am ready to sacrifice the chair of a chief minister to free the country from corruption.' Arvind spoke as per the script.

The Jan Lokpal Bill could only be introduced after the approval of the lieutenant governor. Defying the lieutenant governor's advice, the AAP government tabled the Bill before the assembly. Almost in conjunction, for strategic reasons that would soon be clear, a criminal case over gas pricing was filed against Mukesh Ambani of Reliance.

In the assembly, trouble broke out immediately with the BJP and the Congress vehemently opposing the government's attempts at tabling the Bill—they claimed that the party was violating the Constitution. AAP's proposal for the introduction of a Lokpal Bill was struck down.

In response, Arvind thundered, 'When we tried to pass the Delhi Jan Lokpal, the Congress and the BJP ganged up to stall it. Why did this happen? Because three days back, we registered an FIR against Mukesh Ambani who runs this country. For the last ten years, he was backing the UPA [United Progressive Alliance] government, but for the last one year, he is behind Narendra Modi. From where does Mr Modi get so much money?' Arvind was alleging that there existed a nexus between the Congress and the BJP, and powerful industrialists.

He continued, 'People from the Congress and the BJP know if this law is brought in, their leaders will end up in jail. They realized that after we booked Mukesh Ambani [. . .], if we pass the Jan Lokpal Bill then other senior leaders [. . .] may be next in line.'[12] As always, Arvind had found a way of singling out a powerful industrialist to highlight a socio-political cause.

Amidst such chaos, Arvind went on to resign: 'For

the first time in the history of the country, someone has stepped down from power to uphold the principles for which people had voted for him. We have resigned to take the fight against the corrupt to its end. The Delhi assembly should be dissolved and re-elections should take place.'

This was a premeditated move. The idea was that with the upsurge of support due to AAP's stand, the party would be able sweep the national polls. Delhi would now be under President's Rule.

Meanwhile, Parliament wanted to get Lokpal out of the way. In a smart move, the Congress, with the tacit approval of the BJP, met Kiran Bedi and showed her a watered down version of the Lokpal Bill. Among other things, this draft did not make the CBI autonomous; rather, the CBI continued to remain under the government's control. Kiran, who during the IAC days had been uncompromising regarding the need for CBI autonomy, somersaulted and found nothing objectionable in the provisions of the new diluted Lokpal. Salman Khurshid and some others, meanwhile, met Anna clandestinely and got his approval for this weak Bill with compromised provisions.[13] My respect for Anna nosedived after I heard about this from reliable sources. Prashant Bhushan, questioning the effectiveness of the new Bill, rightly called it 'Jokepal'. The country lost and politicians won. But the story was not yet over . . .

While Arvind had resigned as Delhi's chief minister after just forty-nine days in power, there was the wide open national arena.

14. The Lok Sabha: And Then There Were Four

As we eyed the national stage, our target ceased being the Congress; it was the resurgent BJP and its supreme leader Modi. From anti-corruption, the agenda was now anti-communalism. AAP was quietly certain that it would bag at least 100 seats in the Lok Sabha elections. If not the king, we could certainly be the kingmaker. Arvind said in a press conference: 'There will be a fractured mandate . . . there will be another election, within two or three years.' Our confidence was sky-high.

But, perhaps, our self-assurance was misplaced. The BJP was fast gaining support. The anger against the system, and especially the Congress that had been cultivated by the IAC movement, was helping the BJP gain a strong foothold across the nation. Narendra Modi's advance toward Delhi was near effortless. Rivals within his party fell easily by the wayside. His slogan, '*Na khate hai, na khane dete hai*,' (loosely translated as 'We don't steal, not do we let others steal') became a leading campaign tool for the party, which adopted our anti-corruption plank. His reasonably good stint as the two-time chief minister of Gujarat worked in his favour. The riots of 2002 were almost forgotten.

The BJP ran a very smart, high-octane and focused

campaign promising 'acche din' ('good days') and decisive governance. Their election machinery was well-oiled and brilliantly managed. Thousands of crores were spent on media and outdoor advertising.

The election was less about issues and more about personalities—it was all about comparing Rahul Gandhi and Manmohan Singh, the faces of the Congress, to Narendra Modi. And when pitted against these Congress leaders, Modi seemed miles ahead.

AAP, on its part, decided to do what it did best—attack. We adopted the campaign line, 'BJP-Congress bhai-bhai'—'the BJP and Congress are brothers'—highlighting the fact that mainstream political parties had sold their souls to corruption and crony capitalism. We tried to project ourselves as being unlike them. We also began naming and shaming practically every powerful person—from Adani to Ambani—accusing them of being corrupt. We shouted out every possible allegation with merry abandon, from Godhra to Snoopgate. Where the Congress was the proverbial kettle, unable to call anyone 'black', AAP was new, without history, and therefore perfectly positioned to play the aggressor.

Yogendra Yadav announced, 'We have decided to take on the BJP and Modi frontally. To begin with by consistently asking questions that has not been asked in the public domain. Perhaps the Congress doesn't feel it is in a position to ask these questions. We will raise certain issues. We will use the social media, which is a big platform now. We will raise these issues and go to the streets demanding answers. Modi is, after all, seeking to be PM of India, so the questions will have to be raised everywhere across India.'[14]

*

When news spread in Maharashtra that AAP had national ambitions, other local parties, especially those that were extremely corrupt, became concerned. Anjali Damania, the AAP Maharashtra convenor and an indomitable fighter against the dishonest, had locked horns with ministers from the NCP and had gathered major documents exposing scams totalling tens of thousands of crores. Cases were filed, and a vociferous and high-profile campaign was run.

I was in a meeting in the new AAP Mumbai office, when I got a call: 'Mayankbhai, our old Chakala office has been assaulted by goons. They entered, burnt an effigy of Arvind Kejriwal, and splatted black ink across our premises and banners.' I rushed to the Chakala office to find that the police had taken away the goons—it emerged they were from the NCP—to the police station.[15]

I took a stand that we would not resort to violent counter-protests. Rather, in a Gandhian manner, we decided to walk to the NCP office with brooms and clean their premises. Many volunteers joined us en route, gathered brooms and started marching towards the NCP office. Onlookers and the media began rooting for us. The police wished to stop us, but did not know the section under which they could to prohibit us. After all, the Indian Penal Code did not prevent people from quietly cleaning offices.

Finally, after great deliberation, the police alleged that we were responsible for a 'possible disturbance of peace'. We were taken to the MIDC police station. By this time, lakhs of text messages had travelled across the city, and hundreds of volunteers and supporters gathered outside the police station shouting slogans like '*Bharat Mata ki Jai*' and '*Vande Mataram*'. AAP leaders, too—from Medha

Patkar to Meera Sanyal—watched the proceedings closely and remained supportive.

The Assistant Commissioner of Police (ACP) told us that he would release us, provided we went home silently. We refused; we wanted to clean the NCP offices! The crowds, in the meantime, kept burgeoning, and the media ran this live. Finally, at midnight, at their wits' end, the police let us go and sweep the NCP office, which we did. It was a symbolic gesture but demonstrated how committed our party was to countering violence in a Gandhian way.

*

Yogendra Yadav launched the Maharashtra Lok Sabha campaign with a huge rally comprising all the candidates from Mumbai.

A few days later, Arvind was to visit India's business capital for campaigning. We decided that we'd take him by auto-rickshaw from the airport to the train station and, from there, he could catch a Mumbai local to Churchgate. Our organizers had purchased several train tickets to accommodate our volunteers.

It was a hot and sweaty day, and thousands of supporters milled around Santacruz station, shouting slogans; boot polish workers and railway coolies welcomed Arvind.

When we entered the local train, I softly asked him, so the media wouldn't be able to overhear our conversation, 'Shazia and Kumar Vishwas, with their media utterances about AAP, are vitiating the atmosphere. What is the real issue here?'

My question emerged from the fact that both Shazia and Kumar had expressed their unhappiness to the media with PAC and the ticket distribution mechanism we had in place. While Shazia griped that she did not wish to run against Sonia Gandhi from Rae Bareli, Kumar was fairly vocal about the choice of candidates not being up to the mark. My view was exactly the opposite; I applauded AAP for choosing candidates across the spectrum, from businessmen to farmers, from activists like Medha Patkar to bankers like Meera Sanyal.

When he heard my question, Arvind's voice grew grave. He said, 'Shazia keeps calling me every day, asking for sundry party positions, cribbing that she has been marginalized or has not been invited to a PAC meeting. It would be good for the party and for my peace of mind if she quit.' He aired similar views about Kumar as well.

Our journey ended. Arvind's arrival at Churchgate, and his trip to Mumbai as a whole, created quite a stir, with massive support from religious minorities, Dalits and women. His presence added great value to what was already an exciting and innovative campaign in Mumbai and Maharashtra.

In the State Executive meeting of Maharashtra that followed, it was decided that I would contest the elections, while Anjali would not. She would, instead, campaign across the state. Roughly fifteen days later, however, Arvind called Anjali and persuaded her to contest from Nagpur against the BJP's Nitin Gadkari.

While each candidate had his own style of campaigning, in Mumbai's north-west constituency, from where I was standing, the campaign was ingenious. Tapping into what we had understood about the art and science of elections, we plotted out a huge map of the constituency, tracking every locality in a scientific manner, and allocating teams for each pocket. The voter list was like our Bhagavad

Gita, which we continuously referred to for names and demographic details. We had dedicated volunteers who navigated streets, local trains and buses, covered over 50,000 households, and talked to perfect strangers for the cause of a corruption-free and secular nation. The back-office team consisted mainly of students—from IITians to chartered accountants. And for rallies, padyatras and door-to-door campaigns, we often roped in celebrities.

Among the celebrities whose help we sough were singers Kailash Kher and Vishal Dadlani. I had heard rumours about the two not being the best of friends. So, I asked them individually if they'd consider coming together for my final public meeting. Both of them agreed: 'No problem, we will set aside our differences for you.' On stage, they hugged one another and sang *Allah ke Banday* in one voice. Consumed by national fervor, they abandoned past misunderstandings. That was the day I lost my father—I learnt he was no more as *Allah ke Banday* ended. How strange to have a moment of joy and deep pain entwined.

Speaking of celebrities, since my constituency consisted of Juhu and Lokhandwala, which housed several Bollywood and TV artistes, I found myself contesting against various stars. Film-maker Mahesh Manjrekar represented the Maharashtra Navnirman Sena (MNS); actor-producer Kamaal R Khan (KRK) stood from the Samajwadi Party; and actor Rakhi Sawant was an independent candidate.

This mix of candidates grabbed eyeballs. KRK, notorious for being abusive, carried a series of filthy tweets about women—there were complaints against him and he was asked to be replaced. As for Rakhi Sawant, she was most entertaining. Her election symbol was a green chilli. She'd periodically organize a large rally of open trucks, and she'd stand atop one and shout to those on the road: '*Ae, lal shirt walle, ae takle, mereko vote dena!*' ('You, man in the red shirt, you, bald fellow, vote for me!') She even twisted an innocent remark I had once made so it sounded downright misogynistic.

In this fray, I was convinced I stood a solid chance of victory. However, destiny had other plans. During the campaign, I had made it a point to reach out to minority leaders. When I approached Muslim opinion-makers, I told them that AAP had a three-fold agenda for the community—one, it wished to fast-track the cases of Muslim youth accused of terrorism and, if they had been framed, punish those actually responsible; second, it aimed to reduce poverty and the huge gap between genders; and third, it hoped to treat all individuals equally and involve AAP's Muslim leaders with the party's decision-making processes. These ideas were heartily welcomed by the community's leaders, who, in any case, were disenchanted with the Congress' habit of using them as vote banks.

However, just a day prior to the elections, there was a message sent out to the Muslim community from mosques and madrasas. They were asked to vote strategically for the Congress since the belief was that this was ultimately a race between the BJP and the Congress. Even though AAP's stance was appreciated, the perception was that a vote in its favour was a wasted vote.

The next day, when I saw long queues of people at a polling booth, most of whom knew nothing about my candidacy, I realized my chances were dim. How had I misjudged the mood of my constituency earlier? It struck me that during rallies, when people used to stop our car and give us a thumbs up signal, it possibly wasn't meant to be a sign of encouragement—rather, this was a local gesture that conveyed nothing, zero, thenga.

As it happened, the Shiv Sena won in my constituency. The Congress came second, and I lost my deposit, standing fourth with just over 50,000 votes. It was a rude awakening.

*

When my election campaign ended, I knew it was time to join a larger scuffle. Varanasi was calling. It had become the center of a battle of proportions that I had not envisaged—a battle of ideologies, a battle between money and power on one hand and pure passion on the other. Arvind had chosen to contest against Narendra Modi. This was his attempt at showing his defiance before the BJP.

The campaign in Varanasi attracted people from all parts of India. Thousands of volunteers quit their day jobs to help with the goings-on. Trains to Varanasi were sold out, flights became exorbitant—still, people kept rushing in, spending their savings on air tickets or squeezing into packed general compartments.

When I landed in Varanasi, the air was charged. Porters, airline employees and passengers welcomed AAP volunteers with broad smiles.

However, as I entered the city, I saw that Varanasi had become polarized. We witnessed almost an equal number of people wearing AAP and BJP caps. Both sides were passionate, both shouted slogans. The rallies of the BJP and AAP passing through the circuitous streets of Varanasi were some of the longest and most enthusiastic I had seen. There was no trace of the Congress, the Samajwadi Party or the Bahujan Samaj Party. This seemed to be a battle between Arvind Kejriwal and Narendra Modi.

Or was it? We lacked the muscle of the BJP. As a new organization, we didn't have assembly level, ward level or polling booth level management, and our volunteers included those who had no experience in the arena of politics. This means, as time progressed, we couldn't keep pace with the BJP's might and momentum. Our mood grew increasingly despondent.

I told a journalist from Rediff: 'On May 13, one boy sent me an SMS at 2.35 am: "Mayank sir, only five seats [for AAP are] shown in the opinion polls, what will happen?" There will be a lot of [. . .] kids who want a quick transformation that may not happen. We will have to mentor them. We will have to explain to them that nations cannot be changed like that.'

The journalist asked, 'What do you think is going to happen on May 16 [the day the results of the general elections were expected]?'

I answered: 'I think the NDA [National Democratic Alliance] will form the government, led by Modi. The UPA will be in a bad state and the Aam Aadmi Party will get 5 to 10 [seats], which is not a small number in our first election. What is most important is that the thought processes that AAP is talking about has found a place in the hearts and minds of the people. Maybe we were not able to convince voters that we would be able to become a serious contender.'[16]

Finally, it was counting day. As I went from one counting station to another, the extent of AAP's loss became obvious. Arvind had lost. And the story repeated itself across the nation as a Modi tsunami took over. Yogendra Yadav was routed, and Kumar Vishwas, who fought against Congress Vice President Rahul Gandhi and the BJP's Smriti Irani in Amethi, ended fourth, winning just about 3 per cent of the votes polled.[17] If there was a saving grace, it was AAP's performance in Punjab, where it secured four seats.

During the Delhi elections, all parties and the media took us lightly, but the voters supported us. This time, the parties and the media considered us serious contenders, but the voters did not. What went wrong?

It was time for a postmortem. Besides not having a firm organizational structure to win national elections, we realized we had made tactical blunders. For one, during the 2013 Delhi assembly elections, Arvind had tried to win over BJP supporters by subtly suggesting 'Modi for PM and Kejriwal for CM'. Not surprisingly, many BJP voters voted for AAP in Delhi assembly polls, and many AAP supporters voted for Modi in general elections.

Second, we realized that the decision to take on the BJP instead of the Congress in the national elections was a mistake. In the 2013 Delhi elections, most of our votes had come from traditional Congress supporters. The Congress confronted anti-incumbency, and the BJP took advantage of that sentiment. We should have as well.

Third, the BJP, taking complete advantage of the anti-corruption mood of the country, presented a strong case for rejecting a corrupt Congress, while AAP projected itself as a party that wanted to defeat the party that wanted to defeat the corrupt. Our approach was flawed.

Fourth, the general election had got converted into a presidential election, with votes for or against Modi as prime minister. Crores voted for this decisive leader—not for the BJP, not for its allies, not for its candidates. In fact, I believe a lamp post could have won in that atmosphere as long as it had an association with Modi. The other major contender, a corruption-stained UPA, with an indecisive leader, was rendered irrelevant. If at all people voted for the UPA, it was only because they didn't want Modi as prime minister—in other words, the Congress gathered negative votes while the BJP secured positive ones.

Fifth, none of the contenders could keep pace with the marketing and advertising machinery propping Modi.

Sixth, and most significantly, perhaps, voters felt that AAP had been given a chance in Delhi and it quit in forty-nine days. How then could the party be trusted to lead a nation that needed a strong central government? Only diehard AAP loyalists forgave us for vacating our seat in Delhi.

The entire Lok Sabha experience was teaching us important lessons. But were we listening?

15. Pre-2015: The Night Before the Day

THE POOR 2014 LOK SABHA RESULTS DEMORALIZED A LOT of volunteers. While, to them, we'd enthusiastically say that as first-time contenders we had done marvellously, internally we remained glum, keenly aware that this was a major setback.

I remember, in the first NE meeting after the results, speaker after speaker congratulated the party for securing votes and a handful of seats even though it was our first election. Arvind listened, sullen and angry, while staring at his mobile phone. After some time, he exploded: 'I have not come here to talk like a loser. Nor do I plan to be happy with what we have achieved. Either we win, or we stop the party and go back home.' Everyone was taken aback at this outburst. While I could appreciate his indomitable spirit, I could also see a kind of coldness in Arvind's eyes that I hadn't witnessed earlier.

Sanjubhai and Pankaj Gupta tried insisting that we follow demarcated procedures in the future to improve our performance. Arvind grew even angrier. He got up and shouted, 'Is the party made for procedures or are procedures made for a party?' His abhorrence for set processes was well known. Structures and systems were anathema to the 'anarchist' in him. He was a destroyer, not a builder.

We realized that we had miscalculated the timing of our resignation from the Delhi government. We had incorrectly assumed that the lieutenant governor would call for re-elections in Delhi within a few months. However, the lieutenant governor did no such thing and delayed elections. AAP remained out of power and had no platform to demonstrate its competence in matters of governance. The BJP, meanwhile, had a wide open berth, and displayed a winning streak across Delhi and beyond. There were now rumours that the BJP was trying to form the Delhi state government by luring some of the Congress MLAs who had won the 2013 elections. Things seemed to be slipping away.

This was when, my hero, Arvind, began to truly falter. His impatience to change the nation for the better now turned into a desperation for power, no matter what happened to be at stake—principles, people, or PAC and NE members. Arvind became terse and ruthless.

He had long discussions with his small band of supporters—Manish Sisodia, Sanjay Singh, journalist-turned-politician Ashutosh and Ashish Talwar—and they decided that AAP ought to get into an alliance with the Congress, and stake claim to form the government again. I got a call late at night from Delhi confirming this. I argued, 'Impossible. As IAC, and now AAP, we have been against the Congress. Arvind had targeted the party in the Delhi elections; he had challenged and defeated Sheila Dixit. When we allowed the Congress to lend outside support to our government, we burnt our fingers. There must be some mistake in the news you relay.' But no . . . there was no mistake.

I called almost all the PAC members, requesting them to stop this preposterous move. A PAC meeting was called the next day, and five of the nine members voted against forming a government with the Congress. But nothing was going to stop Arvind. He said, 'The PAC is an advisory body while I am the convenor of the party. I have listened to your advice, but the final decision rests with me. I am going ahead with the process of forming a government with the Congress.' The PAC was shocked. How could Arvind rule against the majority opinion of the highest decision-making body of AAP? Before our eyes, a democratic party was transforming into a dictatorial one.

The PAC members finally coerced Arvind into considering the opinion of the NE members. A conference call was made, and the NE members were told to convey their views by the next morning. After the conference call was done, Arvind made individual calls to every NE member, trying to influence him or her, and get each to sign off against his point of view.

Arvind insisted when he spoke to me, 'Mayank, if we do not do anything, the BJP will form the government in Delhi, and then we will be thrown out of equation.'

I protested, 'Arvind, our entire movement and party has been built on the anti-corruption plank, and the Congress is probably the most corrupt party in the country. Forming a government with them will be unpalatable to all our volunteers. Personally, I may not be able to continue as part of the party if we choose to go with the Congress.'

Arvind seemed disappointed with my response and said, 'Okay, think about it.' Then, suddenly, he added emotionally, 'Everything will get over, we will be finished, and we'd have killed the hopes and aspiration of millions of people . . . simply because some of us choose to remain stubborn.'

Since I do not like being emotionally blackmailed or bullied, I said, 'Arvind, if we go with the Congress and compromise on all our principles, we'd have already have killed the hopes and aspirations of people, and their desire to see alternative politics at play. It is better to stay in the wilderness and fight for the truth rather than destroy everything that we stand for.'

In a temper, Arvind disconnected. It was either his way or the highway.

This was the biggest impasse between Arvind and me. Arvind was concerned about the party, while I was concerned about the nation. He wanted AAP to survive, and I wanted honest politics to survive.

Despite Arvind's personal appeal to everyone, the majority of the NE members opposed his decision to form an alliance with the Congress. Arvind ignored the democratic will of the majority. He sent a letter to the lieutenant governor, asking him not to dissolve the assembly.

That's when there was a sudden twist in the narrative. The Congress, getting wind of our plans, rejected AAP's overtures. We were saved from the repercussions of AAP forming the government with the Congress.

Recently, when I had gone to meet Prashant Bhushan, he confessed to me that he blamed himself for the deterioration of the party. During an argument regarding the ongoing plans to seek the Congress' support, Arvind told Prashant that, for him, only the end mattered, not the means. Prashant said, 'Even then I had understood Arvind's desire for power, but I hoped that he would change. I should have done something to stop him then.'

In the meantime, the BJP persisted with its attempts

at forming a government in Delhi. Rumours emerged that it was now trying to poach some of the Congress' Muslim MLAs—Mateen Ahmed, Asif Mohammed Khan and Hasan Ahmed. Arvind grew even more worried on witnessing these manoeuvrings. He also grew increasingly obsessed with stopping the BJP, no matter the price. Posters were made anonymously and plastered across the locality where the Congress MLAs lived—these posters referred to the MLAs as 'traitors of the community' and called for protests outside their residences. The Delhi police swung into action, removed the prints, registered a case under sections of the IPC for promoting enmity between two groups and for the defacement of property, and arrested Dilip Pandey, AAP's Delhi unit secretary, along with a few AAP volunteers. Arvind went on the defensive, claiming that the BJP was framing his party after failing to form the Delhi government. He further suggested that someone named Amanatullah Khan, an erstwhile member of the BSP, had put up the posters and had even confessed to it, but the police seemed to wish to target AAP volunteers. What exactly was going on? It wasn't hard to join the dots when, soon after, Amanatullah Khan was given an AAP ticket and was designated in-charge of the Okhla constituency. He was to play a much larger role in the future. Like Naveen Jaihind, he'd become Arvind's go-to man.[18]

*

At this point, the rift between the Yogendra-and-Prashant team, who were leading the no-compromises-with-principles school of thought, and Arvind, who led the come-to-power-at-any-cost brigade, was increasing. Arvind's team was sharpening its claws.

Yogendra was very interested in contesting the Haryana elections. To checkmate him, Arvind stationed his loyal follower Naveen Jaihind there. In NE meetings, Naveen Jaihind started attacking Yogendra—the rudeness and aggression were unwarranted. An ugly spat began brewing between Yogendra and Naveen.

Pushed to the wall, Yogendra sent out a strongly worded letter. In it, he raised a number of issues that were troubling, among them the total centralization of power, the tendency to skip consulting volunteers, the creation of a coterie within the PAC, the neglect of state leadership teams and organization building, a policy deficit, and finally, the worrying shift towards a culture that valued a supremo over a leader. He said:

> There is no one who doubts that Arvind bhai is the undisputed leader within the Party. He has richly earned this stature and we would not be where we are without his leadership. But there is a difference between a Leader and a Supremo. Love and affection for a leader often turns into a personality cult that can damage an organization and the leader himself. This is what appears to be happening to our Party. Major decisions of the party appear to, and indeed do, reflect the wishes of one person; when he changes his mind, the Party changes its course of action; proximity to the Leader comes to substitute for organizational roles and responsibilities.

Manish Sisodia drafted a response, in which he made charges against Yogendra Yadav:

> After the fall of the Delhi government, a survey done on your instructions projected that the party would get 23% votes in Haryana. However, six weeks after that, the party got mere 3% votes under your leadership.

> The reasons for this have to be analyzed. Now that the PAC and party workers want an answer to why did this slide take place [*sic*], you are trying to divert the issue by labelling Arvind as dictatorial.[19]

The party was splintering into two camps. As had now become the norm, both letters reached the media.

The NE meeting in June, that followed this exchange of letters between Manish and Yogendra, was expected to be intense. But no one had anticipated the kind of melodrama that unfolded, with Arvind crying and offering to resign for being called a 'supremo'. He attempted to walk away from the meeting—until he was placated.

All the while, Ashutosh had been observing his boss closely while he had been crying. Was he learning something for the future?

It seemed like the party was at the brink of a disaster. I prevailed upon Yogendra and Prashant to visit Arvind's house the next morning. As expected, matters were patched up. But nerves remained frayed, and an explosion was waiting to happen.

*

Meanwhile, Maharashtra and Haryana had elections around the corner, and the party had to take a call on fighting them. While many volunteers were keen to contest from Maharashtra, some of us strongly felt that AAP was far from prepared.

We went to Delhi, and I tendered my views on my state to Arvind at his house. 'Arvind, let me categorically state that the time is wrong. We may not be able to make any major impact in the coming elections in Maharashtra, and a failure to do so could jeopardize our chances in the forthcoming Delhi elections. The goal of winning the capital has to remain firm,' I said.

In another meeting a few days later, Yogendra (who was with Arvind and me) presented a different opinion, 'Mayankbhai, while Maharashtra and Haryana are entirely different states, and I respect your thoughts on Maharashtra, we need to contest every possible election. Otherwise, the party will start losing its base, and we will soon become a Delhi-centric force, with no sway elsewhere. Besides, let the volunteers of each state take a call on whether they want to contest elections.'

Before I could present my viewpoint, Arvind interrupted, 'We don't have to keep consulting volunteers for everything. How much do they know? Their opinion can easily be changed. I don't want to contest any election that we are not confident of winning before the Delhi elections. This is, and will be, my final decision.'

Yogendra had his heart set on fighting the Haryana assembly elections, and when a final decision was taken that it was best not to contest from there, he was very upset, especially with me. But there was little to be done—Arvind had made up his mind.

*

In the midst of all this, it was time for organization building. Two years had passed since the formation of the party, and there was urgent need for internal elections—be it for polling booth volunteers or convenors, from the district to the national level. Mission Vistaar was launched—led ably by Prithvi Reddy and Atishi Marlena—which was to create an ad-hoc committee in each state. This committee had to work towards the initiation of a strong statewide organization and conduct internal elections.

As Maharashtra was one of AAP's strongest states, Prithvi and Atishi decided to personally create a committee. They did a thorough job, travelling and interviewing volunteers across all the districts of the state. They also recommended replacing the existing convenor in Maharashtra, Anjali Damania, with Subhash Ware. I was not in favour of this decision and argued that Anjali's energy and passion were commendable—but the Mission Vistaar team felt differently.

Troubled by this new development, when I met Arvind in Delhi, I commented that I would have liked Anjali to continue as convenor and that Subhash Ware would make a good co-convenor. Arvind, who had always been suspicious of those from socialist backgrounds, was at once wary of Subhash—after all, he had been an ex-socialist. Arvind, at once, agreed that it was best for Anjali to continue as Maharashtra's convenor.

Understandably, Atishi was upset when she learnt that I had jumped protocol and made a direct recommendation to Arvind. I saw her point and apologized for my mistake. To make up for the error—and to soothe a very annoyed Maharashtra Committee—I told Arvind when he visited Mumbai a few days later, 'The committee does not appreciate my suggesting Anjali's name. I would like to take back my recommendation.' Arvind nodded. The next thing I knew was that Subhash Ware had been declared the convenor. He proved to be an extraordinary leader and led the Maharashtra AAP team with great maturity and skill.

Mission Vistaar also travelled to Gujarat, where it was to be handled by Sanjay Parmar—my close friend, the treasurer of Maharashtra and one of the most balanced and committed people I have met—and me. We travelled across the state, meeting and interviewing various volunteers. With the exception of Surat, we felt that the volunteers coming in were not very inspiring. We were also concerned since the existing convenor of Gujarat, Sukhdev Patel, seemed somewhat unpopular with one segment of the party. Therefore, we suggested a committee with a new convenor and co-convenor, but with Sukhdev Patel as one of the committee members.

Arvind liked the recommendation but said, 'I don't want Sukhdev in the committee. Just because he was the founding member does not mean we should continue with him.'

I replied, 'While there are those who do not like Sukhdevbhai, there is a significant section of volunteers in favour of him. Removing him from all positions of authority will only destabilize the party in Gujarat.'

At this Arvind grew irate: 'I just do not want Sukhdev Patel, and if there is any problem, let us just close AAP in Gujarat. We do not need a party in every state.'

I did not like Arvind's attitude. I was quiet and, from then on, kept my distance from Gujarat's Mission Vistaar.

What I focused on were the upcoming Delhi elections—this would prove to be the real test.

16. Delhi Elections, 2015

On 4 November 2014, the lieutenant governor of Delhi declared that the Delhi assembly would be dissolved; he called for fresh elections. That was the war cry all of us were waiting for. A thrill passed through us. AAP would, at last, be a challenge to the BJP which had been winning relentlessly.

In one of my public meetings, I had promised: 'AAP will stop the Ashwamedha of the BJP in Delhi.' This was a reference to a practice in ancient times, where a white horse would be let loose. It would pass through multiple kingdoms, and its kings would either have to challenge the army following the horse or accept defeat and lose their kingdoms. After a year, if no enemy managed to capture the horse, the king would be declared as the undisputed ruler. Our task was to stop the BJP's Ashwamedha.

We began by assessing people's opinion of the party. What we learnt was eye-opening. The BJP, the Congress and the media had consistently branded Arvind as a 'bhagoda'—as someone who had ran away from his responsibility of governing Delhi—and common people echoed that view. We had thought that voters would admire us for relinquishing power to uphold party principles, but instead, voters were convinced that we had insulted their vote by shirking responsibility. We had our task cut out for us—we had to work hard to change this impression.

Thus it was, AAP began its preparations for the Delhi elections by doing something that it would seldom do later—admitting that it had been wrong. Arvind asked voters for forgiveness and promised that next time, if elected, he would not quit. That was how the song and slogan, 'Paach saal Kejriwal'—'Five years of Kejriwal'—was born. Arvind assured the voters that, if elected, the AAP government would complete its full term.

During the 2013 elections, the nation had been furious, and Arvind, in turn, projected himself as an angry young man taking on the system. Irate slogans rent the air, with Arvind leading the brigade, shouting, '*Niklo bahar makaano se, jung lado baimano se*' ('Get out of your houses and fight the dishonest'). This time, since the nation was optimistic, we decided to project a friendly, approachable, positive image. Arvind was presented as a smiling, positive leader rather than as a livid one.

*

Unknown to the public, the differences between the two factions were growing. One day, I was discussing the candidate selection process with Prithvi and Pankaj Gupta, when Arvind joined us. Out of the blue, Arvind began a diatribe against the Bhushans: 'What do the father-son duo think of themselves? They have done nothing for the party. They have made no sacrifices at all. I know all their inner dealings. I will expose them and show them their place!' I had never seen Arvind attack someone in such a vitriolic manner. His tone and body language were dripping with poison. I was taken aback.

On the way back to Pankaj Gupta's house, I told Prithvi and Pankaj, 'I am shocked with Arvind's demeanour. This kind of attitude will spell disaster for the party. I have never heard one man speak against another with so much venom.'

There was viciousness all around. Once, Arvind's personal assistant Bibhav Kumar made me listen to a recording between him and a journalist; the journalist spoke about Yogendra Yadav planting a story in her newspaper against AAP's mode of functioning while criticizing Arvind remorselessly. The altercation between Team Arvind on the one hand, and Yogendra and the Bhushans on the other—an altercation that began with Arvind wanting to form a government with the Congress—had now become an inferno, threatening to engulf the party and all our dreams.

I had no interest in taking sides, but was deeply concerned about the party's future. I told Bibhav, 'You claim that Yogendra Yadav has been working against the interests of the party for months, and you say you have evidence . . . why is he continuing as the spokesperson of the party?' He had no answer.

The fact was AAP needed Yogendra Yadav's skills to present the party positively to the media. And Arvind had every intention of using the man till the elections were done. After that, he could be thrown out. This kind of ruthlessness did not appeal to me.

*

In the 2013 elections, the operating plan guiding the decision-making of the core team had been made with Yogendra's help. The same strategy was to be used for this election, too. Every morning, at 6 o'clock, there was to be a conference call of a small team to take day-to-day decisions about the Delhi elections. I used to join the conference call daily, and every topic, even the minutest one, was discussed threadbare. Things started falling into place, and the right roles were allotted to the right people, whose work was then meticulously monitored.

As with 2013, we had a calling campaign—though the scope expanded as also the degree of professionalism we introduced. People from across the world made telephone calls to complete strangers in Delhi, requesting them to support AAP. On my part, I made over 1,500 calls to gauge the kind of support we had. The response, in most cases, was overwhelming—the common man seemed willing to not just forgive us but also back us all the way.

Arvind was a superlative manager and was especially good at micro-managing. All official memos from the party were scrutinized by him, and every line of advertisements and press releases first went past his eagle eye. Arvind worked relentlessly, sustaining the same levels of energy morning and night. He was a hard taskmaster and refused to tolerate sloppy or lazy work. I admired Arvind's work ethic—though, admittedly, I wasn't a fan of him throwing tantrums and using emotional blackmail to get things done.

In addition, Arvind was extremely smart while managing and manipulating the media. He used the press to garner tremendous amounts of prime time attention. Ashutosh once told me: 'Mayank, one must keep on saying and doing things which can make a story. Good news and bad news is not important, we should be in public limelight all the time.' Therefore, almost every evening, we had stories and spokespersons across panel discussions. A small party like AAP, which had only a handful of MPs and a miniscule percentage of national votes was getting more attention than the political behemoths—and this worked to our advantage.

Sanjay Parmar, Shrey—a brilliant, young law student, my closest confidante and the co-author of this book—and I reached Delhi a month-and-a-half prior to Delhi's elections for campaigning. I was fifty-six years old, Sanjaybhai was thirty-six, and Shrey was twenty. Ours was an unlikely bond, but together, we worked well. We stayed in the house of a volunteer and lived the lives of bachelors—Sanjaybhai took instructions from his wife and cooked delicious food, while Shrey and I washed dishes and clothes. Together, we'd head out in Delhi's cold to the closest metro station, about a kilometre away from our home, and travel across the city, reaching out to strangers, while urging them to vote for AAP.

We also took complete charge of bringing in outstation volunteers. A special website was designed by us where thousands from across the country could register. Our primary aim was to arrange for their lodging and boarding, allocate campaign work to them in various constituencies, and monitor their work. The response was phenomenal. While there were around 2,500 volunteers in Delhi working within their own constituencies on a part time basis, the real strength came from the 6,000 outstation volunteers (especially from Punjab and Maharashtra) who had ventured into Delhi with the single purpose of campaigning. I have to say, they displayed unparalleled energy, vigour and passion, sometimes devoting over eighteen hours a day to AAP. Today, the tragedy is that the contribution of these outstation volunteers has been forgotten, with everyone congratulating the 'faces' of the party.

For the 2015 elections, a local volunteer along with an outstation one was appointed as in-charge of each district of every assembly constituency. These in-charge volunteers would directly report to me, providing me with daily updates—be it the support a candidate enjoyed, or the need for additional volunteers in a constituency; be it the number of people attending rallies, or the kind of impact a speech had. In the evening, we'd prepare a report, which would be forwarded to the central campaign team, the campaign managers and the candidates. The next day, we'd ask each of them if the suggestions and the reported deficiencies were being addressed.

Along with sending volunteers to various constituencies, we created powerful 'buzz teams'; common citizens would go to public places, distributing caps and pamphlets, shouting slogans, singing and dancing to the beat of '*paach saal Kejriwal*'.

In the beginning of January 2015, internal data suggested that AAP would win 10 to 15 seats. But because of the extraordinary influx of volunteers and the buzz campaign, the seat percentage only kept increasing in favour of AAP. The streets, markets and metros were abuzz with support for our party. Something remarkable was brewing.

*

In this time of renewed optimism, Arvind remained edgy. His win-at-any-cost team was not willing to leave anything to chance. Victory was the new mantra. How was an electoral triumph to be assured?

First, by getting candidates that could win elections. Unlike 2013, when a blemish-free character was a selection prerequisite, this time the litmus test was 'winnability'. AAP had a team led by Ashish Talwar which would go to every constituency to identify candidates who had the maximum support. These candidates were fielded. If they were rich, it increased their chances of winning; if they were caste or community leaders, still better. It no longer mattered if a candidate was part of AAP or had other loyalties. Out of the seventy candidates finally selected, twenty-three were those who belonged to rival parties and, for many of them, buying of seats, engaging in criminal or corrupt activities, and winning votes by keeping caste and communal considerations central, was normal.

This troubled me. When Manish Sisodia called me to campaign with him in one of his sabhas, I told him, 'We are not the typical lot of politicians; we did not enter politics for power but to create an alternative, honest political force. Instead of setting an agenda that will force other political parties to improve, we have started following the agenda of others!'

Manish smiled and told me, 'Mayankbhai, principles sound good on paper. What we are now in the middle of is a war. We will have to let go of certain things. Once we win the Delhi elections, we will get back on track.'

Now, I was even more disturbed. Where once we had championed the lofty goal of *sampoorna kranti*—a complete revolution—we now consoled ourselves with the thought that we were marginally better than the BJP and the Congress. Rather than being the solution, AAP was happy to commend itself for being the lesser evil. We were slipping down a slippery slope.

This is the downward slide that had transformed the BJP and the Congress, too—no doubt, like us, they had begun their political journey with idealism, but now, they had an easy justification for every compromise. They had to win!

Someone who was as troubled as me was Prashant Bhushan. While I don't always see eye to eye with his stances, I have always admired his courage and sense of justice. Prashant began raising the issue of candidate selection and even threatened to expose to the media the compromises being made by a party that claimed to stand for principles. He started telling some of us that his hope was that AAP would not secure a majority—because if it did, it would reaffirm Arvind's new stance that compromises alone could win elections. When people close to Prashant asked him if they could make donations to the AAP campaign, his response became a categorical 'no'. 'Until the party gets back on track, no donation should be made,' he'd assert. I was aware that Prashant felt betrayed, and a lot of his anger sprung from a place of deep love for the AAP he had rooted for. To ensure that he didn't do anything impulsive, there were times that I'd rush from Mumbai by the earliest possible flight to urge Prashant to wait until the elections were done before releasing exposés. More than me, it was Yogendra Yadav who managed to keep Prashant away from the media.

A development that especially angered Prashant was that Amanatullah Khan (of the communal poster fame) had been given a ticket to contest elections from Okhla. He longed to expose AAP's volte-face. He was placated with the promise that within two to three days of the results of the Delhi assembly elections, an NE meeting would be called, and the party would create models of transparency, accountability and participation.

But while Prashant could be reined in, his father could not. One night, Yogendra called me: 'Mayankbhai, please come to Delhi immediately. I'm given to believe that Shanti Bhushan is going to speak against Arvind. Prashant is trying to convince him to wait till the elections are through, but knowing Shanti Bhushan, even his son will not be able to stop him. He won't listen to anyone. Let us all meet at his house and stop him from going to the press.'

I knew that no one could change Shanti Bhushan's mind. Nonetheless, I took the early morning flight and reached the Bhushans' home in Noida. The whole house was swarming with journalists, and Shanti Bhushan kept giving statement after statement against Kejriwal and the absence of any kind of internal democracy within AAP.[20] No one else was there in the house. The media felt that I had come to support Shanti Bhushan and rushed towards me for my comments. I distanced myself from him, as did Prashant Bhushan.

I rushed to Atishi's house, where everyone had gathered. I called up Arvind and informed him about what had happened at the Bhushans' residence. As had now become typical, Arvind started yelling: 'This is a planned conspiracy. Shanti Bhushan may be making such statements—but Prashant and Yogendra are the ones supporting him in the background.' Besides the fact that I could sense that Arvind was posturing, I knew that Arvind's conspiracy theory was not true. I had personally seen Yogendra fighting tooth and nail with Prashant to prevent him from leaking anything contentious regarding AAP to the media. Yet, given the party supremo's stand, Arvind's supporters started instigating other volunteers, stating that Yogendra and Prashant were working against the party's interests.

I confronted Arvind with the question: 'If Yogendra is anti-AAP, why has the party appointed him as the spokesperson? If Prashant is anti-AAP and wants to engineer the party's defeat, why had he only *threatened* to go to the press, without actually following through?' Arvind had no reasonable reply to offer.

*

Oblivious to these developments, the voters of Delhi began falling increasingly in love with AAP's façade of honest politics. Very subtly, Arvind once again planted the idea of Modi as prime minister and Kejriwal as chief minister to woo BJP voters.

Given the rising tide of popular support for AAP, the BJP started growing jittery and began making tactical errors. Its biggest mistake revolved around Kiran Bedi. As we know, Kiran Bedi had always had a soft corner for the BJP—going so far as to publicly support Modi during the 2014 elections.[21] Mere months after Modi's victory, she joined the BJP, and the BJP, in turn, made her its chief ministerial candidate. She was paradropped into the party's core group. She did not enjoy the support of ordinary BJP and RSS workers.

Initially, we were worried that the BJP would get a massive fillip with her entry—for, Kiran Bedi was popular in the capital, and was particularly loved by its women. But expectedly she started making a series of bizarre statements. She was, at heart, a policewoman; she was a stranger to politics and its idiom. Social media (including the AAP online team) started mocking her utterances and behaviour; the media caught on. The BJP started looking like a caricature.

On the last day of campaigning, thousands of us, led by the women's wing of AAP, landed in Kiran Bedi's Krishna Nagar constituency and held huge rallies in the neighbourhood all day long. I met some senior BJP leaders of the constituency who said that they wanted to teach a lesson to BJP's central leadership team for having planted Kiran Bedi as the chief ministerial candidate. They planned to vote for AAP in large numbers, as did several others across the rank and file of the BJP and RSS. Victory for AAP seemed close.

*

The campaign was through. The votes were to be cast. I returned to Mumbai, tired but happy.

With the IAC movement, and later AAP, I was aware that the churning that had begun would bring forth amrut (nectar) and vish (poison). That's how it is with all major transformations. Yet, the venom spilling out—the dirty politics, the lies and viciousness—was unlike any I had anticipated.

Besides, I had joined a movement, not with the intention of staying on forever, but with the desire to sow the seeds of change. I felt that, now, my role as an initiator or a catalyst was over.

It was time to exit politics and go back to a more spiritual quest.

I shared this desire with Sanjaybhai, Shrey and my children. I also sent an email to Prithvi and Atishi, conveying my plans to quit soon after Delhi went to the polls. I carry the letter verbatim:

> Subject: Resigning from politics
>
> Just wanted to put this on record now, so that it does not get clubbed with anything that may happen. I shall resign from active politics on the next day after Delhi voting, so that there is no adverse impact and it [will] not be colored with victory or loss. This decision is for personal reasons and independent of the future of AAP. Thanks for everything.

My daughter Khushvi and my son Manaan, who were privy to my restlessness and discomfort, were of the view that I ought to resign on the evening of voting day itself—there was little reason to prolong my agony. But Shrey and Sanjaybhai were convinced that I had far more to offer, especially in Maharashtra, and that it was best to continue in politics and guide the party.

There were some rather interesting emails exchanged between Shrey, who wanted me to continue, and my daughter Khushvi, who thought that it was time to say goodbye to politics.

Shrey wrote that while he recognized my reasons for wanting to quit, he believed staying on was important because, among other reasons, I could not break the trust of thousands of volunteers who relied on my feedback. He argued that no matter the field one chose, there was always dirt and muck—so one fraught arena would only get replaced by another. Equally, he urged to me to, at the very least, continue my political pursuits for two more years—so, I could steer a victory in the forthcoming BMC elections in Maharashtra.

In response, Khushvi said:

> A long time back, dad contemplated whether he should enter public life, whether he was ready for the adventure,

whether he [should] take the plunge. I believe he had set a deadline for himself till the end of 2014. Much has changed, agreed. Decisions are flexible with situations, sure. But I still believe that this prophesized deadline is the proper time for an exit. Why? [. . .]

Movement's [fading] charisma [. . .]: The charismatic stage in any movement is irresponsible, it is freedom seeking, it is inspirational. People make enormous sacrifices, hope is instilled, and it is this stage that has the power to move mountains. Charisma requires some essential ingredients to survive—an adamant opposition, a public ready for change, a system that people are sick and tired of, a simple choice between black and white. Movements come but once in while, and they touch the life of the participants completely. Inspiration is rare to come by, and when it does, you find life has a direction beyond money-making or hedonism. So everyone wants to hold on to it. But in a wave there are crests and troughs. Movements cannot be held within a structure, yet to survive they need to be organised. Charisma by its very nature is organisation breaking. The bondage of organisation defeats its very purpose. Mayank Gandhi, to my mind is sheer charisma. [. . .] Roles do not fit him. AAP is at a stage where party structures need to be built. This job is not meant for him.

Unison of thoughts and action: [For] the past few months, there seems to be discord in dad's life. It feels like his association with AAP is holding him back from his potential. His disinclination to be a part of the party, yet his passion for its work [. . .] is making him a reluctant politician. [. . .]

What of those who joined seeing him? There could be arguments that each person joined to see a better India—not due to a Kejriwal or Mayank Gandhi. There

> could also be a thought that no one is indispensable, so it won't affect the party if Mayank leaves. But it's not true. People put their trust, their money and devotion to support dad. If today, he feels that he's had a change of heart, many will feel disheartened. But that cannot be a reason to hold on. Mayank Gandhi has a lot more to offer to the world, Shrey. Politics is but a path.
>
> According to me, he has walked his bit. It's time to try something new. Something more challenging. Something more exciting.

I was so fortunate to be surrounded by people who cared so much about my decisions. Sanjay came over for a long discussion with Shrey, my children and me. Throughout, I mulled over my daughter's letter, then Shrey's—especially paragraphs of this kind in Shrey's email:

> AAP in Maharashtra is Mayank's baby. The baby is still growing and it needs to be groomed. The father has, in this case, decided: [. . .] "Let everybody hurt my baby, I'll leave it alone for it to [grow] on its own at a very young age." Maybe he could wait for some time till the baby reaches at least such an age where the father's support is not needed. [. . .] If Mayank resigns, there is no right leader to take over the party [in Maharashtra . . .]. So, for the sake of this baby, the father has to stay, till the baby is ready to walk.

After much deliberation, I finally decided to continue my stint in the party for a while, albeit reluctantly. Perhaps it was my destiny to watch it corrode and degenerate.

*

Delhi voted. In Mumbai, confident of a victory, we booked a hall with a large screen in Dadar and invited volunteers and the media to watch the results with us. As the results trickled in, we could not believe our eyes. For the first time since independence, a new party—our very own AAP—had secured 95 per cent of the seats and 54 per cent of the votes. The Congress was reduced to zero seats and the BJP bagged only 3 seats.[22] Kiran Bedi, the BJP's chief ministerial candidate, lost in Krishna Nagar.

It was unbelievable. All around me, I could hear people saying: *Bharat zarur badlega.* India will change.

Tragically, this unprecedented victory was a curse in disguise. In it lay the seeds of arrogance and the disintegration of the party. It's hard to tell if Bharat changed, but the people who came to change Bharat certainly did.

17. A Tale of Two Meetings: The NE Meeting

'*BHARAT MATA KI JAI, VANDE MATARAM, INQUILAB ZINDABAD*.' The crowd roared back, echoing Arvind's slogans. We all had goosebumps.

Arvind said: 'Friends, when one gets such a victory, arrogance can creep in. And if one gets arrogant, everything is lost. That is why all of us—me, the ministers, MLAs, families, volunteers—must be on guard. We'll have to introspect constantly and question ourselves to ensure we don't turn arrogant. If we turn arrogant we will never complete our mission. In the past few days, I've been hearing our people say on TV we will fight elections here and there, we will contest in five states, ten states.'

Arvind paused, then said something very interesting—something that will possibly continue to haunt him: 'I see some arrogance in these statements. I don't think this is right. Why did people vote out the Congress? It's because the Congress became arrogant. The same BJP, which got such a handsome mandate in May, was humbled in Delhi. They, too, became arrogant. The last election, we won 28 seats, but we, too, became arrogant and decided to contest elections across the country. God punished us for our arrogance and the Lok Sabha election results made that clear.'[23]

Ramlila Maidan, the familiar location of the IAC movement, was bursting with people. There was no place to stand as women, children and men gathered for a moment that might never come again. Here was the oath-taking ceremony of a young, fledgling party that had swept aside a thirty-five-year-old behemoth which had overwhelmingly won the national election.

Little did we know then that we'd err precisely the way we said we wouldn't. Winning 67 seats sowed the seeds of conceit. Sometimes, I wish we had got a thin majority. It would have kept AAP on its toes. A strong opposition ensures that the ruling party is in check.

*

After the swearing-in ceremony, the Delhi government got down to work. There were unresolved questions about the party's mode of functioning, raised by Yogendra Yadav and Prashant Bhushan. Issues of institutional reform like inner party democracy, swaraj, transparency and accountability had to be addressed. The NE meeting that had been promised post-elections (when Prashant had threatened to go to the people with the inner dealings of AAP) could not be delayed.

However, basking in his massive victory, Arvind lost interest in discussing any of these subjects. He had no genuine desire to pursue decentralized decision-making within the party. He felt, now that the people had voted for him in such large numbers, he was accountable to the people alone, and not to his party members.

Yogendra and Prashant, however, refused to let matters lie. They sent persistent reminders to Arvind, which only made him increasingly irritated. Finally a call was taken:

'Enough is enough!' Yogendra and Prashant needed to be thrown out of the party once and for all.

Arvind's team charted out a ruthless strategy to get rid of Yogendra, Prashant and their supporters. An NE meeting with many guest invitees, mostly Arvind's acolytes, was called on 26 February. Before the agenda suggested by Yogendra, concerning reforms within the party, could be announced, Pankaj Gupta read out a note by an absent Arvind. In this note, Arvind accused Prashant and Yogendra of anti-party activities; he offered to resign as AAP's convenor. Arvind's offer of resignation hijacked the agenda of party reforms. As had been orchestrated, some members stood up and spoke out against Prashant and Yogendra, using language that has no place in decent debate. Each brought up a discrete episode, with the singular purpose of humiliating the duo. The hope was that they'd feel so insulted that they'd quit of their own volition.

I cringed in my seat as all limits of decency were crossed. One politician from Punjab, Fateh Singh, said sardonically, 'This really is a party with a difference. After such a glorious victory, anybody else would celebrate . . . but because AAP is different, we are fighting amongst ourselves.'

I mulled over the situation. On the one hand, I could see where Arvind was coming from. Now that AAP had won, and won so handsomely, he wanted to work without irritants—and Yogendra and Prashant, for whatever reason, were in constant conflict with him; PAC meetings had become routinely stormy, and there was a huge trust deficit.

On the other hand, I was appalled at the manner in which the senior party men were being treated. Equally, I strongly felt that AAP suffered from a dearth of high calibre people—and Yogendra and Prashant were among the few who came with stellar credentials. We could not afford to let them go.

I stood up in the meeting and said, 'As with life, in politics, there are times when we can't get along with some people . . . and that is okay. The solution lies in having different working groups for the immense task before us. Let Arvind not interact with Prashant or Yogendra on a regular basis—then, surely, all three can co-exist in one party. Let us structure AAP such that tasks are well distributed and everyone has a specific responsibility.' Many clapped in approval. Some members of Team Arvind mistakenly perceived my remarks as being in their favour and against Yogendra and Prashant. The fact is, I belonged to neither camp. I was simply being objective and true to myself.

After the meeting, late that night, most of the members of the NE (including me) went to Arvind's house. Arvind had just woken up. He seemed to be in a foul mood, shouted for no apparent reason, and was rude to Prof Anand Kumar, who was supposed to be part of Yogendra's camp. Then, he looked at me and asked me for my views. I told him that I was in favour of a divorce—if a divorce meant that the aggrieved parties would not interact extensively with one another—but Yogendra and Prashant had to remain in the party and be given senior responsibilities. Arvind smiled at me. He mistook my stance on separation as an acceptance of his plans.

The wheel started moving towards the final confrontation on the 4 March NE meeting.

*

I believe that in a political party, there should be a tapestry of views, so decisions emerge from debate. Indian democracy, warts and all, has always stood for this. In a dynastic Congress, Sonia Gandhi, who disagreed with Sitaram Kesri and a few others regarding a range of issues, found a way of managing her power equation with them. In the BJP, a party viewed as being authoritarian, L.K. Advani and Murli Manohar Joshi coexisted for over forty years. And even today, Yashwant Sinha, Arun Shourie and Shatrughan Sinha subsist alongside Modi in the BJP.

In the early days of the IAC movement, Arvind and I used to discuss the dangers of authoritarianism in Indian political parties, the need for politicians to embrace collective leadership, and the merits of ensuring that the main leader was a first among equals. Now, the Arvind who had once decried despotism was its strongest votary. Where once he had been able to tolerate a range of viewpoints, these days his prime desire was to keep rigid control over AAP members and quash dissenting voices.

This was entirely linked to the 2015 election results. Arvind likely thought: 'Neither Prashant nor Yogendra have ever been able to influence voters . . . why then should I listen to them?' The fact is that the 2015 victory heightened Arvind's contempt for the views of the 'intelligentsia'—this only widened his rift with such scholars and thinkers as Yogendra, Prashant, Anand Kumar and Ajit Jha.

Now, if anyone approached Arvind with suggestions, his chief concern, even while appearing attentive, was: 'Will this person or his comments secure more votes? Or can he at the very least get me a donation?'

Arvind cultivated loyalists—members who were coached to execute each of his plans. This coterie started moving in like a pack of wolves. When we used to travel together, Manish Sisodia and Bibhav would engage with Arvind, constantly relaying dangerous gossip about AAP members Manish felt threatened by. In some ways, Arvind was just like Anna—those in his inner circle could easily manipulate him.

Nobody was safe.

Today, one must ask: is Kumar Vishwas next?

*

To target Yogendra and Prashant, social media platforms were used as the first line of attack.

The AAP social media team, led by the poet-politician Kumar Vishwas, consisted of impressionable, highly charged patriotic youth. Some of them were paid and some worked pro bono. Almost all of them had multiple fake accounts, and on receiving a signal from the party 'high command', they would chase their target like bloodhounds.

Yogendra Yadav and Prashant Bhushan began to get 'branded' in a particularly insidious manner. The impressionable social media team would be fed stories about Yogendra's interview against Arvind or Prashant's pre-election statements or Shanti Bhushan's support for AAP's opponents. They were portrayed as traitors or 'gaddars'. Fabricated narratives, too, emerged out of nowhere, and they did their damage. The social media team went hammer and tongs after the Bhushans and Yogendra, trolling them incessantly and using the worst possible language.

These youngsters were unaware of Prashant's body of work, or Shanti Bhushan's service to democracy, or Yogendra's in-depth knowledge and love for the nation.

Rather, driven by propaganda, they tweeted ruthlessly. My heart broke. I felt like going up to those naive boys, holding their hands and telling them the truth. I wanted to heal them by letting them know that one man's political ambition was not the be-all and end-all.

*

AAP supporters sensed that something unpleasant was about to happen in the NE meeting scheduled for 4 March. Desperately, they created a hashtag 'United AAP' group; they called up and petitioned each member of the NE, pleading with him or her to keep the party united. I was besieged by calls throughout the night from different parts of the world. Some volunteers were in tears. I promised to do my best to keep the party intact. But I knew that the die was cast.

The meeting started in a resort near Delhi; there were twenty-three members who had voting rights. The sole agenda was the removal of Prashant and Yogendra from the PAC. Arvind, as usual, stayed away from the meeting while tutoring his team to 'do the needful'. Desperate, I sent a message to Arvind. I repeated my alternative plan. I urged him to retain Yogendra and Prashant as senior active members, even while removing them from the PAC. But Arvind did not reply.

I was asked to present a resolution for the removal of Prashant and Yogendra. I proposed that both be removed from the PAC but be given some other key responsibilities. On hearing this, Manish Sisodia got angry and said, 'Mayank, you do not know what to say . . . let me say it instead!' He proposed a one-line resolution: Yogendra and Prashant must be removed from the PAC.

At this, Yogendra stood up and tried to salvage the situation: 'People across the world are concerned about what is happening in the party and want a United AAP. I also understand that Arvindbhai does not like to work with us in the PAC. Let me suggest two alternative proposals that can address his concerns. Firstly, we can hold a PAC election in the next month, in which neither Prashant nor I will contest . . . or secondly, let the PAC continue its regular meetings till elections scheduled for October and we will not attend any of these meetings. This will allow Arvindbhai to function smoothly . . . because he has to take a lot of decisions now, and he should not be diverted by our intervention. This will also address the concerns of the supporters.'

Kumar Vishwas, who was chairing the meeting, immediately said, 'Yogendrabhai, you have solved the matter with your excellent proposal.' He congratulated him for his statesmanship. A lot of us witnessing this turn of events felt that the conflict was resolved, now that Yogendra and Prashant themselves had decided to stay away from the PAC.

But little were we aware that the original plan for calling an NE meeting was different. Manish looked grim and said, 'Let us take a break and reconvene in about an hour.' In hindsight, it was evident that Yogendra's suggestion was unexpected and Team Arvind's strategy had to be redrafted.

Team Arvind went to one of the suites in the resort. Ashish Khetan, Ashutosh, Durgesh Pathak, Dilip Pandey and others who were not a part of the NE were already waiting there. I also joined them after a while.

When I reached, I heard Sanjay Singh saying, 'Whatever has been suggested by Yogendra Yadav actually solves our problem. The snake will die, and the stick, too, will remain unbroken.'

At this, Manish became furious and said, 'This will not do! We have to kick Yogendra and Prashant out of the party, and in such a manner that nobody will ever have the guts to challenge Arvind in the future.'

Durgesh Pathak intervened, 'Remember how Prithviraj Chauhan had forgiven Mahmud of Ghazni in the first battle, only to be subsequently ruled by him for many decades? We cannot be gentle with such creatures. They have to be thrown out.'

Kumar Vishwas spoke wisely, 'All of you, sycophants of Arvind . . . do you realize that your senseless plans will harm Arvind most of all?' My respect for Kumar Vishwas went up a notch.

Suddenly, Ashutosh, who was on a phone call, said, 'Arvind has already called three times. He has asked us not to argue but to simply execute what has been planned.'

I stood up and told the gathering, 'You know, I had been in favour of the removal of Prashant and Yogendra from the PAC, as long as they were offered important roles in the party. Now I understand that the plan has been simply to humiliate them. I am not in favour of this stupid decision. Excuse me!' I walked out of the room.

I then met Sanjubhai, our decent and soft-spoken treasurer. I told him that since the party's agenda was to demean Prashant and Yogendra, I was going to abstain from voting. Sanjubhai also decided to abstain from a 'yes' or a 'no'.

The meeting reconvened after three-and-a-half hours. Immediately, there was a call to vote. It was resolved that Yogendra and Prashant were to be removed from the PAC—eleven members were in favour of their removal and eight were against such a move. Sanjubhai and I abstained, and Kumar Vishwas, who had the right to veto, did not need to vote.

While I was distressed by what had just happened, it was not the end of the world. In political parties, people come and go. In any case I had to accept the democratic verdict.

I now started thinking about what our volunteers across the world would feel. I wondered how I was to break the news to them that AAP was no longer a united force, and that I had failed to mend the breach. It was best to be upfront and send them the official minutes of the meeting. I asked Pankaj Gupta, the party secretary, 'When will we get the minutes? AAP supporters across the globe are waiting.'

To my surprise, Pankaj Gupta informed me, 'No one should be told about today's event. There is a gag order against informing the media or anyone outside the room about the proceedings of the NE meeting.'

I could not believe my ears. Were we the same party? In our IAC days, transparency had been our calling card; but now, our whole aim was to conceal. I protested against the decision, but it was all in vain.

As I had a flight to catch, I left the meeting early. As soon as I ventured outside, the media surrounded me, seeking updates. I never speak out of turn. So I told the media that after the meeting was done, the party would officially brief them; I could not reveal anything.

Soon after, Atishi and Prithvi called me. They said that they were very upset that I abstained from voting—I should have cast my vote in favour of Yogendra and Prashant. I explained my position, but they were too distressed to listen.

On my way to the airport, I kept getting calls from volunteers and supporters seeking information on AAP's future—was it united or dismembered? What could I tell them? They wanted to know what exactly had transpired . . . but I had been silenced by a gag order. I was shattered from within. On the one hand, I had been unable to secure the party; on the other, I was unable to even speak openly to the supporters. I could understand their anguish and anger. They must have felt so betrayed.

Just before I reached the airport, I noticed a tweet. Aaj Tak had announced that I had voted in favour of Arvind. I tweeted a message to correct the channel; I said that I had abstained from voting. At this, Ashish Khetan, who was not even a part of the NE, threatened disciplinary action against me. He removed me from our internal messenger group. I did not take him seriously; these were the manoeuvrings of someone, who, in the larger scheme of things, didn't really matter.

At the airport, I kept mulling over a couple of existential questions. The first question was: who is the primary force in a party—the leader or the volunteers? The twenty-three people in a room with voting powers or the millions of supporters outside? I recognized the need for a power structure and trust in decision-makers. But we weren't in a boardroom. We were a volunteer-driven party. Therefore, volunteers had to remain supreme. We had to keep them in the loop about key developments. Not doing so was an affront to their dignity.

The second question that confronted me was whether I ought to abide by the diktats of a party or listen to my conscience. Was it important to please Arvind and the few around him, or acknowledge the dignity and rights of lakhs of supporters, by informing them of the day's tumult?

On the flight, it came to me with great clarity that in life one has to take a stand at crucial times, even if one is standing alone. I could not stop the split, but it was my duty to inform my volunteers about what had transpired in that critical meeting. Oddly enough, the Arvind Kejriwal I once knew served as an example. Back in the IAC days, when Kapil Sibal had asked him not to inform anyone about the discussions during internal Lokpal meetings, Arvind had told him that he was a representative of the people and not informing them was wrong. Similarly, I represented the volunteers, and it was my duty to speak to them honestly. Martin Luther King Jr's words rang in my ears: 'There comes a time when silence is betrayal.'

The next morning, I woke up early, and I wrote a blog post detailing the meeting objectively.[24] I was neither in favour of Arvind and his team nor in support of Yogendra and Prashant. I was in favour of the truth; I wished to pursue transparency. A blog was the only long-form communication platform available to me to reach out to lakhs of volunteers across the globe—so I utilized it.

I was aware of the repercussions the blog post would have. My wife Minal and Shrey were not too sure about what I should do; they began discussing the implications with Sanjaybhai on the phone. While the call was in session, I came out of the bedroom and switched on the TV. The news was out.

As the post turned viral, the compound opposite my house saw a host of media vans. Journalists began urging me to reveal juicy bits of information. But I had said what I needed to, so I told the media that I had little else to offer. Some anchors pointed out that as one of the key leaders in the highest body of AAP, I had jeopardized my political career by following the thorny path of truth. I shrugged. It had been a conscious call. I remained unfazed.

All major news anchors called me personally, asking for one-on-one interviews. I declined. Rajdeep Sardesai told me, 'Hats off to you for both your principled stands—to speak up truthfully to the millions of supporters and to avoid publicity.' It felt good to know that I had not betrayed my volunteers or myself. Sanjay Singh, Kumar Vishwas and Ashutosh called me, requesting me to remove the blog post, but I politely told them that I did not think that I could overrule my conscience and retract a factual narration of events.

I sent an email to Arvind. I accepted that I had broken the party protocol and that, as the convenor of AAP, he was free to initiate disciplinary action against me and throw me out. I would have no complaints. I added that I still believed that he was the only person in the party to understand why my conscience would not allow me to keep quiet. He did not reply.

In the days to come, I received a lot of appreciation for being transparent in my dealings. When a few members of the AAP social media team tried trolling me on Twitter, common volunteers came forward to ferociously defend my actions.

The leaders of AAP, however, remained furious with me. They thought they had staged a silent coup, but I had exposed their actions to the nation. Obviously, they had to penalize me. And they did—I had to pay the price for being truthful. And boy, what a price I had to pay!

In the days to follow, I clutched on to Winston Churchill's observation: 'You have enemies? Good. That means you've stood up for something, sometime in your life.'

18. A Tale of Two Meetings: The NC

AAP WAS AGAIN ON PRIME TIME NEWS, BUT THIS TIME THE headlines weren't positive. Media anchors asked, 'Is AAP going the way of the Janata Party, with leaders fighting amongst themselves?'

But Arvind's team had no patience for public opinion; they were determined to take the removal of Yogendra and Prashant from the PAC to its logical conclusion. It was time to eject them from the party. 'We will win over the people's approval with our work later . . . but, first, we must rid ourselves of these irritants,' was the consensus within Arvind's coterie.

The belief that they'd win back public support was entirely misplaced. Not a single election has been won by AAP, except for few scattered seats, after the ouster of Prashant and Yogendra. This is not entirely surprising since AAP is not just another party; it has been a surrogate family for its supporters. 'Us' versus 'them' is not an approach that is accepted. The bond has been not strategic but emotional. Therefore, after the PAC coup, supporters felt terribly letdown. Where once people believed that AAP was their party—they identified with its agenda and trusted the leaders—now, there was general apprehension and suspicion. There was also a great deal of hurt.

AAP made a few feeble attempts to negotiate with Yogendra and Prashant, but everyone knew that this was just a façade. The diktat was clear—throw them out. Yogendra knew his days were numbered; still, he wanted to initiate a few reforms before being told to leave AAP. He called me to say: 'Mayankbhai, Prashant and I have no desire for a post in the party, but unless AAP begins some course correction, Arvind's attempts at hijacking all decision-making will turn the party into just another power hungry and unprincipled outfit. We need to do something, or the dream of alternative politics shared by millions of Indians across the world will be shattered.'

I replied, 'Yogendraji, I know that, right now, you have no interest in a party position. So, why don't you offer AAP your resignation on the condition that it brings in these much needed reforms?'

Consequently, Yogendra and Prashant sent a note to the party leaders stating that they were willing to resign provided the NE set certain changes into motion. The note's contents were twisted to make it appear that Yogendra and Prashant had simply agreed to resign, no strings attached. Shanti Bhushan was of the strong view that Arvind could not be trusted any more. Given the jangled lines of communication and the suspicion harboured by both sides, talks broke down.

Now, with the smokescreen of negotiations out of the way, it was time for the final showdown. Both teams started flexing their muscles.

Prashant began reaching out to most of the NC members for support. There was a point where both Yogendra and Prashant seemed confident of defeating the proposal for their removal. On the night before the NC meeting,

Yogendra and Ajit Jha came to meet me and briefed me about their preparation and their chances. I remained silent. While Yogendra was optimistic, he was seriously underestimating the cunning of the other side.

Meanwhile, Sanjay Singh and his team travelled extensively, meeting various volunteers, NC members and MLAs throughout the night. The evening prior to the NC meeting, the security company in charge of organizing bouncers were ordered to send twenty-four men, instead of the original eleven. Placards against Yogendra and Prashant were made in large numbers. All MLAs were given express instructions to bring in busloads of supporters to shout slogans outside the venue of the meeting.

28 March 2015, the day of the NC meeting, dawned. Just a few hours prior to the meeting, Admiral (Retd) L. Ramdas, who served as AAP's Internal Lokpal, was asked by the party general secretary, Pankaj Gupta, not to attend the NC meeting so as to avoid any kind of confrontation. In a letter to NC members, Ramdas expressed his disgust: 'I hold our leadership collectively responsible for this, and for our failure to be able to rise above personal egos, to resort to leakages—the cheapest form of stings—and spreading conspiracy theories which should put us all to shame.'[25]

By the time I reached the venue, there were large numbers of people shouting, '*Yogendra, hai, hai . . . Prashant, hai, hai,*' and holding printed placards that referred to the duo as traitors. It was obvious that every action was well choreographed. As I hopped out of the car, I realized that I'd have to pass hundreds of volunteers to reach the gate. Would they heckle me for my previous blog post? Far from it. Instead, when they saw me, several volunteers started clapping, patting me on my back, thanking me, even while making way. There were young boys shouting, '*Mayank Gandhi zindabad*!' Even while being consumed by a sense of gloom, I was reassured that the volunteers appreciated my work.

I entered the gates. I was asked to hand over my pen, mobile phone, etc, at a counter. Considering that we had had multiple episodes of news leaks, I found these precautions justifiable. As I turned around, I saw Arvind coming towards me. I waved at him and smiled. He frowned in response and turned away. It was churlish. I remembered his body language and the words he had chosen when he had criticized Prashant a while ago; I was almost certain that I would be relegated to the same category.

Meanwhile, as I walked in, I saw senior volunteers of the party whisking away NC members into a room to sign a predesigned resolution seeking the removal of Yogendra and Prashant. My views were out in the open, so no one asked me to sign the resolution. There were bouncers everywhere. As I settled into my chair, four bouncers stood around me. When I went to the washroom, two of them traipsed behind. I was amused that the party was taking such care of me.

Arvind came and spoke with great gusto, pointing out that Yogendra and Prashant had betrayed the party. Then, looking at Shanti Bhushan, he changed his pitch and tone; he was rude and angry. He asked NE members what ought to be done to someone who chose Kiran Bedi over the party—referring to a moment in time when Shanti Bhushan had announced that Bedi would make a good chief ministerial candidate.[26] In what seemed like a pre-rehearsed move, some workers, led by Kapil Mishra, ran towards Shanti Bhushan shouting, '*Gaddaro ko hatao*'—remove the traitors! For a moment I grew nervous. It seemed like things would go out of hand and a ninety-year-old Shanti Bhushan would get physically assaulted.

Fortunately, things calmed down, and Arvind continued his emotionally charged speech. He ended his rabble-rousing outpouring by narrating the story of two women who were fighting over a child. 'The women took the child to the king and asked him to decide who the mother was. The king mulled over the situation and said that the child could be cut into two, and each woman could keep one half. On hearing this, the real mother said that the other woman could keep the child.'

Arvind thundered, 'I have given my sweat and blood to this party and will not allow its break up. Either get rid of Yogendra and Prashant or release me from all responsibilities and positions within the party.'

After this, in what had become his customary melodramatic style, he walked out of the meeting. This was exactly the way I had anticipated the NC meeting going. No decorum, no rules, just bullying.

As Arvind walked out, AAP member Ramzan Chaudhary[27] tried asking him why, as the leader, he wouldn't stay back and listen to the volunteers. Arvind brushed him away and stomped off. In front of my eyes, some bouncers drew forward, caught Ramzan by his legs and hands, and carried him out of the meeting. It was alleged that he was punched outside.

A resolution to remove Yogendra, Prashant, Prof Anand Kumar and Ajit Jha from the NC was read out. It was also announced that the resolution was backed by

247 members (with fifty-four abstaining and eight being against it).[28] The irony didn't miss me—a resolution had been signed before it was even read out.

Prashant, Yogendra and co were out. Arvind had won. He had achieved his short-term objective of removing from the party those he felt threatened by.

However, the country was disgusted. All those I knew, who had once been in favour of AAP, withdrew their support. A little over two years prior, we had formed this party to counter other outfits we had accused of impropriety; to uphold the best democratic practices; to bring decency into public life; and to create an alternative political space. All this now seemed laughable.

As I walked out of the meeting venue, Manish Sisodia sarcastically told me, 'Why don't you stay back for some more time? You will get more material for your blog.'

I retorted: 'Manish, the more you become anti-volunteers, the more I will speak up. The party belongs not to you but to our foot soldiers.'

With a wry smile, Manish walked away.

Outside, I saw Prithvi sitting alone, sobbing, and repeating to himself, 'Everything is over.' Yes, it was. All that was now left was the politics of power.

Over the next few days, I heard that Admiral (Retd) L. Ramdas was removed as the Lokpal of the party. I also heard that Medha Patkar quit, among many others.

Soon after the NC meeting, Atishi wrote a letter to Yogendra and Prashant (who were her mentors) criticizing them. Among other things, she wrote, '[. . .] I do not believe that our paths can be common anymore. I do hope that they do not diverge to a degree that we may have to stand confronting each other.' As with most letters, this one, too, was leaked.[29] I was reminded of a Bollywood movie where the hero, after infiltrating the villain's gang, was told to kill someone to prove his loyalty. Atishi established her allegiance to her new mentor Arvind Kejriwal. As an aside, I should add that I have immense respect for Atishi's work, and it offers me some consolation that she is still there as part of AAP's education initiative.

After the NC meeting, I did a lot of soul-searching. I used to think that I was working with some of the best people in the country. But now, the illusion was shattered. If this was the least evil alternative before us, I shuddered to consider what the other parties would be like.

I also wondered: 'Had we really hit rock bottom . . . or could things get any worse?'

Well, as it happened, we were to sink further.

19. Maharashtra: Back Home

There were eight NE members who had voted in favour of Yogendra and Prashant. They were systematically thrown out. Now came the turn of one of the abstainers—me. In addition to non-participation, I had also defied a gag order. Strong retribution was the order of the day.

But there were some roadblocks, among them public perception. AAP had ceased being a darling of the media. Negative stories emerged every day regarding the functioning of the party. Volunteers, especially after reading my blog, were very upset with the central management team. The party sensed that, given the general turmoil, it was best to play a waiting game.

In any case, I wasn't an irritant.

*

Atishi and Prithvi, through Mission Vistaar, had created excellent committees in the state and district levels, with powerful and cohesive teams. These committees took up several issues via an Anti-Corruption Helpline, Shetkari Yatra and AAP Ka Samvad. As I was a part of the NE—one of the highest bodies of the party—I was a part of all committees as an ex-officio member.

My management style has always been to empower others and stay in the background. Maybe, subconsciously,

I've always wished to create a team that will continue after my exit. At one level, this is the best way to strengthen the organization. But when things go wrong, or the empowered person starts becoming arrogant, one has to wonder if handing over power (especially to someone who isn't ready) is wise.

The Maharashtra State Executive (SE) Committee, under the leadership of Subhash Ware, was united and principled. It was unafraid of taking a strong, independent position. After the expulsion of Yogendra Yadav and Prashant Bhushan, the 1SE Committee wrote to Arvind Kejriwal that it was pained by the way two senior members were told to leave. It asked the party to introspect and try bringing them back. Incidentally, this was one of the few letters that did not leak to the press. The reasons are obvious.

On 23 June 2015, Pankaj Gupta and Ashutosh from Delhi visited Mumbai and a few other cities and towns in Maharashtra to meet volunteers. They expressed satisfaction that, all across the state, a lot of positive work had been done and the teams seemed strong. Both of them asked me pointedly whether I regretted my writing the blog and whether I would like to apologize to Arvind. It was a no brainer. In a measured and firm tone, I told them, 'It was the correct thing to do under the circumstances. And if a similar situation arises again, I shall do exactly the same thing.'

My response was guided by the philosophy of Immanuel Kant, who held that a 'moral agent does a particular action not because of what it produces (its consequences) in terms of human experience, but because he or she recognizes by reasoning that it is morally the right thing to do'.[30] In some ways, this position was identical to the

Bhagavad Gita's: 'Do your duty without worrying about the outcome.'

The next day, on 24 June, there was a Maharashtra SE Committee meeting. This was attended by Pankaj Gupta and Ashutosh. In that meeting, I conveyed to both of them, on behalf of the SE Committee, that the focus on Arvind in every advertisement and debate, to the exclusion of AAP, was making many of us uncomfortable. I said that we were against the over-glorification of leaders, and we hoped that this sentiment would reach Arvind. While no one was questioning Arvind's position in the party, we strongly felt that personality-driven politics created an unhealthy political atmosphere—it made AAP akin to the BJP and the Congress, which had created a cult around Narendra Modi and Sonia Gandhi respectively. Ashutosh and Pankaj could not believe their ears. They were not used to listening to independent positions from state teams However, AAP was as much our party as the central team's, and we were duty-bound to point out flaws in its functioning, even if what we conveyed annoyed Arvind. Keeping Arvind happy was not our job.

On 30 July, I had to visit Delhi for personal work. I was invited by Pankaj Gupta and Ashutosh for a discussion. When I met them, they confessed that while they were completely convinced about the support I enjoyed in Maharashtra and the positive role I was playing in the party, the 'Delhi team' was hostile towards me due to the blog.

Pankaj suggested, 'On your own, Mayankbhai, you should leave the party . . . and if you do so, maybe after some years, the party will consider letting you rejoin. Or else, the entire thing will become ugly.'

I smiled. 'After so many years of working together, do you guys really think that I will get intimidated when you threaten to make things "ugly"? What can you do to someone who has no desire for a party position and has no fear of losing anything?'

The next day, I sent Ashutosh and Pankaj Gupta a written response in bullet points. I told them (and I paraphrase):

- The position and respect I have earned in the party in Maharashtra is on account of the work I have done at the grass-roots level—not by keeping Delhi leaders happy or by conspiring against the local leaders. I have little reason to feel insecure since I have the goodwill and love of the volunteers. Remember, during the heady IAC days, while the entire central leadership team was in Delhi, the rallies in Mumbai were of the same strength as those in Delhi—and, sometimes, they were larger than the demonstrations in the capital. This was because I had the support of the state team—I was viewed as one of them—not because I had affiliations with Delhi.
- AAP is as much my party as anyone else's. I had worked very hard from the time it was conceived. In fact, for the 2015 Delhi elections, I was leading over 6,000 outstation volunteers who had come to Delhi. One sometimes forgets that outstation volunteers from all over the globe campaigned 24x7 and were critical to the party's victory. While some might praise the 'faces' of our organization, I believe we owe everything to the lakhs of people who acted as foot soldiers. They are AAP.
- My primary role is guiding and mentoring the team

in Mumbai, as per SE guidelines. On my part, I believe that a political party's role is to build future leaders for the country. All along, my attempt has been, not to project myself as a leader, but to work in the background to bring some of Mumbai's best youth to the fore. If you visit any party office, you will not find a single picture of mine.

- I shall continue to take a stand whenever I believe I am bearing witness to something wrong. Our nation and the principles on which our party have been built are much bigger than the short-term benefits that 'practical' shortcuts to power bring. Indeed, power is but a medium to initiate a new political culture. Today, it seems that our dream of 'alternative politics' has been abandoned.
- I have heard that our party maintains 'confidential files' of all senior members. The social media team refers to these files to demolish the character of anyone the central team wishes to oppose. I request both of you to neither start a vilification campaign against me through social media nor disturb Mission Vistaar to get even.
- Just because someone does not like me or is influenced by conspirators does not mean that I will quietly walk out of the party. I am not a coward nor am I a 'ranchod' (deserter). So, if the central team wants me out of the party, it should remove me. I am willing to be crucified for speaking the truth.

I shared a version of this response with my colleagues in Maharashtra, and they unanimously agreed with my stand. My volunteers stood by my side, refusing to get browbeaten. They told Pankaj that the party had to reconsider its decision to ease me out. The entire SE team, including Meera Sanyal, Subhash Ware, Raju Bhise and others, decided that if the central leadership team decided to throw me out, all of them would resign. I appreciated their sentiments but advised them against such a move since the party was bigger than an individual.

In every party, there are those who play dirty politics. Sadly, AAP not only identified this lot but also encouraged them to conspire against Maharashtra's team. For a while, we refused to believe that this was possible within a party like ours. But then reality caught up.

Arvind had decided that by end-September, all of Maharashtra's committees would be dismantled. An alternative 'probable' committee list was being planned, consisting of those removed by Mission Vistaar. What emerged, therefore, was a disgruntled alternate faction. Rumours began to surface that a watertight case against Maharashtra's convener Subhash Ware was being created, in a bid to remove him. The central team seemed to be conspiring against its own state party.

False statements began to get issued against the Maharashtra SE Committee. The SE Committee complained to Delhi. No reply. Thrice, the SE Committee asked for an appointment with Arvind. No reply. I called Arvind on multiple occasions, but my call would be cut. I sent messages to him. Once more, there was no reply. There came a point where I considered quitting the party, so that my colleagues would be spared some grief. I even sent messages to Arvind to this effect; I said I'd leave without rancour, but I'd like to speak to him once. As usual, there was no reply.

Subhash Ware and Raju Bhise (the co-convenor) were called to Delhi and told that the high command wished to dissolve the Maharashtra team, and the two of them could reconstitute new committees. To their credit, they refused to be a part of this exercise. Instead, they asked Delhi to send a team to Maharashtra to review the committees; if there was cause for concern, a joint decision could be made to solve the problem.

This was the third time the Maharashtra SE Committee was defying the central team's diktats—the first time was when the SE Committee asked Arvind to reconsider throwing out Yogendra and Prashant, and the second time was when it pushed for an end to personality-driven politics. The central team was fuming.

End-September was drawing close. Something had to give. On 1 October, there was a small entry on the AAP website announcing that all committees in the state of Maharashtra had been dissolved, and Pankaj Gupta had been given charge of making new teams. This was precisely the kind of culture—a high command approach—that we had opposed when we had formed a new party.

I was deeply saddened. How could an outfit that functioned remarkably well be dismantled? After all, Maharashtra was the only unit in the country to have had internal democracy; we were known to promote causes rather than people; we had helmed several successful campaigns including one against the Adarsh scam; and our financial prudence was well known. Indeed, our treasurer Sanjubhai had told Kumar Vishwas in an NE meeting, 'You talk so much about proper accounting systems, yet except for Maharashtra, no one has given their accounts!'

But there was nothing to do—the empire had struck back. It has now been almost two years, and we're yet to find a committee of calibre in my state. It feels as though there is no AAP left in Maharashtra. And to think this was a state that had some of the tallest leaders, that had given humungous donations, that had offered the largest pool of volunteers, and that had campaigned tirelessly for the Delhi elections . . . today, it is all gone in a haze of anger and arrogance.

Soon after the committees were dissolved, I went to a small village in Maharashtra. The local volunteers came up to meet me, and one boy, with tears in his eyes, asked, 'Sir, what was our fault?' What could I tell him? If AAP was upset with the SE's stances, why was the SE Committee alone not dismissed? Why did all the committees, across the taluka and district levels, also have to go?

When people tell me that our party has become like the BJP or the Congress, I laugh. 'No,' I reply. 'Can Narendra Modi or Amit Shah dismiss all the committees in Rajasthan with a one-line message? Can Sonia Gandhi throw out everyone in Madhya Pradesh with the stroke of a pen? But AAP and Arvind Kejriwal have done what others could not.' In terms of authoritarianism and arrogance, we had surpassed all competition. Besides, whereas I could still conceive of a Congress or a BJP surviving after a Gandhi or a Modi, I was no longer sure if there would be an AAP without Arvind. We had turned into an outfit with a supremo, where the strengths and the limitations of an individual became the strengths and the limitations of the party.

Yet, I refuse to give up hope. When volunteers, who are upset, seek my advice about what to do next, I say, 'This is as much your party as much as anyone else's. Continue work within AAP; devote yourself to the cause of the nation. Times will change, and real volunteers will get their due. *Satya pareshan ho sakta hai, lekin parajeet nahi ho sakta.* (The truth can tire, but cannot be defeated.)'

20. Resignation

THERE IS A SAYING THAT GOES: 'DO NOT WRESTLE WITH pigs in the mud, you will get dirty and they will enjoy it.' I felt there was a lesson for me in this expression. I could not be part of AAP any longer; I needed to get out and inhale some fresh air. I decided to quit.

On 11 November 2015—it was Diwali—I dispatched a letter conveying my decision to resign from the NE:

11th Nov 2015, 12.19 hours

Dear Arvind and my other friends,

I have been losing interest in politics for some time, and I think that it is unfair to continue to be a member of NE with this mindset. You are requested to please accept my resignation from the NE with immediate effect. Hope that you will find some capable representatives from Maharashtra.

It has been a wonderful experience working with many of you from Jan 2011 and being part of the change in this country. I pray and hope that this transformation continues and accelerates in the coming months and years and leads to a resurgent India. Arvind, India has a lot of hopes from you.

Jai Hind.
Love
Mayank Gandhi[31]

But Pankaj Gupta and Ashutosh had already given me a clear signal that things would get 'ugly'. So, there came a letter:

To
Mr Mayank Gandhi
Mumbai

Date: 18th November 2015

Subject: Show Cause notice and suspension of primary membership

Dear Mr Gandhi,

The party has received a copy of an FIR filed against you, lodged in Varanasi wherein you have been charged with very serious IPC sections, namely 323, 504, 506, 427, 452, 392, 307, 376, 326, 120V, 354B, 366A and 372. A copy of the FIR is attached in the documents called FIR Page 1A, FIR Page 1B and FIR Page 2.

Aam Aadmi Party takes charges of such heinous crimes very seriously.

You have also been making baseless allegation on the party and its leadership [sic] on various public fora like social media and the media with a purpose to damage the party and confuse party volunteers. Some of your utterances are attached in the subsequent files. These acts amount to misconduct and violate the Code of Conduct enshrined in the Party Constitution.

Accordingly, you are hereby required to show cause on both counts, the FIR against you and the misconduct in baseless criticism and allegations on the party in public forum, on or before 20 November 2015, as to why disciplinary action should not be taken against you.

Since the charges levelled against you are of [a] grave and serious nature, your primary membership of the party is suspended pending further proceedings.

Regards

Pankaj Gupta

Chairman, National Disciplinary Action Committee

CC:

1. Dilip Pandey

Member, National Disciplinary Action Committee

2. Deepak Bajpai

Member, National Disciplinary Action Committee

The charges were completely baseless, the crimes imaginary. I had sufficient evidence—from tweets to documents to recordings—to establish that these cases were false and malicious.

In response to the show cause notice, I wrote to Pankaj:

Dear Pankajbhai,

One of the perils of public life is that one becomes an easy target for false complaints, allegations and blackmail. Some of our leaders can attest to that. The FIR that you refer is over one-year-old and is completely false and filed as a counterblast because we were trying to help our friend MP Singh [. . .] Both Arvind Kejriwal and Manish Sisodia have stayed a night at the same MP Singh's place in Varanasi and would have [been privy to] the simplicity and depth of knowledge of this pious person. Many volunteers from all over the country stayed at his house during Arvind's campaign and they know of his piety. Helping [a man] who is in [the] 2nd stage of leukemia, who has lost his vision and who was being duped financially is the only crime that I and Sanjay [who had also been accused] have done. [. . .] The law is at work and will soon prove us innocent of these charges. For AAP party [*sic*] to use these old charges to "settle scores" is unfortunate.

[. . .] Some journalists from Delhi call[ed] to say that

they had been told [by] the party office about the FIR. Is it right for a party with principles to leak information to [the] media before even asking an explanation from the person concerned? Or was this exercise done to corner me and to ensure that I step out of AAP? Was it done keeping the National Council meeting in mind? Was it done to ensure that I am humiliated? If your anger was because I was raising some uncomfortable issues, you should have simply sacked me. I had sent messages to Arvind that instead of removing the entire Maharashtra Committee, please ask me to step down and I will do so easily, without rancour. But looks like it has become the party's operating style to humiliate a person before he exits. I had come into this movement to change the country and change the politics of my country but [I am] deeply disturbed with the viciousness in the party.

'Silence becomes cowardice when occasion demands speaking out the whole truth,' says Mahatma Gandhi, one of the greatest dissenters of modern times.

[. . .] In a democratic society, including ours, the need to accept difference[s] of opinion is an essential ingredient of plurality. In that sense, the right of dissent also becomes the duty of dissent. Tactics to suppress dissent tend to diminish the democratic essence. [The] Party command will always be uncomfortable with dissent and label it as "Indiscipline", but that is counter-productive [. . .]

Individuals do not matter—you may expel me if it serves your purpose. But, remember, AAP is the hope of the nation. Please do not break the heart of crores of people by becoming arrogant [. . .] Stay humble and serve. Sabko sanmiti de bhagavan. [Bless everyone with this wisdom.]

JAI HIND

Love

Mayank Gandhi

As expected, there was no reply.

One senior national member from Maharashtra, known for her closeness to the core team in Delhi, and also famous for her viciousness, circulated a copy of the FIR to the media to implicate me. Fortunately, most of the journalists knew me well enough to see that the FIR lacked credibility.

Anjali Damania fought like the tigress on behalf of Sanjay and me, calling up journalists and explaining how false the allegations were. Eventually, in 2016, the police, after an intense round of investigation, filed a final report in which we were found completely innocent.

Meanwhile, Arvind was to travel to Mumbai for a court case. Possibly worried that some supporters would try meeting him to speak on our behalf, the disciplinary committee suspended us from primary membership of the party a day before Arvind was to arrive.

Once again I was sustained by the overwhelming love and respect of the volunteers. The Twitter army of AAP rebelled against the diktat to discredit me; it either supported me or did not write against me. As I read each tweet of support, as I received one message after another of love, as I got calls thanking me for upholding the truth, I was overwhelmed.

Some volunteers from the interiors of Maharashtra, Karnataka, Gujarat, West Bengal, among other states, went to Delhi and personally asked the core party leaders to stop attacking me.

In May 2017, when key entities within the party began targeting me, they were severely rebuffed by hundreds of AAP volunteers on social media. Some senior leaders from Delhi later phoned me and apologized; they said they were ashamed of the turn of events.

I was left with a thought that consoled me: there were still a few decent men.

*

Abraham Lincoln had once said, 'Nearly all men can stand adversity, but if you want to test a man's character, give him power.'

The political arena we had come to change had changed us. It was heartbreaking. We used to think that we had no option but to enter the gutter of politics to clean it; now, the gutter had soiled us.

The leaders who tried maligning me were the ones I had worked with to build a movement and a party. These were supposedly my friends; many had stayed in my house; we had spent a substantial part of our lives fighting for the country shoulder-to-shoulder. All of a sudden, power had become more important to them than integrity, loyalty and simple decency.

What disturbed me even more was what we had done to the youth who had joined us. Instead of offering them hopes and dreams, we had made them fearful. We had broken their inner spirit for our power games.

I was uncomfortable. Osho used to say that in life, there is ugliness and beauty, there is poverty and richness. One has to choose what one wants to be with.

I was choosing to walk away from the ugliness.

21. The Game Plan

Notwithstanding the vituperative NE and NC meetings, we were not yet prepared to completely let go of the faith we had once invested in AAP. While I was not a part of the party any more, I was unwilling to abandon the mission we had started.

If the party could not pursue alternative politics, could it at least show signs of exemplary governance in Delhi?

During the swearing-in ceremony at Ramlila Maidan, Arvind, with his customary flair, had roared, 'Since God has instructed me, Delhi's people have instructed me, people have put their faith in me, for the next five years I'll live in Delhi and serve people of this city and put my heart and soul to fulfill my responsibilities.'[32] And his responsibilities were many. He had to prioritize soft infrastructure like education and health, empower mohallas, attack corruption, and institutionalize an anti-corruption machinery by passing a powerful Lokpal Bill.

It seemed like a great plan. Arvind became the chief minister but did not take any portfolio. Every day, the cabinet would meet in his cabin and take quick decisions under his personal supervision. Arvind was micro-managing beautifully, as always.

Some of the government's moves were noteworthy—

among them, reducing the electricity rate in Delhi, fulfilling the promise of providing up to 20,000 liters of free water per household per month, offering a boost to education and health by increasing budget allocation in these spaces, and placing Atishi in the education sector to help Manish Sisodia. The first financial budget was perceived as being pro-poor and progressive. Tax collection was simplified, and this resulted in an increase in the taxes collected.

Satyendra Jain, who held some of the most important portfolios, including health, industries, home, public works, power and urban development, was in a tearing hurry to show results. He wished to push for serious reforms for healthcare and industries, and accelerate urban development. Back then, since I was still a part of AAP, he asked me for support. I introduced him to the ex-chairman of HUDCO, who offered to work for the government gratis, and to Hafeez Contractor, a renowned architect from Mumbai. Satyendra Jain discussed building thousands of vertical small industrial estates to attract industry from neighbouring states. He also wished to construct affordable houses for the poor.

The aspirations of the Delhi government seemed just about right.

This is when Arvind made *the* classic mistake.

He started believing, or was made to believe, that the nationwide support the party was enjoying was not because of the 'idea' of AAP—its policies, its freshness of approach and its principles—but because of Arvind Kejriwal, the individual. He assumed that he was the Pied Piper who enchanted people, when, in fact, it was the music of a new political culture that had the public enthralled. He also assumed that if the nation needed to be salvaged from the Congress and the BJP, he alone could come to the rescue. Having 'saved' Delhi, his task was to become the messiah of India. These were clear strains of megalomania—a quality displayed by all the world's dictators and one-man parties across time.

There is a popular story of a wise man entering a village on his donkey. The villagers were ready with garlands and music to welcome him. On witnessing the reception committee, the donkey thought that the public had gathered to welcome him; it started braying and bounding with pleasure, thus unseating the wise man. Even as the wise man fell, the crowds chased the donkey away.

Was this story going to repeat itself in a fresh avatar when AAP approached voters in Punjab, Goa and the Municipal Corporation of Delhi (MCD)?

While Arvind grew increasingly self-absorbed, AAP became smug. With Delhi in its pocket, it decided to 'go for India'. I am convinced that if the party had won a small majority in the Delhi elections, it would have governed Delhi sensibly for a few years and only then considered expanding its presence across other states. But a 67-seat victory deluded the party into believing that Arvind could aim for the post of a prime minister in 2019.

It was against this backdrop that the core team met and took some decisions that would have a far-reaching impact on the party and the future of the country.

- Manish Sisodia would handle the Delhi government, while Arvind would focus on the rest of the country. To challenge the BJP and Narendra Modi, AAP would start the process of creating a nation-wide coalition—a 'mahagathbandhan'. Concurrently, it would try to win a few more states—Punjab, Goa and Gujarat to begin with. Once AAP was the ruling party in more than two states, it could become the leading partner in this 'mahagathbandhan' and challenge Prime Minister Modi in the 2019 general elections. Feelers were sent to Nitish Kumar, Mamata Banerjee, among others, to prepare for a future coalition.

- Narendra Modi had won 282 seats in the 2014 Lok Sabha, with around 31 per cent of the national votes. This meant that 69 per cent of the voters voted for parties that were against the BJP. AAP decided to position itself as the best alternative option. Already, the Congress, the main opposition party in the Centre, had been discredited as being corrupt—it had secured just 19.3 per cent of the votes and 44 seats in the 2014 Lok Sabha elections,[33] and zero seats in the assembly polls in Delhi. Since, in Delhi, AAP had benefited from voters who had defected from the Congress, it expected the trend to repeat itself across other states.
- A corollary: The concept of hyphenation and de-hyphenation is relevant to political power games. Till now, at the national level, India had a two-party hyphenation model, with the BJP and the Congress. AAP wanted to de-hyphenate the Congress and replace it, so as to make this an AAP-BJP contest.
- There wasn't enough time for AAP to build a strong grass-roots network across the country by 2019. Therefore, AAP decided to convert the Lok Sabha elections into a US presidential style contest by pitting Arvind Kejriwal against Narendra Modi.

Rahul Gandhi was perceived as being relatively weak, so the belief was that if Arvind was projected well, anti-BJP votes would rally around him. That Arvind had secured more votes than the Congress in Varanasi when he had dared to contest against Modi offered the party some hope.

- If Arvind had to win this contest against Modi, an early step had to be showcasing the work of the Delhi government while projecting Arvind as the central force behind it. Advertisements (paid for by the Delhi exchequer) that had emotional appeal—with Arvind as the face, rather than AAP or its principles—had to be chosen.
- But this wasn't enough. If Arvind had to fight Modi, his image had to match that of India's prime minister. Fearlessly confronting Modi would make Arvind look like a serious competitor and create a place for him in the hearts of anti-Modi voters. Arvind and his team, therefore, had to blame Modi for everything conceivable. (In the days to come, Arvind went overboard, calling the head of our nation a coward and a psychopath,[34] and releasing a public message through video that Modi was planning to kill him.[35] Arvind's aim was to project himself as being so powerful that even the prime minister wanted to target him.)
- The epicenter of AAP has always been Delhi. Since Delhi was an urban city-state, it could be won without invoking communal and caste issues. But the same strategy could not be adopted for states like Punjab. After all, large swathes of India were used to voting on the basis of the 4Cs. Therefore,

to achieve its target, AAP had to bend its values. It had already started compromising by selecting candidates of questionable repute for the 2015 elections. This would have to be taken to the next level. Given that a significant chunk of anti-BJP votes came from minorities and backward classes, minority appeasement and caste politics would be a prerequisite for electoral success. This was especially necessary since a strong party base right up to the polling booth level was missing; the 'winning potential' of candidates based on their caste and religion was AAP's best hope for victory.

*

These decisions changed the way AAP and Arvind Kejriwal functioned.

AAP quickly became a one-man party, with Arvind taking all key decisions and his small coterie of loyalists implementing them. Ashutosh told me: 'There should be a single voice in the party, and anyone contradicting it should be dealt with summarily. No one should have the guts to oppose Arvind.'

Arvind's greatest strength soon became his fatal flaw. He has always been ruthless in the pursuit of his goals—going so far as to put his life at stake on the two occasions when he fasted. While this quality can win wars, it also translates into a kind of cold-bloodedness. People, their emotions and feelings, ceased being of concern to Arvind once he began chasing a target. When the aim was the betterment of the nation, one could admire this streak—but when it became self-aggrandizement, it spelt doom.

As personality cults took root, one witnessed the

rapid disintegration of state squads. Given that the core leadership team did not have faith in those who weren't a part of the Delhi coterie, loyal MLAs from Delhi were given the task of securing AAP's interests pan-India. These MLAs from the capital, appointed as state observers, would reach the designated state's capital with their entourage. They would stay at luxury hotels, call loyalists from the state to their rooms and create informal committees with local yes men, who, in turn, would ensure that the volunteers they selected were non-threatening and docile. These committees would be remote-controlled from Delhi. Obviously, this impacted the calibre of state teams. Gone were the days when talented individuals with opinions were frontrunners. Rather, there now emerged a band of mediocre people working under one angry, impatient man who wanted to control the smallest of actions. What was equally disturbing was the impact this had on the capital, as Delhi MLAs, who were supposed to take care of their constituency, began focusing on other states!

The lack of local talent impacted even those decisions that would otherwise have earned AAP dividends. For instance, one of the interesting resolutions AAP made was to select the states it would contest from such that there would be a direct fight between the BJP and its allies on the one hand and the Congress and its allies on the other. The aim was to supplant a weak Congress and become the main contender. Punjab, Goa, Gujarat, Madhya Pradesh and Rajasthan were the first line of states being eyed. This smart strategy fell through because of the poor quality of local leadership.

What also hurt the party was the unwarranted noise that it was generating. Crores were spent for promotions across the nation. The ads released extolled the virtues of Arvind Kejriwal to the virtual exclusion of all else. One series of advertisements actually had a woman saying, '*Bhagwan, Arvind ko lambi umar de*'—'Please grant Arvind a long life, God'. The PR machinery, far from helping AAP, made it seem like a caricature.

It didn't help that AAP was attempting something that was impractical. It was trying to contest elections across the length and the breadth of our vast country without understanding local dynamics, challenges and structures. If AAP was successful in Delhi, it was because (among other reasons) it was dealing with a small, urban centre, and the core team was intimately aware of the ground conditions. Now, with the new policy of paradropping leaders from the central office to manage various state teams, there was no possibility of being attuned to the inner workings of a state outside the capital.

22. Sliding Down the Slippery Slope

While AAP doggedly focused on winning the 2019 general elections, core values became an immediate casualty.

This came to the fore when allegations surfaced that the law minister, Jitender Singh Tomar, had a fake law degree. Here was an opportunity for Arvind to show true statesmanship by sacking Tomar; instead, AAP spokespeople were sent to prime-time news channels to defend the indefensible. Where, once, the party had harboured the dream of having a standard operating procedure for serious allegations, even creating an internal Lokpal for impartial investigations, it now witnessed AAP leaders playing judge and jury. Arvind announced: 'I am not Tomar's relative or friend. I had sought an explanation from Tomar on the controversy. He gave a satisfactory answer and said he wasn't at fault as his degree is genuine.'[36]

It was only when Tomar's lie was caught that Arvind stopped defending him. He announced that Tomar had kept him in the dark about the validity of his degree. The statement meant one of two things—that an activist who had repeatedly taken on the most corrupt leaders of the country, could not spot the bad apple within his own party; or that Arvind selected his cabinet without doing his due diligence.

Things kept going downhill. Alleged scams repeatedly came to light—those involving the purchase of onions, medicines, sugar[37]—the list was endless. There were scams reported in the Public Works Department and in Mohalla clinics.[38] A cabinet minister was embroiled in a sex scandal, and a cloud of suspicion hung over a few others.

The Shunglu commission pointed out various anomalies including nepotism.[39] But by now, the party had become brazen—justifying everything and blaming others. Much had changed in a short period, and it wasn't a pretty sight.

The CAG passed strictures against the AAP government regarding ad spend, inadequate dengue preparedness and other lacunae. During the IAC days, we used to confront those against whom there were CAG strictures or allegations.[40] But now, we chose to keep quiet or blame others.

It was alleged that many volunteers were appointed across posts without due processes being followed—this included twenty-two counsels, forty advisers, 940 estate managers in schools, and eighty-five representatives in the Delhi Commission for Women and 200 in the Delhi Jal Board. Many leaders were made chairmen of various boards. Twenty-one MLAs were appointed as parliamentary secretaries; laws came to be disregarded.[41]

There were allegations of financial impropriety.[42] While the party had been scrupulous about the use of public money when it had been conceived, increasingly there were accusations of AAP ministers using these reserves for travelling first class for foreign tours and spending public money lavishly.[43] The line between public and private interest grew blurred. The decision to pay lawyer Ram Jethmalani roughly four crore from public funds for

Arvind's personal case was an example in point.[44]

One of our volunteers from Mumbai, Sonia Punjabi, offered a chunk of her savings to Arvind, saying, 'Arvindji, this is our family's hard-earned money. We had saved this with great difficulty. I hand it to you with our blessings.' She wasn't the only one to donate generously; I know of others who had smaller weddings or cancelled parties, and dispatched their savings to a party that promised to be transparent. Yet by the end of 2016, AAP had removed its donor list from the website, offering two reasons—one, that other parties did not display their list, and second, that the Income Tax Department was harassing donors.[45] By now, AAP had started justifying everything. It had started sliding, and it was a slippery slope.

Sometimes I think the stupendous victory in the Delhi election was a classic case of 'Operation Successful, Patient Dead'—power had been gained but principles were gone.

*

When justifications could not be found, AAP assigned blame.

For all its faults, Indian democracy has its virtues. One of them is that governments in the Centre and state generally work in a collaborative manner, irrespective of the party in power. For example, Naveen Patnaik, Nitish Kumar, Chandrababu Naidu, Sheila Dixit, despite belonging to different parties, have worked well with the Centre.

Initially the Centre did try to cooperate with the AAP government. Venkaiah Naidu announced a Rs 3,250 crore urban development budget for Delhi. Piyush Goyal worked hard to fix Delhi power distribution issues, and, as far as I know, the ministry is also paying part of the power subsidy. Uma Bharti stepped forward to clean the Yamuna. Maneka Gandhi met Arvind to start support centres for women in the capital.[46] But given AAP's unwillingness to view others with anything but suspicion, and its usual habit of hurling unfounded allegations, rival politicians began to retreat.

Instead of mending fences, AAP became confrontational—to the detriment of Delhi. For electoral benefits, the chief minister of the capital played to the gallery. The authority of the lieutenant governor came to be routinely questioned—with Arvind announcing that the 'lieutenant governor will go crawling if Amit Shah's peon calls'[47]—which only widened the breach between the lieutenant governor and the state government. As expected, the powerful Centre and lieutenant governor, with all their resources, hit back at AAP very hard.

But the biggest betrayal of the party was when it reneged on its commitment to pass the Lokpal immediately after coming to power. The Delhi Lokpal was purposely designed for failure. Some of its provisions—such as taking action against central government employees—were proposed knowing full well that the no government would ever pass this Bill. If the intention of the Delhi government had been honest—in other words, if Arvind had wished to pass the Bill, instead of simply blaming the Centre for rejecting a Bill that no government would concede to—it could easily have adopted the state version of the Jan Lokpal Bill—the Uttarakhand Lokyukta Bill (passed during the height of the IAC movement). But no such attempt was made, and when Prashant Bhushan challenged Arvind to a debate on the matter of the Jan Lokpal Bill, Arvind dodged.

*

No one could question the marketing will of AAP—but beyond catchy ditties and popular slogans, was anything being delivered? Instead of focusing on getting work done, a great deal of time was spent discussing people—what they did and what their intentions happened to be.

Expectedly, a number of articles stating facts and figures on the misgovernance of AAP began to get published—with one detailing the many promises of Budget 2015-16 which were yet to be met in March 2016. I list out the salient points in this article titled 'Delhi, Beware of Kejriwal's Misleading Budget' by Aman Panwar in *DailyO*:[48]

1. The Kejriwal government had barely been able to spend Rs 11,900 crore out of the Rs 19,000 crore budgetary allocation earmarked for the planned projects in financial year (FY) 2015-16. This was a significant decline in the deployment of planned expenditure—almost 65 per cent—when compared with the performance of the Delhi government in the previous years—80 per cent in FY15, 87 per cent in FY14 and 88 cent in FY13.
2. Out of planned budget of Rs 3,051 crore, about 40 per cent remained unspent.
3. Out of the Rs 30 crore the Kejriwal government received from the Centre for the advancement of the Right to Education (RTE) programme, only 2 crore was disbursed.
4. AAP in its manifesto had promised building 500 new schools, with a special focus on secondary and senior secondary schools, and opening twenty new colleges. None of this was pursued.
5. 40 per cent of public health budget remained unutilized. 60 per cent of the allocation for medical

institutions remained untouched.

6. 40 per cent of the total budget allocated for the transport sector remained unutilized, with zero buses purchased that financial year.
7. 94 per cent of the money allocated for the advancement of the tourism sector remained unspent.
8. 94 per cent of the total budget for civil supplies (such as ration and food grains) stayed untouched.
9. 80 per cent of the labour welfare budget remained unutilized.

A cursory look at the budget of 2016-17 presents a similar story. Instead of the recruitment of 20,000 teachers that had been promised, it was revealed that 5,500 teachers were being employed. Instead of 500 mohalla clinics, just one was started. The commitment to provide 100 emergency CAT ambulances and ten advanced life-support ambulances was not met at all. Ditto for the assurance that 1,380 low-floor buses, 500 mini-buses, and another 1,000 buses under the cluster scheme would be organized—these remained words on paper.[49]

It must be admitted though, that in the midst of such negative news, the focus of the government on soft infrastructure like health and education has been heart-warming. Even though much more needs to be done in these sectors, this can become an example to be emulated by other governments.

*

In an environment of tall claims and zero performance, how were AAP's volunteers to survive?

The foot soldiers we had nurtured were those who had committed themselves to the party on ethical grounds.

They had no desire for power and position but were fierce upholders of justice. Most importantly, they were driven by love for the land, for a higher calling. Once, during an AAP rally, I had spotted a young man riding a bike with a flag in his hand; he was shouting patriotic slogans. Something prompted me to stop him and ask after his life. He told me he had just quit his job a few days earlier—this, despite having a young son, a wife, a mother and a sister to care for—because he was convinced that the country needed him. For me, he represented the volunteers we attracted.

In December 2013, during an interview, I had been asked: 'Power can be corrosive; how will you ensure your candidates stick to the straight and narrow?'

My reply was simple: 'That is one of the biggest fears that we have. I completely agree that it is very difficult. We have created a system by which the Lokpal [. . .] can control corrupt or criminal behaviour. But the best antidote, I think, is the kind of volunteers we have. We don't have the BJP/Congress [variety of] volunteer[s] who will toe the line. Arvind used to say, "*Hamara sarkar banega aur pandhra din mein Lokpal nahi aaya na, toh aur koi marega ke nahi, hamare volunteer humko pakadke maarenge*" ("Once we come to power, if we don't pass the Lokpal Bill in fifteen days, our volunteers will take us to task"). Do you think any of our MLAs in Delhi have the guts to become arrogant? Our volunteers will immediately bring them down a few notches.'[50]

But as I write this, towards the end of 2017, my belief that our volunteers were warriors who would stand up to the core leadership team and challenge all wrongs, seems preposterous.

The harsh manner in which courageous AAP members

who dared to speak for the truth were treated, pushed others towards mute submission. Even as AAP leaders elevated themselves to the position of demi-gods, volunteers found themselves getting manipulated, exploited and used.

I remember, once, during a contentious NC meeting on 23 November 2015, Kumar Vishwas delivered a long speech, where he spoke eloquently to all members, detailing the sacrifices made by Manish Sisodia, Sanjay Singh, Durgesh Pathak, etc. I felt like standing up and telling him that while he could appreciate the work of those on the stage, it was incumbent on him to also acknowledge the immense sacrifice of the supporters, who, while not being leaders, had given equally of themselves, if not more. Already, there appeared to be an incestuous clique of leaders; the volunteers were forgotten. This was our tragedy.

In spite of my disillusionment with the volunteers' inability to fight back, I felt their pain. When I'd meet former colleagues, I could tell that they were torn between their dreams and reality. Perhaps, as a defence mechanism, they justified AAP's slide, saying that a compromised AAP was still a lesser of all possible evils in the political arena. Their arguments lacked conviction.

I used to believe that supporters were our party's last bastion. Alas, it all now seems like a mirage.

23. Waterloo

AAP HAD PLACED ALL ITS FAITH IN PUNJAB. AFTER ALL, this was the state that had secured the maximum support for AAP during the 2014 Lok Sabha elections, with four MPs—Dr Dharamveer Gandhi, Prof Sandhu Singh, Harinder Singh Khalsa and the comedian Bhagwant Singh Mann—getting elected to power.[51]

AAP was convinced that, as a precursor to a nationwide blitzkrieg, it would sweep this state. Support for it appeared to be growing rapidly; public meetings seemed packed with enthusiasts. There was a groundswell across the state in favour of the party, and some independent opinion polls gave AAP over 100 out of 117 seats in February 2017. An AAP leader, thrilled by the verdict, went to the extent of promising to quit politics if AAP won less than 80 seats.

Smugness, overconfidence and arrogance don't bode well for any party. AAP was poised to make mistakes in Punjab.

And mistakes were made. For one, as had now become the norm, all decisions for the Punjab elections came to be taken from Delhi.

The Delhi team had little knowledge of the sentiments of Punjab, and this led to a series of gaffes—for instance, AAP posters emerged with the party symbol, the broom, placed alongside the Golden Temple; and, at another point, AAP leader Ashish Khetan compared the AAP manifesto with the sacred Guru Granth Sahib. None of this went down well in Punjab.[52]

Second, AAP strategized that it would focus on a candidate's 'winning potential'. Several veteran IAC volunteers were sidelined in favour of those who had money—never mind if they had defected from a rival party—or those who were caste leaders. Harinder Singh Khalsa grew concerned: 'The Delhi leadership team [. . .] are promoting moneybags who are deserting their traditional parties and joining AAP with ulterior motives.' Dharamveer Gandhi, in turn, warned that the party leadership's current policy of giving preference to 'turncoats from traditional parties'[53] would only pave the way for the return of the Akali Dal in Punjab. By end August 2015, instead of introspecting, as was now its new standard operating protocol, AAP suspended both Harinder Singh Khalsa and Dharamveer Gandhi for alleged 'anti-party activities'. Arvind announced that if AAP won, the deputy chief minister of Punjab would be a leader from the Dalit community.[54] If AAP truly wanted to empower, it could have declared a Dalit as the chief ministerial candidate, or it could have announced a Dalit as the chief minister/deputy chief minister of Delhi. This entire episode reeked of casteism, with caste arithmetics having taken precedence over principles.

This brings us to the third mistake AAP made. Arvind had his heart set on becoming the chief minister of Punjab—he wished to show his administrative might in a full-fledged state. So, AAP refrained from announcing a chief ministerial candidate.

Fourth, the central team deputed Sanjay Singh and Durgesh Pathak to lead the party in Punjab, but there were multiple claims that they were misusing their powers. Early on, Harinder Singh Khalsa had shot off an email to Arvind stating that Sanjay Singh had inducted 'dubious' leaders into the party. 'I think they are out to destroy the spirit of the party. What about the respect for the party's constitution? Is Sanjay Singh bigger than the state executive? And what is the party; is it only Sanjay Singh?'[55]

Fifth, the growing perception was that AAP did not have a definite ideological position vis-à-vis Punjab. When the contentious issue of the Sutlej-Yamuna Link canal was brought up, Arvind remained non-committal.[56] Similarly, while raising funds, AAP did not weigh the implications of getting donations from Khalistani supporters in Canada and the USA.[57] In a state that had strong memories of the bloodbath of the 1980s, AAP's apparent flirtation with Sikh radicals led to the alienation of urban Hindus.

Sixth, there emerged all kinds of allegations—of corruption, of the sale of tickets,[58] and of seeking sexual favours from ticket claimants.[59] AAP Punjab chief, Sucha Singh Chhotepur, was removed under dubious circumstances, which made the fissures within the team obvious. AAP Punjab no longer seemed like a stable alternative.

Last, word got out that the Delhi government was offering sops to appease Punjabi sentiments in Delhi and to influence Punjab's voters—in full-page advertisements published in several newspapers, Arvind had declared that Punjabi would be taught in all government schools in Delhi; that each school would compulsorily have to hire at least one Punjabi teacher; and that the salaries of

Punjabi language teachers would increase.[60] The common man isn't naïve; the growing impression was that there was now no real difference between AAP and the other mainstream parties. 'We' had become 'them'. Or as George Orwell put it in *Animal Farm*: 'The creatures outside looked from pig to man, and from man to pig, and from pig to man again; but already it was impossible to say which was which.'

*

AAP still wanted to consolidate its position in Punjab. An opportunity seemed to present itself when, in response to an attack on our soldiers by Pakistan in Uri, the central government executed a successful surgical strike. Here was an issue that evoked strong national sentiments, and if played right, it could improve prospects.

Arvind Kejriwal at once sent a congratulatory tweet to the Indian army without crediting the role of the Indian government, knowing very well that no military action could be done without the government's directions. It was churlish at best, and diabolic at worst

Then, when Pakistan began questioning the authenticity of the surgical strike, AAP felt it had a masterstroke. The strategy was: 'Let us sow doubts in the minds of all people, so that anti-Modi votes come to us, and Punjab can be won.' Therefore, in a video that tried too hard to be clever, Kejriwal glorified Modi and the army, but then, asked the government to unmask Pakistan's lies and provide proof of a strike.[61] The assumption was that secrecy laws would prevent the government from furnishing evidence and, therefore, it would lose credibility.

But the strategy backfired. For one, it was perceived

that AAP was questioning the army's credibility. Then, Pakistan itself used Arvind's video as proof that the chief minister of India's capital had serious doubts about the Indian government's announcements. Finally, the media in India worked behind the scenes, and News18 got an expose from Pakistan's side establishing that there was indeed a surgical strike.[62] In other words, the strike was proven without the government or the army having to disclose classified information.

After this episode, people began wondering if AAP had stooped so low as to trade national interest for votes. Within Punjab, where multiple families have a firm connection with the army, common people were fuming. AAP supporters were aghast. Personally, I was shocked that those with whom we waved the Indian flag passionately were choosing political one-upmanship over national interest.

*

Five years of misgovernance and corruption had made the Akali-BJP combine one of the least popular coalitions since independence. A growing drug menace, rising unemployment and farmer suicides had created an impassable breach between the Akali-BJP and the general populace.

The Congress, too, was in trouble. The Sikhs had not forgiven the party for the 1984 riots. While the stage, therefore, seemed set for AAP to win Punjab—despite all the internal party chaos and poor strategizing—the Congress had other ideas. Under the direction of a brilliant strategist, Prashant Kishor, the Congress declared Captain Amarinder Singh as its chief ministerial candidate. The veteran politician energized his party and started attacking the weaknesses of AAP. Labelling this as a fight between Punjabi pride and outsiders, he started making inroads within AAP's support base.

To counter AAP's Bhagwant Mann and Gurpreet Ghuggi, who drew huge crowds for their comic acts, Amarinder Singh got Navjot Singh Sidhu on its side. Neither Mann nor Ghuggi had Navjot-Amarinder's stature, and the Congress increasingly became a lethal force.

It also helped that Amarinder Singh was intimately aware of the state's needs and sentiments. Conscious that farmers formed the backbone of Punjab, he undertook kisan yatras. Sensitive to the drug menace impairing the lives of the state's youth, he started a flagship programme that promised employment to one member in the 18-35 age group in each family. Unlike Arvind, who sat on the fence when the Sutlej-Yamuna Link canal was brought up, Amarinder Singh was quick to assert that not a single drop of water would leave Punjab. 'Brand Captain' was a wave that seemed unstoppable.

*

Soon, it was time for Punjab to go to the polls.

AAP's hopes of victory were built around the 69 seats in the Malwa region[63]—it was assumed that the Akalis would be destroyed in their citadel. But not only did the Akalis manage to cling on to some of their strongholds, AAP's conviction that the anti-Akali votes would come only to them turned out to be completely false. For instance, Sangrur—from where AAP's Bhagwant Mann won the 2014 Lok Sabha elections with a majority of roughly two lakh votes—saw AAP losing badly and the Congress winning.[64]

AAP eventually secured all of 20 seats.[65] The Congress won emphatically. Amarinder Singh became Punjab's chief minister.

In the days to come, AAP's base in Punjab began fragmenting even further. Its volunteers had lost heart. The results of the Gurdaspur assembly by-elections, where AAP came third with just 6 per cent of the votes, after the Congress and the BJP,[66] seemed like the final nail in the coffin.

*

After Punjab, AAP selected Goa as the next state to contest assembly elections from. Even though there were very few volunteers there, the party believed that it had a strong chance of winning. After all, the BJP was confronting anti-incumbency, and the Congress seemed ill-prepared. With the media raging against corruption in the ruling government, AAP, as an anti-corruption party, felt it could make serious inroads. Besides, Goa was tiny—how hard could it be to win votes?

However, as in Punjab, old mistakes came to be repeated in Goa. Delhi remote-controlled the campaign in the state. Pankaj Gupta and Ashish Talwar were dispatched from Delhi to build the party and win the elections. There were very few homegrown volunteers, as we know. The few recruited had no real understanding of politics and were not trained. Volunteers from Maharashtra and Karnataka were sent to Goa to campaign; they were in no way connected with the electorate. AAP was soon branded as an 'outsiders' party', taking on a battle-hardened BJP, Congress and Maharashtrawadi Gomantak Party (MGP).

AAP typically relied on noise and bluster. It exaggerated

the significance and reach of small meetings on social media. It also banked on its most potent weapon—internal surveys. Opinion polls were published suggesting that AAP's vote share in Goa would be 41.9 per cent, the BJP's would be 21.5 per cent, the Congress' would be 14.4 per cent and the MGP would secure 12.2 per cent. It was advertised that AAP was poised to sweep the Goa polls.[67]

One had to question the veracity of such polls when, on 11 March 2017, AAP got 6.3 per cent of the popular votes across the state—less than a fifth of what the winning BJP got—and zero seats. It lost its deposit in 38 of the 39 seats it contested. The chief ministerial candidate, Elvis Gomes, not only came fourth in his race but also lost his deposit.[68]

The battle of the polls is as much about ground strength as about perception. The BJP had at least one volunteer on each of the (approximately) twenty pages of the polling booth booklet in the states it contested from. The Congress had around ten workers per polling booth. AAP wanted to win Goa without feet on the ground, relying purely on Arvind's name, questionable surveys, and social media/press presence.

*

After the Punjab and Goa debacle it was time for AAP to claim its karma-bhoomi, Delhi, in the forthcoming MCD elections. After all, just two-and-a-half years ago, AAP had won 96 per cent of the assembly seats in Delhi with 54 per cent of the votes. The BJP had performed terribly during the decade it had been in power in the MCD. AAP had a chance if it played on the shortcomings of the BJP's work in the MCD. It felt that it had the possibility of a victory.

But what AAP hadn't factored in was the mood on the street. People were furious about the allegations surfacing almost every day against AAP and about the transformation of the party from one representing the 'aam aadmi' to one serving the 'khas aadmi' ('the privileged').

When I took a cab from the Delhi airport, I asked the driver, 'How is the AAP government doing?'

What followed was pure rage: 'My entire family voted for AAP, expecting change. Nothing has changed. Corruption has only increased, the roads have deteriorated, and the leaders are busy playing politics.'

'What about schools and mohalla clinics?' I pressed.

'*Arre saab*,' the driver complained, '*kuch nahi hai. Sirf publicity hai*—it's nothing, it's all publicity. The mohalla clinic is closed for the most part. The one time it was open, I took my wife. She was simply given a note and sent to a hospital.'

Over the next few days, I spoke to auto-rickshaw drivers, shopkeepers, taxi drivers—once the chief supporters of AAP—asking the same questions. Each time, I received similar responses. While I knew that some of the complaints were unwarranted—the mohalla clinics and schools were doing good work—the mood was such that no one wanted to concede ground or forgive. All those I spoke to unequivocally said they wished to teach AAP a lesson.

How did this miss AAP? Possibly because it had turned into an echo chamber, where every member of a coterie praised every other member. There was no access to the truth. When the media's polls screamed that AAP would fare poorly,[69] the party's spokespeople kept repeating the figures of an internal survey that projected 218 seats to AAP out of 282, hoping perhaps that this would be a self-fulfilling prophecy.

Worse, AAP decided to run a campaign propped by one figurehead—Arvind Kejriwal. He was pitted against the BJP's leaders across posters and banners. Instead of focusing on misgovernance in the MCD, voters were asked to choose between Arvind and the BJP. While people were undoubtedly upset with the BJP-driven MCD, they were even more disappointed with AAP—a party they had once invested all their faith in.

It was election day. In several localities, old supporters, topis perched on their heads, were conspicuously absent. They had been replaced by professional, power-seeking politicians.

When the results were announced, the BJP emerged victorious, with 181 wards. The biggest gainer was the Congress, with its vote share increasing from 9 per cent in 2015 to over 20 per cent in the 2017 elections. As for AAP, it got around 26 per cent of the votes—less than half the votes that it had secured from the same set of voters just over two years ago.[70] What should have been a negative vote against the BJP-led MCD, became a negative vote against Arvind.

This was a terrible strategic mistake. A party that had taken pride in its connection with the aam aadmi somehow seemed to have lost its way.

24. After the Drubbing

For all his limitations, Arvind is one of the best individuals I have known. As a true well-wisher of the party, and a founder and ex-member of their highest decision-making body, I have genuine interest in its survival and success. I hoped that AAP's shock defeats would bring Arvind back to the path we had once walked. Besides, I strongly feel that India needs AAP—not in its the present avatar but as one representative of its founding principles.

If AAP had soul-searched, it would have realized that part of the problem with its mode of functioning was that Arvind had retained far too much power—he was Delhi's chief minister, the convenor of AAP, a hands-on decision-maker—and he was failing everywhere. The party was floundering, the Delhi electorate was disappointed with AAP, and a coterie was manipulating all power positions.

The other problem was that there was complete lack of accountability. Sanjay Singh, Durgesh Pathak, Ashish Talwar, Pankaj Gupta and Dilip Pandey should all have resigned for the poor performance in Punjab, Goa and in the MCD. But, like their boss, they held on to their posts.

The question of accountability is a tricky one. It has puzzled even the likes of the former chairman and CEO of Wells Fargo, John Stumpf. I carry a part of his inquisition before the senate banking committee hearing on 20 September 2016. Elizabeth Warren, senator of the US Congress, gave Stumpf the severest dressing-down for an unauthorized accounts scandal.[71]

> Warren: You have said repeatedly, 'I am accountable.' But what have you actually done to hold yourself accountable? Have you resigned as CEO or chairman of Wells Fargo?
>
> Stumpf: The board . . . I serve . . .
>
> Warren: Have you resigned?
>
> Stumpf: No, I have not.
>
> Warren: Alright. Have you returned one nickel of the millions of dollars that you were paid while this scam was going on?
>
> Stumpf: Well, first of all, this was by 1 per cent of our people.
>
> Warren: That's not my question. This is about responsibility. Have you returned one nickel of the millions of dollars that you were paid while this scam was going on?
>
> Stumpf: The board will take care of that.
>
> Warren: Have you returned one nickel of the money you earned while this scam was going on?
>
> Stumpf: And the board will do . . .
>
> Warren: I will take that as a no, then. Have you fired a single senior executive? And by that, I don't mean regional manager or branch manager. I'm asking about the people who actually led your community banking division or your compliance division.

Stumpf: We've made a change in our regional . . . to lead our regional banks . . .

Warren: I just said I'm not asking regional managers. I'm not asking about branch managers. I'm asking if you have fired senior management, the people who actually led community banking division, who oversaw this fraud or the compliance division that was in charge of making sure that the bank complied with the law.

Stumpf: Carrie Tolsted . . .

Warren: Did you fire any of those people?

Stumpf: No.

Warren: No. OK, so you haven't resigned, you haven't returned a single nickel of your personal earnings, you haven't fired a single senior executive. Instead evidently your definition of 'accountable' is to push the blame to your low-level employees who don't have the money for a fancy PR firm to defend themselves. It's gutless leadership.

Replace Stumpf with Arvind—and one can see an identical trajectory in the ensuing conversation.

After the three-state debacle, instead of taking responsibility, reflecting and redrawing strategies the only visible change in AAP proved to be a knee-jerk response—the party stopped invoking the name of Modi constantly. Was this the only lesson that the party had learnt from the defeat?

Another ill-thought-out tactic used by AAP was challenging the highly credible and autonomous Election Commission (EC). It was accused of keeping faulty electronic voting machines (EVMs) to favour the ruling party. Arvind further called the EC 'completely shameless' and 'spineless', and charged that the EC was Dhritarashtra, willing to do anything to help the BJP, which was Duryodhana, win.[72]

Even our faulty democratic setup, has some redeeming features. One of them is the elegant exchange of power between parties and governments. The one who is vanquished in an election is graceful, congratulates the winner and promises to serve well in the opposition. But the sullen AAP went on the offensive.

Every argument it made against the EC was a blow to the very foundation of our democracy—free and fair polls. While Kumar Vishwas distanced himself from his party's stance, most others contributed to the general clamour.

The EVM hacking theory was flawed for several reasons. Let's list them out:

1. AAP had won nearly 96 per cent of the seats in the 2015 elections with precisely the same EVMs. If the machines were hacked, were re-elections to the Delhi assembly the order of the day?
2. I was a candidate in the 2014 Lok Sabha elections, and few days before the poll, scores of our volunteers were called for 'EVM checking'. They were allowed to randomly select one of over a hundred machines, press a button and confirm that their votes were being registered correctly. Some volunteers pressed an assortment of buttons across various machines, and each time the result was correctly registered. Of all the machines we tested, only one proved to be faulty—when volunteers repeatedly pressed the button against my name, the vote was transferred to a nondescript independent candidate. As soon as we pointed this out, the officer promptly replaced

the machine. That's when I came to understand the kind of care that was taken to ensure that elections were fair. Even if there happen to be a few faulty machines, this does not amount to a case of massive rigging.

3. During the 2014 Lok Sabha elections, 9,00,000 EVMs were being protected day and night by the Central Reserve Police Force (CRPF), election officers and political workers across all parties. To suggest that EVMs, despite being under such scrutiny, were having their motherboards tampered with, was unrealistic.
4. As a corollary, there were thirty-four lakh permanent and temporary employees as part of the election exercise. It is impossible to conceive of any party being able to arm-twist all of them into ignoring faulty machines.
5. In several constituencies across Punjab and Goa, where AAP made allegations of the ruling party hacking EVMs, the maximum seats went to the Congress. Did the BJP manipulate the results so the Congress could win?
6. AAP (whose support base is strongest in Delhi and among the youth) was decimated in the 2015 Delhi University polls where no EVMs were used. Chhatra Yuva Sangharsh Samiti (CYSS), the student arm of AAP, got just 18 per cent of the votes,[73] and in 2016, it did not fight the elections. The party was losing its voters in Delhi rapidly.
7. Almost every opinion and exit poll run by the media (and EVMs have nothing to do with such polls) showed AAP faring poorly.

8. All 1,642 polling stations in the 40 assembly seats of Goa as well as those in 33 assembly seats in Punjab had VVPAT (voter verified paper audit trail)—an independent verification method in a ballot-less voting system which allows voters to check that their vote has been cast correctly. Connected to the EVM, the printer-like apparatus generates a receipt indicating the symbol and name of the candidate a voter votes for. After being visible to the voter from a glass case in the VVPAT for some seconds, the ballot slip is cut and dropped into a drop box in the VVPAT machine and a beep is heard. VVPAT machines can be accessed by polling officers only. The VVPAT rolls are taken out for counting only if a candidate, his election agent or counting agent (in the candidate's absence) applies in writing to the returning officer (RO) to count the printed paper slips in any or all the polling stations.[74] As per counting data of the 33 VVSAT constituencies of Punjab, the Congress got the largest number of votes in 20 seats, followed by SAD (Shiromani Akali Dal) and AAP which emerged victorious in 6 constituencies each. A lone seat went to the Lok Insaaf Party. This showed little variation with results in other constituencies having EVMs without paper trail. As we know, while the Congress emerged as the single largest party with 77 seats, AAP got 20 seats and SAD secured 15 seats.[75]
9. Neither AAP's candidates nor AAP itself approached the courts with their complaints, which should have been the obvious course of action.
10. When the EC, to call AAP's bluff, scheduled an

> open hacking challenge for EVMs, AAP did not participate. Instead, it sought permission to change the internal circuitry of the machines, which was turned down by the EC on grounds that it was 'irrational and implausible'.[76]

As these facts came to be discussed, AAP's attempts at discrediting the very foundations of a democratic voting process did not succeed.

It seemed like things had hit their nadir—till Kapil Mishra happened!

*

Kumar Vishwas and Arvind had a long-running feud. And the rift became obvious when Kumar's name was found missing from the list of party campaigners for Punjab.[77] Insiders tell me that Arvind was waiting for victory in Punjab or Goa to eject Kumar from the party.

Contrary to Arvind's plans, AAP lost in Punjab and Goa. Kumar is arguably the second-most popular leader of AAP, and given the spate of losses, Arvind likely felt he needed all the popular leaders he could retain. A decision was taken to postpone the removal of Kumar.

Meanwhile, in the political circles of Delhi, it was said that the BJP was in touch with AAP MLA Kapil Mishra, and Kapil was trying to rope in Kumar, and Kumar, in turn, was trying to rally together other AAP MLAs. Gossip has a way of spreading, and it's entirely likely that Arvind got wind of these murmurs. He had to plot a counter-attack. And he did this through Amanatullah Khan.

Amanatullah Khan alleged that Kumar Vishwas was an RSS stooge. Left with little room for manoeuvre, Kumar cobbled together support and demanded the removal of Amanatullah from the PAC, and also demanded a position of leadership in Rajasthan. To retain Kumar, Arvind accepted his demands.[78] Yet, even as Amanatullah quit, Arvind made him the chairman of a panel of the Delhi Assembly and a member of seven newly constituted committees, including the Special Inquiry Committee.[79] 'Take that,' Arvind seemed to say.

Four months after Kumar took over Rajasthan, in an interesting development, the CYSS fared remarkably well in the state's university elections. Kumar gave a clarion call for AAP to 'go back to basics'[80]—subtly defying Arvind by suggesting that the party had lost its way. The Delhi coterie of AAP was left stunned by Kumar's conquest and acted churlishly by not even congratulating the victors—for, this would mean advancing Kumar's image. Further, cocking a snook at Kumar, they inducted Amanatullah Khan back into the PAC.

Apparently, Kumar was keen to wrench a Rajya Sabha seat from the party.[81] He publicly announced his candidature for a Rajya Sabha seat, and as expected AAP's social media team branded him as 'power hungry'. When I talked to Kumar over the phone, I said, 'Kumar, your days in the party are numbered. And if you have to exit, why don't you raise the principled issue of the compromises made by our party, rather than focusing on yourself and your ambitions?'

Kumar, whose hero is—guess who?—Kumar himself, thought differently. He told me, 'Mayankbhai, as the date of the Rajya Sabha nomination draws close, the entire nation will stand up and demand that Kumar Vishwas be made a Rajya Sabha member . . . Kejriwal will be forced to do so.'

I shook my head. People really take themselves far too seriously.

As it happened, in spite of the machinations of the party, Kumar got an opportunity to speak at the thinly attended and lacklustre fifth anniversary public meeting of AAP, where he spoke his heart out: 'The party wants to finish me off, but like Abhimanyu [a warrior in the Mahabharata who died fighting], I will become famous by my demise.'

'Unlike what transpired with Prashant and Yogendra's exit, we will create conditions such that you will be forced to leave the party—but without becoming a martyr (*marega zaroor, lekin shahid nahi hone dunga*),' Arvind told Kumar in one of the meetings. Recounting this conversation, Kumar continued with another episode: 'In a stormy meeting, Alok Agarwal proposed that I should be removed from the PAC, and even though Pankaj Gupta tried to calm the situation, Arvind interjected, "I second the proposal to throw this gaddar [traitor] out of the party."' Sanjay Singh brought peace back to the meeting, but not before Arvind and Kumar promised to show each other their 'aukat' (place). This was the level that we had descended to.

As the time for Rajya Sabha nomination came closer, Kumar asked me to arrange a meeting with Yogendra and Prashant. I had no confidence in Kumar Vishwas, but I decided to at least hear him out. I called Yogendra to apprise him of Kumar's stand. Very wisely, he warned me, 'Mayankbhai, Kumarbhai cannot be trusted, and even if we just meet him to hear his views, he can go to the media and use our name to increase his prominence in the party and pressurize them. Let us just stay away.'

And that is exactly what happened. Kumar told the media that he was in talks with Prashant, Yogendra and me for a AAP version 2.0. It was a statement without any basis. My disenchantment with politics and politicians increased.

Meanwhile, Kapil Mishra was caught in the crossfire. While Kumar was a big fish and needed to be handled with care, Kapil, could be discarded. He may have been a close confidant of Arvind at one point; he may have even led a group of fuming party workers towards Shanti Bhushan in the infamous internal meeting that led to his ouster. Now, however, it was time for him to go. He was removed from a minister's post and was publicly humiliated.

Arvind perhaps underestimated Kapil—for, he is a man of immense energy. He started attacking the AAP convenor and a few ministers, making allegations of corruption and the misuse of power.[82] While some of his claims may be exaggerations, Kapil had opened a can of worms.

What followed was uncharacteristic. Arvind and his clique refused to address the allegations. A party that had always been quick to go on the offensive suddenly chose quiet. The karmic circle seemed to be complete.

25. What Just Happened?

How did a man—a man who was once my hero—suddenly become the most disliked Indian?[83] How did a protagonist steering national change become a people's antagonist?

Let's recall the Arvind I had first befriended. He was a man who cared for the poor and the underprivileged—so much so, he would stop key conversations with colleagues if a beleaguered auto-rickshaw driver happened to approach him. He was a man who quit a reasonably well-paying job to work in the Sundar Nagari slums. He was a man committed to changing the nation, without any desire for power or any inclination to engage with messy politicking.

Yet, by 2014, the same man had surrounded himself with unsavory people, built a coterie, and abandoned all that we had stood for.

What just happened?

Having closely observed Arvind, I think that some of his biggest failings have been his insecurity, impatience, anger, lack of faith in others and most importantly the arrogant belief that he knows best, and worse, that no one else does.

Since Arvind believed he had the answers, he came to view most people as expendable. In the first NC meeting after AAP's creation, Arvind had said: 'This party is not the property of 300 founding members but of the lakhs and crores of people in this country.' This refreshing stance shifted over time, got corrupted by power . . . till, one day, the party became the domain of a small clique. Unilateral decisions soon became AAP's hallmark. And gullible volunteers and the media were manipulated to show Arvind in the light that he wanted to project.

The first turning point, that changed Arvind's approach entirely, was AAP's 28-seat conquest in the 2013 elections; it was an episode that made him confident of his ability to win elections. The second turning point was when he listened to Shanti Bhushan and others and tried to campaign across 400 Lok Sabha seats; he may have fared miserably, but now, his ambitions had been stoked. The final turning point was 2015, when he won big after sidelining all senior leaders and taking almost all decisions with is coterie. Now, he was convinced that he did not need anyone and he alone knew what was best.

Arvind told me, 'I do not want intellectuals in the party, just people who say "*Bharat Mata ki Jai*".' Much like Anna who used to assume that the IAC movement circled around him—that *he* was IAC—Arvind started believing he was AAP, and everyone else was merely an extension of his image. If party members protested, they were to be removed—which is what happened to both Yogendra Yadav and Prashant Bhushan. If volunteers left, it was absolutely okay—'*Ek jayega to dus ayenge*,' Arvind used to tell me—'If one goes, ten will come forward as replacements.' From the outset, he was clear that people and principles served a purpose—and they could be discarded once the purpose was served. This stance only grew more ruthless with time. What emerged, consequently, was a coterie of yes men. Instead of debate, there was constant assent. Instead of a discussion of ideas, there was talk of the doings and misdoings of others.

The megalomaniac in Arvind gained ascendance. 'Modi and the Congress are evil,' he seemed to say, 'and unless they are removed or replaced by me, the country will collapse. I am the messiah who can deliver.'

And to deliver, he believed the ends justified the means. If principles had to be compromised, so be it. The larger goal mattered. 'One cannot have too much idealism, one needs to be practical,' Arvind would say.

But beyond pragmatism, what seemed to grow in Arvind was the desire for power. He had flirted with it already—and now, he couldn't conceive of a future without it. During a meeting where we opposed AAP's proposed dalliance with the Congress, Arvind shouted: 'If we do not do something, we will become an NGO!' That is when I saw the writing on the wall: he was willing to go to any length for clout. Like a businessman counting his money, Arvind began calculating votes all the time—with people reduced to the constituencies they could bring in.

At such times, I was reminded of the IAC days. When a decision was taken to withdraw the call for donations (we had collected enough to sustain the movement), and a few workers protested, Arvind said, 'We are not shopkeepers or businesses to collect money for the future. If our movement is good, people will give money whenever we ask. And if it isn't, what reason do we have to exist?'

*

As I saw Arvind surrounding himself with a clique, using the resolve I had once admired to capture power within the party, and moving away from a vision of alternative politics, I was left distraught. Someone had to speak up.

For me, personally, the 'up' in AAP does not signify electoral victories. Rather, it connotes a battle for the nation, for integrity. Lalu Prasad Yadav wins elections; so does Mayawati; the Congress ruled for over six decades. For me, electoral victories have never been the parameter for being 'up' or 'down'. A party that fights for the truth, no matter the cost, is 'up'.

The 'down' points to the loss of a moral compass.

The way I see it, a downward slide is in progress within AAP.

This is not an epitaph of this young fledgling party, which has shown a beacon of light to the nation. It is a transitory state of affairs, which can still be corrected. The future will determine whether the party will continue to slide as it tries to expand its footprint beyond Delhi and Punjab. It could either get into a 'mahagathbandhan' with tainted parties and become one of them, or it could do a course correction, return to its core concepts of nation-building, and tread alone on its path to redemption. Whether 'AAP and Down' becomes 'AAP and Down and Still Further Down' or 'AAP and Down and AAP' remains to be seen.

What also remains to be seen is whether Arvind learns to function as a leader should. Like Anna and Kiran Bedi, Arvind has been functioning at the gut level. Anger, jealousy and impatience have been a part of his operating style. However, for any major transformation to take place, I strongly believe that decisions should be driven by the intellect.

The nation has been looking for a statesman in Arvind.

Who is a statesman? Someone who is interested, not in himself, but his constituency; who displays the qualities of balance, calm and intelligence; who cultivates a team of qualified people with independent opinions; who has the courage to cultivate and assimilate different viewpoints; and who, most significantly, stands steadfast by core values.

Instead of a statesman, the nation has got a politician in Arvind—someone who flip-flops on issues; succumbs to rage and impatience; and chases one goal alone—getting elected. Arvind's motives are not evil. But a desperation for power has made him and his coterie adopt morally questionable modes and stances.

*

I'm often asked, 'What do you think will happen to AAP in the future?'

In my view, AAP will remain a potent force in Delhi—after winning 67 (of 70) seats and 54 per cent of the votes, it cannot but have a firm footing in the capital. While it has lost a chunk of the electorate due to the scandals, scams and fights that have come to light, its work in the space of education and health has been noteworthy, and this might still ensure that a sizeable number of voters vote for the party in the future. What might also hold AAP in good stead is that it has addressed the needs of the poor, be it by reducing the power tariff or by lowering water bills.

Beyond the capital, AAP had an opportunity in Punjab—but this was frittered away. Now, without a strong leader in the state, and without a discredited Akali-BJP combine to secure anti-incumbency votes, AAP's chances of becoming a potent force in Punjab seem dim. The Gurdaspur assembly bypoll of October 2017, where AAP fared miserably, is perhaps a sign of the times.

As for expanding its footprint across other states, a lot depends on whether AAP soul-searches and realigns itself with its core values. AAP's model of controlling and running the party from Delhi has been a proven failure, and is likely to come in the way of securing any major election beyond the borders of the capital.

AAP's task of becoming a national force is complicated by the fact that the BJP has been gaining ground rapidly after its 2014 victory. It has begun asserting itself in parts of India where it has had a marginal presence so far—be it the South, the East, or the Northeast—and is well on its way of becoming a pan-India party. Whereas, traditionally, the BJP's appeal had been restricted to upper/middle class Hindus (and the Congress has found supporters in the SC/ST and minorities segment), the BJP has now tried winning the trust of the backward classes and the poor. Indeed, the selection of a Dalit president is proof of the party's desire to be perceived as inclusive. That the party has a strong network, right down to the polling booth level, makes it a behemoth that will be hard to conquer.

That said, despite its obvious strengths and the rapid expansion of the party, the BJP's failure to meet its promises of 'acche din' has created a feeling of disenchantment among voters. Corruption continues unabated, and communal and caste politics rule the roost. Even as the BJP flounders, the Congress seems more and more like a party without a leader. The Left is left with a failed ideology.

There is an opportunity to fill the vacuum. Will this challenge be taken on by the Congress or AAP or someone else? That is the big question.

Right now, it seems as if AAP will remain no more than

a regional power—much like Mamata Banerjee controls West Bengal, or Jayalalithaa once led Tamil Nadu, or Amarinder Singh administers Punjab. Indeed, this might be AAP's best hope.

If AAP manages to become the ethical political party the country yearns for, the scenario might well change. In fact, after every show of the film on AAP, *An Insignificant Man*, the audience would break out into a spontaneous applause. Nothing could signify the underlying desire for change better.

*

Hypothetically, what would I do if I were Arvind Kejriwal and wanted to regain the support of the nation?

To begin with, while remaining the convenor of AAP, I'd resign as the chief minister of Delhi and hand over the reins to Manish Sisodia. I'd recognize the quantum of work that still needed to be done to consolidate the party's position across vast swathes of the country; I'd realize that I'd be able to focus on this only if I relieved myself of the responsibilities of a top post. I'd have a one-man one-post policy in the party.

I'd call for a meeting of supporters in Delhi and apologize to them, as also to volunteers and donors, for some of the ill-thought-out decisions of the party. I'd request all IAC volunteers and old AAP members to return to the party's fold. I'd personally meet Prashant Bhushan and Yogendra Yadav, let go of past anger, express regret, and ask them to join forces with me.

I'd appoint a team for each state. As the convenor, I'd travel to each of these states to meet volunteers and strengthen the party's organization; I'd also hold internal elections right down to polling booth level, and entrust key responsibilities to local leaders to empower them. I'd be firm that state elections cannot be fought without a robust organizational base. I'd start small—by fighting Zilla Parishad and Municipal elections. I'd recognize that age and time are on our side, and wisdom lay in building the party and the nation step-by-step after great deliberation, without compromising on principles.

I'd restructure the PAC. I'd remove some of those who had consistently failed the test of integrity and efficiency as well as issue a strong message against corruption by taking decisive penal action against offenders. I'd replace wrongdoers with new, capable, honest people. Merit, not loyalty, had to guarantee growth within the party.

As a corollary, I'd surround myself with those who displayed guts, courage of conviction, and the ability to put forward clear views. Those with opinions unlike my own would be treated as allies rather than adversaries.

I'd also appoint a two-tier Internal Lokpal—the first tier to examine the seriousness of the complaints against MLAs and senior members of the party, and the second tier (comprising a three-member Lokpal) to investigate and pass judgement.

I'd reinstate the donor list on the party website.

I'd work on our communication and, at all times, keep anger and impatience in check. I'd recognize that I was now a part of the system that I wished to reform from the inside—no longer could I act as the 'outsider' making unsubstantiated allegations. My task, while in power, was to display maturity and strong leadership. My task, while out of power, was to act as a diligent but responsible opposition, criticizing the ruling party only when the situation demanded negative feedback. Balance was key.

The aim was not to attract media attention by entering a negative news cycle; the aim was to do good work, so the press would be compelled to approach us. To this end, it was vital to regularly interact with the media, answering their queries and taking journalists with me on a journey to propel change.

Most of all, I'd create an agenda for alternative politics. I'd remind volunteers that power would come to us as long as we continued working hard and working ethically. I'd repeat JP's slogan: 'The solution to bad democracy is more democracy.'

I'd remind myself: there are no shortcuts to nation-building.

26. Ruminations

We have a tradition of ruminating in the midst of battle. The Bhagavad Gita was conceptualized at the height of the Kurukshetra war.

When I look back at my life as an AAP member, I perceive four key lessons:

1. *Leaders are not as they appear.* I had the good fortune of working with (and observing closely) some of the finest activists of India, including Anna Hazare, Arvind Kejriwal, Medha Patkar, Yogendra Yadav, Prashant Bhushan, and spiritual leaders like Baba Ramdev and Sri Sri Ravishankar. As I saw each of them in close proximity, I realized that there was a gap between the way they were presented and how they really were. This is not to say that they were being duplicitous; it's just that they were unlike the way they were being projected. Unlike Gandhiji, who was brutally honest with himself and others at all times, the limitations of these individuals became visible only when one went up close. At such times, personal ambition, anger, idiosyncrasies and prejudices coexisted with all the good they stood for.

2. *Many leaders veil their ambitions behind loaded terms like 'service to the nation'*. The country and the public are mere pegs to climb the ladder of personal ambition and aspiration.
3. *As leaders gain in popularity, they start believing the lies used for image building*. Flatterers and loyalists become trusted friends, and anyone speaking openly against them is perceived as a threat. Except for a rare Gandhiji, history is filled with instances of leaders who embrace a false persona and surround themselves with those who prop it up.
4. As a corollary, *there is a tendency to devote far more attention to those who complain than those who silently do their work*. To maintain the integrity of the group, these 'cribbers' are kept in good humour, while the hard workers get taken for granted. This sows the seeds of resentment within an organization.
5. *Fame, adulation, power and money are like opium*. They're a heady mix. They fool the best of leaders and make them believe they are invincible. The fact that the public hangs on to every word, every tweet, and every comment makes frontrunners feel invulnerable.

The public eye works like a microscope. It overstates individual qualities. Dormant traits suddenly get exaggerated. Perhaps this explains why Arvind changed so dramatically after becoming the chief minister of Delhi.

*

Periodically, I used to observe myself minutely, so as to keep negative tendencies in check. Once, on 'Newshour' on *Times Now*, I derided Renuka Chowdhury from the Congress. She had been trying to block all arguments against Robert Vadra, and, in response, I mocked her for 'rolling [her] eyes and making faces' instead of answering the nation. She was understandably angry, but many viewers were highly tickled. For the next two days, there was a flurry of emails, texts, Facebook posts and tweets that expressed amusement and applauded me for an 'apt retort'. I began gloating over my sharp riposte.

It was on the third day that I suddenly realized what a monster I was becoming! Instead of apologizing to Renuka on air, I had taken delight in offending her.

My ego was getting the better of me; I was bursting with self-importance.

During the height of the movement, I used to participate in TV panel discussions almost every night; in public places, people started recognizing me, praising my arguments or making suggestions. One day, at the Mumbai airport, I caught myself trying to make eye contact with people, hungry for recognition. I had to stop myself. What was I doing?

All my life, I had mocked those who took themselves far too seriously, who were pompous and sought the limelight. A white khadi shirt-clad politician with gold rings on his fingers and thick gold chains around the neck was my idea of the absurd. While I had not yet become *that* man, I recognized that my attitude needed a complete rethink.

There is a Marathi poem that goes: 'There was once a man who peed into the sea; he spent his life measuring how much the sea level had risen because of his pee.' Was

I travelling to the point of becoming that man?

I had erred in a similar manner as far back as 2007. While reconnecting with my spiritual self, through a process called 'sun gazing', I had energized my mind and body to such an extent that I had no desire to consume food. Instead of acknowledging the science guiding this, I gave all credit to 'my spiritual evolution'. My family started broadcasting my 'powers', and as people started visiting me with wonder, my conceit only grew. When, after a twenty-eight-day fast—which left me feeling, not depleted, but energized—I got a call from my mother-in-law, I found myself gloating, full of pride at my achievement. Suddenly I stopped myself. I approached my wife Minal and said, 'This is not my true path. Siddhi—miraculous power—has a way of distracting one from the goal of self-realization. I have strayed.' Instead of humbling my mind before a higher power, I had allowed myself to grow vain.

I had brought myself in check back then; it was time to fashion myself again. I had to stop being an attention-junkie. To bring balance back to my life, I had to embrace anonymity—till such time that I learnt equanimity. I informed the media management team of the party that I had no desire to appear on television shows henceforth. The party wasn't pleased—they believed I added value by being a spokesperson—but deep within I knew I'd turn into a liability for myself and the party if I remained self-obsessed.

For over a year, I did not appear on television debates. It was only when I grew confident that I'd be able to handle recognition without digressing from my path that I resumed media appearances—and that too, very rarely. I had moved on.

One day, Manish Sisodia and I had gone to address

a large public meeting in Pune. Manish, who could not stop smiling, asked me, 'Mayank, how does it feel to be *this* famous?' I felt nothing . . . except perhaps humility. I was grateful I had an opportunity to serve. That day, I was glad to realize that in the battle between my ego and my self, the latter had triumphed. I no longer sought acknowledgement, recognition or approval through others; I was secure.

The reason I narrate this is to highlight that public life is a minefield; there are temptations everywhere. Money, fame, flattery—there are far too many traps, and only someone who is aware of himself every minute can avoid these landmines.

These days, when I see AAP spokespeople on television panels, I realize that if I hadn't stopped myself when I did, I'd have become just like them. These were spokespeople who, during the IAC and initial AAP days, sounded honest and upfront; their candour was refreshing. Today, they're not unlike BJP or Congress spokespeople, trying to defend every act of injustice.

*

Sometimes, I am convinced there is a script that has been written for me. And that I am merely playing a role assigned to me.

Without my full awareness, my scriptwriter—who has a wry sense of humour—was fashioning another dramatic twist. As an urban dweller, who had never seen a village in his life except in the movie *Lagaan*, I was about to become a rural activist.

It all began in September 2015. I was off to Trimbakeshwar in Maharashtra to participate in the

Kumbh Mela. There were pilgrims from all across India, and I was fortunate to be among the first few to take a plunge in those holy waters at 3.30 am, along with my spiritual guru and some friends.

It was daybreak by the time we reached the hotel. From the balcony, I could see hundreds of villagers trudging along with their families towards the river. They seemed to have walked great distances, some carrying huge bags, others children. 'Who are these people?' I began to wonder. 'What do they think and feel?' I had no answers; I started questioning myself. 'Do I really understand my countrymen? As a politician, I was supposed to represent people . . . but without knowing anything about 65 per cent of this nation—the denizens of rural India—what right did I have to speak for a country?' I felt phony and pretentious.

Also, it was a matter of great regret that despite spending fifty-seven years in Maharashtra, I had not cared to pick up basic Marathi. This had to be corrected.

A few months passed. In April 2016, I read of a terrible drought in Marathwada, Maharashtra. While authorities were trying to supply water to Latur, the neighbouring district of Beed (sometimes referred to as the Bihar of Maharashtra for its spiralling crime rate) was getting neglected. I heard of several people dying. The news disturbed me.

I reached out to those I knew from AAP in Beed, and with the help of a local surgeon, Dr Wange—he remains an inspiration—we tied up with water tankers and started supplying water immediately. All arrangements had been taken care of at the ground level. It was now time to collect funds.

My guru used to emphasize the need to embrace bhiksha

(supplication, or quite literally, begging, to let go of the ego). While, as part of IAC and AAP, I always felt just a little uncomfortable asking for donations, now, as I focused on Beed, the ability to ask came naturally. In a little over a month, we had collected enough money to supply 1.57 crore litres of water to thirty-six villages of Beed. As I saw a parched village coming to life—and, equally, when I witnessed the helplessness of villagers during the brief spell when I was unable to arrange water—something within me stirred. I made up my mind.

With the help of local friends, we selected and attended to some of the worst affected villages in Parli within Beed district in Marathwada—roughly 530 kilometres from Mumbai. Ambitiously, we named our mission 'Global Parli'; we believed that even the villagers of a remote Parli could have global aspirations. I was back to nation-building . . . but this time, it was through rural transformation. Developmental politics instead of confrontational politics became my motto.

Gandhiji said, 'India lives in its villages.' We focused on a cluster of fifteen contiguous villages, with a population of around 35,000 people. We wished to create a sustainable model of growth, development, prosperity, self-reliance and happiness, that could then be replicated across the country. After around three years, the hope was to set up an institution where people from all over could come and learn.

In the last year-and-a-half since this mission began, some extraordinary work has been done in our adopted villages. One can probably write a complete book about our experiences—but for the purposes of this book, a summary must suffice.

One of the first lessons we learnt was that villages

suffer from a multiple organ failure. If we worked on the heart, the liver would give way, and if we worked on the liver, the lungs seemed to fail. We had to attend to all parts at the same time. Therefore, what was needed was a 360 degree development model.

We divided our work into five major verticals:

1. Water: One of the main reasons for the four droughts across seven years in the fifteen villages in Parli, Beed district, Marathawada was that the 32-kilometre-long River Paapnashi, emerging from the Bodhegaon Dam, was not replenishing the land. During the monsoons, Paapnashi would overflow and destroy hundreds of acres of the surrounding fields. The rain-water would then flow into the Godavari, leaving the area as dry as before. The hardened river bed would not allow water to percolate, and therefore the water table was very deep.

With funds from villagers and the government, Global Parli started deepening and widening 10.2 kilometres of the river bed with the help of machines and men. The process allowed the bed and the margins of the river to soak in water, leading to higher water table levels. Already five check dams have been built on the river and many more are being proposed.

The river banks, made with the material removed from the river bed, have been converted into bullock cart tracks, with bamboo and other trees planted along the sides. In total, around 14,000 new trees have been planted on the river banks and another 12,500 in the villages. We hope that in subsequent years, green cover will attract more rain.

This year, the water table has risen, wells are full, and the river filled with water that will last till mid-December.

Water supply for the rabi crop, and for drinking and usable water will be adequate. Life has become so much better!

Drip irrigation, rain water harvesting, compartmental bunding and other water management techniques are planned to make this area water-sufficient.

2. Economy: The second vertical revolves around increasing the per capita income by 250 per cent in three years. Training, training and more training has been our mantra. Agronomists, scientists and successful farmers have been giving lessons regarding how to increase yield, change crop patterns, adopt horticulture or inter-cropping, experiment with mushroom farming or initiate stronger marketing strategies to increase financial dividends. Field visits, lectures at agricultural institutions and better loan- and financial-structuring have been started. Besides farming, animal husbandry is being encouraged, along with sericulture, cottage industries like stitching bags, and small-scale industries.

3. Education, health and human development: There are nineteen schools, with a total of 4,357 students, for which we have taken up the following work:

- E-learning kits have been offered across each of the schools, along with an audio-visual syllabus in Marathi. This has improved the quality of education and increased attendance, with class stragglers getting more attentive and involved.
- Tablets are being given to bright students.
- Compounds have been cleared, and compound walls for schools have been built.
- Water filters have been supplied across some of the

schools; toilets have been built and solar pumps have been installed.

- Libraries have been set up in some schools, as also computer and chemistry laboratories.
- School bags, stationary and footwear are being distributed to children.
- Sports and gym equipment are being supplied to schools. Sports tournaments and bi-monthly local sports events are being organized. We have pushed for the creation of sports infrastructure, be it for football, wrestling or kabaddi.
- Private tuitions have been started at the village-level for top students so that they can excel.

The students of these villages are bright and intelligent; they just need opportunities.

To attend to their health needs we have started offering free medicines within medical camps and low-cost medical insurance. The 'bori bagicha' scheme (household gardens) has helped reduce household malnutrition. Skill development, capacity building, cleanliness drives in villages are being worked on; there is a move to ensure that there are toilets all across.

4. Social reforms: The fourth vertical, have curbed the sale of illegal hooch. Because of an andolan in every village by the womenfolk, there is not a single drop of liquor being sold in our fifteen adopted villages.

5. Gram swaraj: The villagers themselves plan the development of the village; they work to improve their community's life without our help. Our goal has been to make villages self-sufficient rather than simply prosperous.

Our role is that of a catalyst.

The government has huge funds and immense manpower to execute development plans in villages. Therefore, we work very closely with the administration—and we have, in turn, received proactive support from it—to deliver various benefits to villagers.

The collector of Beed (who has 1,405 villages under him) and the divisional commissioner (who has eight districts and over 9,000 villages under him) believe that our project is probably the best model in Marathwada (which sees the highest number of suicides in the country) for rural transformation and nation-building. They are supporting the mission along with their officers. My reputation as an anti-corruption activist is also helping.

United Phosphorus Limited (UPL) is our main supporter and takes care of monthly expenses. We do not seek donations. Already many corporates and individuals are working directly for the villagers.

Nowadays, I spend much of my time in the fifteen

villages in Parli. I speak fluent Marathi, and I understand what it means to live with villagers. From a confrontational public life to one of quiet development—my reality has shifted drastically. What I can say with confidence is that this is the best phase of my existence.

At a personal level, I continue to harbour the same feelings—like IAC and AAP, Global Parli is not my life's final destination. Destiny has bigger plans.

Epilogue

WHEN AAP WAS BORN, I HAD TOLD ARVIND, 'I SEE MY role as someone who pushes for transformation. By the end of 2014, I am convinced we'll have a team of strong, young leaders in Maharashtra. I will then leave politics.'

Arvind laughed sarcastically and said, 'Nobody has ever been able to escape the trap of politics. Let us see.'

Confident of my ability to be nirlep (unattached to the material world), I smiled back and said, 'Yes, let us see.'

Today, I have quit politics. I have no desire to return.

*

When I look back, I am content that I played my part during a historic period. I danced, sang, slept on the road, went to jail, delivered rousing speeches and fasted—everything was driven by my love for the nation.

Equally, what makes me content is that after independence—after nearly seven decades of politicians ruling supreme—IAC overturned the hegemonic order. They created a counter-hegemonic narrative, one that asserted that the people of this nation could not simply be treated as voters. They were citizens first, who had a right to involve themselves with the day-to-day aspects of governance. In other words, IAC reminded us that we, the people, were supreme in a democracy; politicians were just representatives of our will.

What IAC (and by extension, AAP) therefore shattered was a mindset that was submissive and fearful. Citizens came to recognize their own power and questioned the system when it faltered. The relationship between the government and the people is no longer one of servility. Rather, the association is one of checks and balances. Citizens stand up, and politicians see that they can't afford to remain brazenly corrupt.

Notwithstanding all that ensued after AAP's creation—the spate of betrayals, the viciousness, the arrogance—what can't be denied is that IAC and AAP together altered the national consciousness, probably forever.

Today, once more, there is need for a strong and powerful civil society movement. While I had been staunchly in favour of IAC going political in the heady days of 2012, these days, when I look back, I wonder if it was the wisest decision. If IAC had continued, we would have been able to exert pressure on the system from the outside. We might have been able to spur reform.

*

I had decided to resign from AAP on the day of the Delhi elections in early 2015. I even conveyed this desire via an email to the party (carried in this book). But, if I stayed on, it was because I was dissuaded by colleagues and friends. Instead of listening to my inner voice, I continued on my path as an AAP activist.

As a result, I got to witness first-hand the machinations of a party that had lost sight of its founding vision. The grime and ugliness was such that I was repelled from politics forever. Despite receiving offers from several key parties, including the BJP and the Congress, I had no inclination to return to the fray after quitting. Life was leading me in a different direction.

Our country is destined for greatness. In the years to come, various governments will come and go, bringing with them events that may seem imposing. However, there is little reason to feel despondent or elated. These are just small hiccups in the over 5,000-year-old history of our nation.

In the midst of such churning, it is our duty to make ourselves 'prachand' or formidable, pick up the gauntlet and fulfill India's destiny. The fight has just begun. Like the poet Piyush Mishra says:

Jis kavi ki kalpana me zindagi ho prem geet
Uss kavi ko aaj tum nakar do
Bheegti mason me aaj fulti ragon me aaj
Aag ki lapat ka tun baghar do

It's time to shun the poet who sings of love;
Instead, harness the fire in your veins, and
Blood pounding,
Leap into the blaze of war.

India can wait no more.

Jai Hind.

Notes

1. A Lokpal Bill was introduced by Shanti Bhushan in Parliament in 1968 but was never entirely passed. Neither the government nor the opposition had genuine interest in creating strong anti-corruption laws.
2. See <https://timesofindia.indiatimes.com/india/Manish-Tewari-regrets-hurting-Anna-still-faces-lawsuit/articleshow/9739234.cms>, accessed on 21 October 2017.
3. See <http://www.firstpost.com/politics/expose-did-swami-agnivesh-betray-team-anna-71576.html>, accessed on 20 October 2017.
4. See <http://www.dnaindia.com/india/report-iac-to-hold-protests-gherao-houses-of-ministers-from-july-25-1709676>, accessed on 20 October 2018.
5. See <https://timesofindia.indiatimes.com/india/Now-Arvind-Kejriwal-gets-breach-of-privilege-notice/articleshow/9850162.cms>, accessed on 21 October 2017.
6. See <http://kashmirwatch.com/kashmir-plebiscite-remarks-by-prashant-bhushan/>, accessed on 21 November 2016.
7. See <https://timesofindia.indiatimes.com/india/Ex-Anna-blogger-posts-Hazares-blog-on-reorganising-core-team/articleshow/10618350.cms>, accessed on 20 October 2017.
8. See <http://www.firstpost.com/india/sad-that-a-corrupt-person-may-become-president-kejriwal-362047.html>, accessed on 23 October 2017.
9. See <http://indiatoday.intoday.in/story/arvind-kejriwal-aap-sheila-dikshit-government-private-discoms-delhi/1/248416.html>, accessed on 21 November 2017.
10. See <https://timesofindia.indiatimes.com/india/Electrician-Kejriwal-begins-power-struggle-dares-the-law/articleshow/16704244.cms>, accessed on 21 November 2017.

11. See <http://www.business-standard.com/article/current-affairs/digvijay-calls-kejriwal-a-self-serving-and-ambitious-megalomaniac-112102000015_1.html>, accessed on 22 November 2017.
12. See <http://www.thehindu.com/news/cities/Delhi/arvind-kejriwal-quits-over-jan-lokpal/article5688528.ece>, accessed on 22 November 2017.
13. See <http://indiatoday.intoday.in/story/lokpal-certainly-not-a-jokepal-says-kiran-bedi/1/331456.html>, accessed on 21 November 2017.
14. See <https://timesofindia.indiatimes.com/interviews/Modi-and-party-our-next-target-Yogendra-Yadav/articleshow/30129401.cms>, accessed on 23 November 2017.
15. See <http://indiatoday.intoday.in/story/aap-activists-held-on-way-to-protest-ncp-attack/1/345032.html>, accessed on 23 November 2017.
16. See <http://www.rediff.com/news/interview/ls-election-mayank-gandhi-india-has-changed-after-aap-emerged/20140515.htm>, accessed on 23 November 2017.
17. See <http://www.mid-day.com/articles/elections-2014-salman-khurshid-medha-patkar-yogendra-yadav-among-prominent-faces-to-lose-deposit/15310171>, accessed on 23 November 2017.
18. See <http://indianexpress.com/article/india/politics/aap-delhi-unit-secretary-arrested-arvind-kejriwal-blames-bjp/>; <http://www.caravanmagazine.in/vantage/mlas-just-beginning-prashant-bhushan-aap-legal-troubles>; <https://economictimes.indiatimes.com/news/politics-and-nation/Posters-against-Congress-MLAs-sellout-to-BJP/articleshow/38534720.cms>, accessed on 23 November 2017.
19. See <https://timesofindia.indiatimes.com/india/AAP-vs-AAP-Full-text-of-Manish-Sisodia-and-Yogendra-Yadavs-letters/articleshow/36156171.cms>, accessed on 21 November 2017.
20. See <http://www.thehindu.com/news/cities/Delhi/shanti-bhushan-hits-out-at-arvind-kejriwal/article6314156.ece>, accessed on 23 November 2017.
21. See <http://www.financialexpress.com/archive/expressed-support-for-narendra-modi-as-an-independent-citizen-kiran-bedi/1217584/>, accessed on 25 November 2017.
22. See <http://www.thehindu.com/elections/delhi2015/landslide-for-aap-in-delhi-bjp-humbled-cong-scores-nil/article6879373.ece>, accessed on 25 November 2017.

23. See <https://timesofindia.indiatimes.com/delhi-elections-2015/top-stories/Read-full-text-of-Arvind-Kejriwals-first-speech-as-Delhi-CM/articleshow/46247444.cms>, accessed on 27 November 2017.
24. See <http://mayankgandhi05.blogspot.in/2015/03/note-to-volunteers-ne-on-4th-march.html>, accessed on 27 November 2017.
25. See <http://www.rediff.com/news/report/not-quitting-as-aap-lokpal-ramdas/20150328.htm>, accessed on 28 November 2017.
26. See <https://www.ndtv.com/delhi-news/kiran-bedi-will-make-a-good-chief-minister-says-aaps-shanti-bhushan-730812>, accessed on 28 November 2017.
27. See <http://indiatoday.intoday.in/story/aap-ramzan-choudhary-police-complaint-kejriwal-prashant-bhushan/1/426321.html>, accessed on 28 November 2017.
28. See <http://www.huffingtonpost.in/2015/03/27/yogendra-yadav_n_6959558.html>, accessed on 28 November 2017.
29. See <http://www.indiatvnews.com/politics/national/atishi-marlena-turns-against-bhushan-yadav-28050.html>, accessed on 28 November 2017.
30. See <http://www.loyno.edu/~folse/Kant.html>, accessed on 29 November 2017.
31. See <http://indianexpress.com/article/cities/delhi/mayank-gandhi-resigns-from-aap-national-executive-citing-losing-interest-in-politics/>, accessed on 29 November 2017.
32. See <https://timesofindia.indiatimes.com/delhi-elections-2015/top-stories/Read-full-text-of-Arvind-Kejriwals-first-speech-as-Delhi-CM/articleshow/46247444.cms>, accessed on 1 December 2015.
33. See <https://timesofindia.indiatimes.com/news/BJPs-31-lowest-vote-share-of-any-party-to-win-majority/articleshow/35315930.cms>, accessed on 1 December 2017.
34. See <https://timesofindia.indiatimes.com/city/delhi/Modi-a-coward-and-a-psychopath-Arvind-Kejriwal-following-CBI-raid/articleshow/50181493.cms>, accessed on 1 December 2017.
35. See <http://www.thehindu.com/news/cities/Delhi/Modi-may-get-me-killed-says-Kejriwal/article14513084.ece>, accessed on 1 December 2017.
36. See <https://www.ndtv.com/delhi-news/arvind-kejriwal-defends-minister-over-fake-degree-row-seeks-public-trial-of-media-houses-760215>, accessed on 1 December 2017.
37. See <http://indiatoday.intoday.in/story/revealed-aap-govt-bought-

onions-at-rs-18-kg-and-sold-to-delhiites-at-rs-30-kg/1/478019.html>; <https://scroll.in/latest/839336/aap-crisis-acb-launches-investigation-into-kapil-mishras-allegations-of-a-medicines-scam>; <https://economictimes.indiatimes.com/news/politics-and-nation/sugar-scam-acb-chief-mk-meena-initiates-probe-against-aap-government/articleshow/49359091.cms>, accessed on 1 December 2017.

38. See <https://www.ndtv.com/delhi-news/bjp-demands-probe-into-arvind-kejriwals-role-in-delhi-public-works-department-scam-1693194>; <http://www.financialexpress.com/india-news/arvind-kejriwals-aap-mohalla-clinics-are-a-big-scam-alleges-delhi-congress-chief-ajay-maken/833204/>, accessed on 1 December 2017.
39. See <http://indiatoday.intoday.in/story/shunglu-committee-report-indicts-arvind-kejriwal-led-delhi-government/1/921577.html>, accessed on 14 December 2017.
40. See <http://indianexpress.com/article/india/aap-assembly-national-capital-4560480/>, accessed on 14 December 2017.
41. See <http://www.thehindu.com/news/cities/Delhi/Delhi-HC-quashes-appointment-of-21-AAP-MLAs-as-Parliamentary-Secretaries/article14628671.ece>, accessed on 15 December 2017.
42. See <http://www.dailypioneer.com/city/i-t-notice-exposes-aaps-transparency-claim-ajay-maken.html>, accessed on 1 December 2017.
43. See <http://indianexpress.com/article/cities/delhi/shunglu-committee-exposed-misuse-of-the-public-money-by-aap-manoj-tiwari-bjp-delhi-4601756/>, accessed on 2 December 2017.
44. See <https://www.ndtv.com/delhi-news/arvind-kejriwal-wants-delhi-government-to-pay-his-3-8-crore-legal-bill-1676875>, accessed on 15 December 2017.
45. See <http://indianexpress.com/elections/punjab-assembly-elections-2017/arvind-kejriwal-defends-move-to-take-off-donors-list-from-aap-website-4461197/>, accessed on 1 December 2017.
46. See <http://www.financialexpress.com/economy/centre-to-give-aap-led-delhi-govt-rs-3250-crore-for-decongestion-development-work/169119/>; <http://www.financialexpress.com/archive/crisis-power-minister-piyush-goyal-warns-delhi-to-brace-for-more-blackouts/1259016/>; <http://www.deccanchronicle.com/150406/nation-current-affairs/article/clean-ganga-not-possible-without-clean-yamuna-uma-bharti>; <http://www.thehindu.com/todays-paper/tp-national/Maneka-ropes-in-DCW-

for-%E2%80%98One-Stop-Centre%E2%80%99-for-distressed-women/article15478267.ece>, accessed on 1 December 2017.

47. See <https://navbharattimes.indiatimes.com › Metro › Delhi › Politics>, accessed on 1 December 2017.
48. See < https://www.dailyo.in/politics/arvind-kejriwal-aap-delhi-government-budget-2016-advertisement-wi-fi/story/1/9756.html>, accessed on 2 December 2017.
49. See <https://www.thequint.com/news/business/delhi-budget-rhetoric-vs-reality>, accessed on 2 December 2017.
50. See <first-thoughts.org>.
51. See <http://radio.aamaadmiparty.org/aap-mps-take-oath-to-serve-the-people>, accessed on 2 December 2017.
52. See <http://indianexpress.com/article/india/india-news-india/aap-apologises-for-using-golden-temple-image-on-cover-of-youth-manifesto-2895660/>, accessed on 2 December 2017.
53. See <http://www.5dariyanews.com/news/150148-AAP-set-for-vertical-split-two-of-four-Lok-Sabha-MPs-to-resign-soon>, accessed on 2 December 2017.
54. See <http://www.hindustantimes.com/punjab/arvind-kejriwal-dalit-to-get-deputy-cm-post-if-aap-comes-to-power-in-punjab/story-PFMHZ5rb8EHtBtl9XXXl5H.html>, accessed on 2 December 2017.
55. See <http://indiatoday.intoday.in/story/aap-arvind-kejriwal-dharamvir-gandhi-harinder-singh-khalsa-prof-sadhu-singh/1/452238.html>, accessed on 2 December 2017.
56. See <http://www.hindustantimes.com/punjab/caught-in-a-bind-kejriwal-mum-on-satluj-yamuna-link-canal-issue/story-7mUEilNCGNiVa83WHGNTPL.html>, accessed on 2 December 2017.
57. See <http://www.hindustantimes.com/punjab/have-proof-of-khalistanis-funding-aap-capt-amarinder/story-mbNOiKQJ6qKpd1iRYV3h2L.html>, accessed on 2 December 2017.
58. See <http://www.dnaindia.com/delhi/report-infighting-aap-member-alleges-sale-of-party-tickets-for-punjab-polls-2278604>, accessed on 2 December 2017.
59. See <http://indiatoday.intoday.in/story/aap-leader-exploiting-women-punjab-ticket-sehrawat-kejriwal/1/756979.html>, accessed on 2 December 2017.
60. See <http://www.indiasamvad.co.in/politics/to-woo-punjab-voters-kejriwal-makes-punjabi-compulsory-in-delhi-govt-schools-14179>, accessed on 2 December 2017.

61. See <http://indiatoday.intoday.in/story/arvind-kejriwal-surgical-strike-proof-bjp-leaders/1/780788.html>, accessed on 2 December 2017.
62. See <http://www.news18.com/news/india/surgical-strikes-full-text-of-conversation-which-exposes-pakistans-lies-1298937.html>, accessed on 2 December 2017.
63. See <http://www.thehindu.com/elections/punjab-2017/In-battle-for-Punjab-Malwa-is-where-the-action-is/article17090125.ece>, accessed on 2 December 2017.
64. See <http://www.elections.in/punjab/assembly-constituencies/sangrur.html>, accessed on 2 December 2017.
65. See <https://timesofindia.indiatimes.com/elections/assembly-elections/punjab/news/congress-wins-punjab-with-77-seats-aap-bags-20/articleshow/57596968.cms>, accessed on 2 December 2017.
66. See <http://www.news18.com/news/politics/gurdaspur-by-election-results-live-congress-candidate-sunil-jakhar-wins-by-over-190000-votes-1546769.html>, accessed on 2 December 2017.
67. See <http://www.india.com/news/india/aap-to-win-goa-elections-with-decisive-mandate-partys-internal-survey-1803110/>, accessed on 2 December 2017.
68. See <http://www.livemint.com/Politics/Ct69xkEPNWaFn384XSsUhL/AAP-debacle-in-Goa-more-stunning-than-it-looks.html>, accessed on 2 December 2017.
69. See <http://indianexpress.com/article/cities/delhi/live-updates-mcd-elections-2017-exit-polls-bjp-congress-aap-4624994/>, accessed on 2 December 2017.
70. See <http://indianexpress.com/article/cities/delhi/delhi-mcd-elections-results-live-updates-2017-ndmc-sdmc-edmc-bjp-inc-aap-congress-aam-aadmi-party-arvind-kejriwal-narendra-modi-list-of-winners-all-wards/>; <https://economictimes.indiatimes.com/news/politics-and-nation/mcd-polls-aaps-vote-share-nosedives-to-26-congress-rises-to-20/articleshow/58388786.cms>, accessed on 2 December 2017.
71. See <https://www.cnbc.com/2016/09/20/senator-warren-on-wells-fargo-ceo-gutless-leadership.html>, accessed on 3 December 2017.
72. See <http://www.hindustantimes.com/assembly-elections/spineless-election-commission-has-surrendered-to-modi-aap-s-kejriwal-accuses/story-vScQ0lRL1HFcwIpZcInXBN.

html>; <http://www.hindustantimes.com/delhi-news/election-commission-dhritarashtra-helping-bjp-duryodhana-win-kejriwal-on-faulty-evms/story-jFNE68OaJHGIK4gw9su9eP.html>, accessed on 3 December 2017.

73. See <http://www.dnaindia.com/india/report-dusu-polls-a-breakdown-of-how-abvp-nsui-and-cyss-fared-2124600>, accessed on 4 December 2017.
74. See <https://timesofindia.indiatimes.com/city/goa/ceo-officials-say-debut-vvpat-feature-not-integral-to-counting/articleshow/57261016.cms>, accessed on 3 December 2017.
75. See <https://timesofindia.indiatimes.com/india/paper-trail-tallies-with-evm-results-in-punjab-and-goa/articleshow/58232422.cms>, accessed on 3 December 2017.
76. See <http://www.hindustantimes.com/india-news/only-one-party-accepts-ec-s-hackathon-challenge-aap-and-congress-stay-away/story-RC2zHwxoshKi0YpbIJU4sL.html>, accessed on 3 December 2017.
77. See <http://indiatoday.intoday.in/story/aap-kumar-vishwas-assembly-elections-2017-aap-campaigns-in-goa-punjab-arvind-kejriwal/1/850883.html>, accessed on 3 December 2017.
78. See <http://www.hindustantimes.com/delhi-news/aap-s-amanatullah-khan-quits-top-post-sisodia-says-kejriwal-hurt-by-vishwas/story-kEJj1RaceaXPRRouZ3XiEM.html>, accessed on 4 December 2017.
79. See <http://www.dnaindia.com/india/report-suspended-from-aap-amanatullah-khan-made-chairman-of-panel-of-delhi-assembly-2429057>, accessed on 4 December 2017.
80. See <http://www.hindustantimes.com/jaipur/student-election-aap-wins-president-post-in-12-colleges/story-PrE2O4KyPZFqqSTzgsNzbM.html>, accessed on 4 December 2017.
81. See <http://www.india.com/news/india/kumar-vishwas-demands-rajya-sabha-seat-from-delhi-says-aap-may-remove-him-arvind-kejriwal-2586046/>, accessed on 15 December 2017.
82. See <http://www.hindustantimes.com/delhi-news/sacked-aap-minister-kapil-mishra-makes-new-corruption-allegation-on-kejriwal-jain/story-SINwdUv4dkizHI08Mqo10O.html>, accessed on 4 December 2017.
83. See <http://zeenews.india.com/news/india/arvind-kejriwal-was-the-most-hated-indian-in-2015-others-on-the-list-are_1842233.html>, accessed on 4 December 2017.

About the Authors

MAYANK GANDHI is an activist from India, leading the initiative Global Parli—a nation-building mission through rural transformation. He was previously a member of the Core Committee in the India Against Corruption (IAC) movement and a National Executive member of the Aam Aadmi Party (AAP).

During his time in AAP, Mayank was responsible for consolidating the party's position in Maharashtra and was also a state observer in Gujarat. In 2015, he resigned from the party's National Executive.

Mayank lives in Mumbai with his wife and children. He can be reached at mayankgandhi04@gmail.com and on Twitter @mayankgandhi04.

*

SHREY SHAH has been a part of his mentor Mayank Gandhi's journey right from the IAC days. He is also a budding lawyer who aspires to be an IAS officer in order to serve the nation.

About the Authors